ZT: In 2012 Dieter Roelstraete wrote an article for the Italian magazine Mousse introducing my work to its readers. The original text has been re-published as a pretext to the conversation held a few years later when Dieter and I met up to generate a text for this book. The idea was to talk, in the way we have often done through the years, the ideas into existence; an analogy to the process of translating thoughts into forms, an opaque simplification that I often use to describe what it is that I do. In this way the abstraction created within the structural confines of a conversation now becomes a tool to develop, or grow, forms that are visually present and take up space - what could suggestively be used as a definition of sculpture. Over the course of a few days we recorded our conversation within, and beside, a variety of outdoor Chicago locales. When editing the transcription a natural segue presented itself that linked the article's conclusion to what we have here: a text addressing the act of formation.

In other words, so as to begin somewhere, why write?

TAYLOR MADE ZIN TAYLOR AND THE STORY OF FORM

The art world is flooded with printed matter, a bottomless hunger for paper that Dieter Roelstraete finds an opportunity to analyze in relation to the work of Zin Taylor, undoubtedly an exquisite narrator. His stories often focus on anecdotes from art history and are patiently excavated, "unearthed", even literally entering the underground realm...

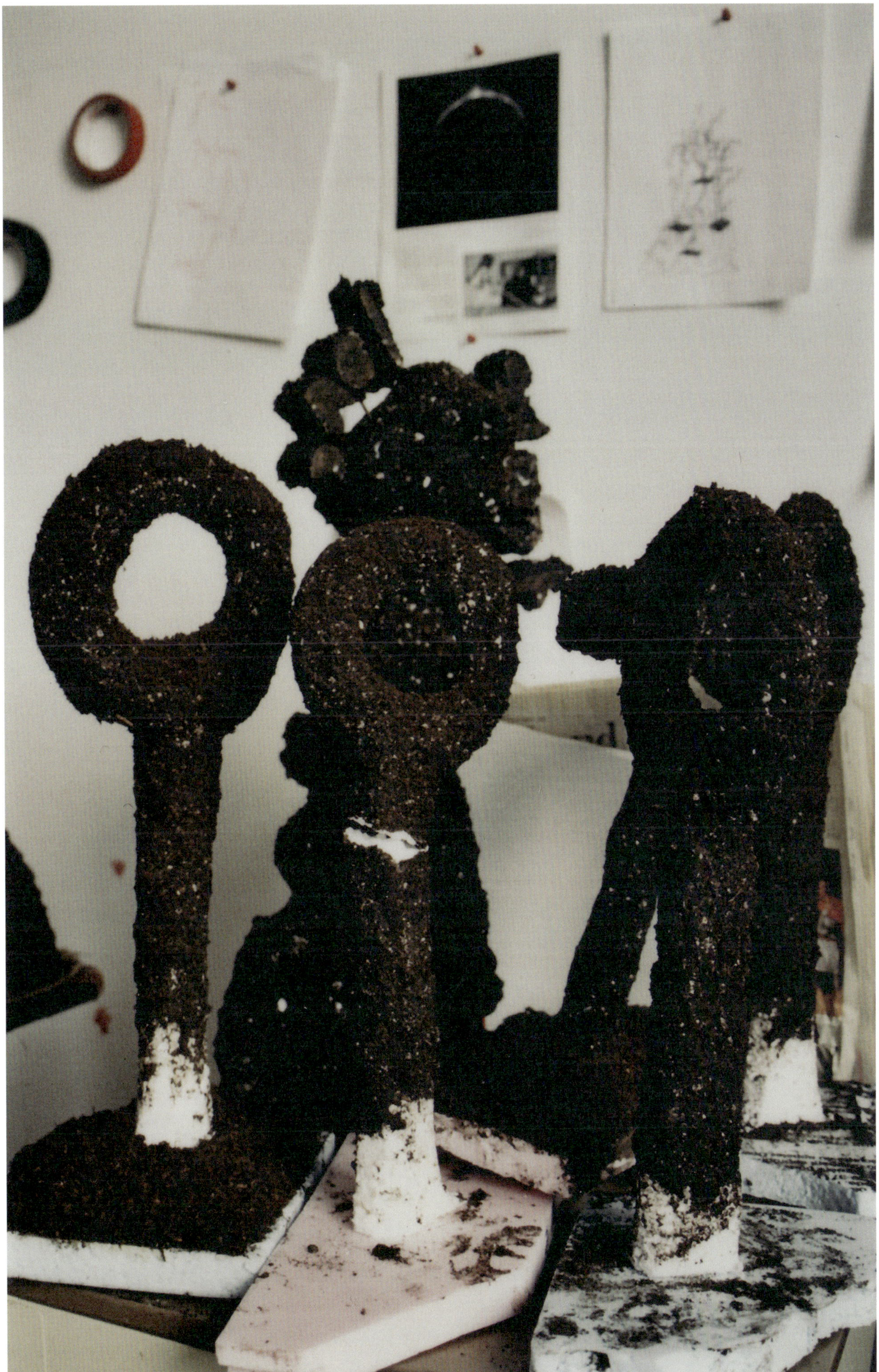

Why are so many young artists interested in storytelling? Why am I, when visiting the art schools of the world, so often asked, in this day and age, to read or listen to work rather than merely look at it? And this, typically, in studios that are cluttered with books and photocopied texts first and foremost, old school art "objects" often a distant second? Why are so many artists writing, and interested in writing? Why etc. – many more questions much like the above could be asked still, and perhaps they shouldn't. After all, artists may well constitute the last truly dependable consumer constituency for that exact type of specialty writing or publishing which the undersigned, among many others, engages in. Indeed, while the mainstream press (that is to say, by and large, the printed word) is continually awash in apocalyptic tidings about the end of print – and they are probably right too – the art world appears consumed, paradoxically (or not), by an unquenchable thirst for printed matter, and the subject of this essay, Brussels-based Canadian artist Zin Taylor, is not notably different in this regard, as the ever-expanding catalogue of Zin Taylor-made artist books seems to attest.

Now anyone who raises the kind of questions like those raised above, must also, even if only rhetorically, attempt an answer of some kind, and my suggestion for such an answer would probably involve the following elements: 1) the increased demand for literacy (both "literary" and theoretical) that has become an essential ingredient of art education; 2) the distinct aura of anachronism and obsolescence that is starting to surround the art of book-making; 3) the artist's typical instinct to come to the rescue of precisely those cultural phenomena that are becoming increasingly marginalized and threatened with disappearance. Somewhat related to this impulse is the intertwined issue of 4) the hypertrophy of image production in our current cultural climate – which has led to a devaluation of the image that the artist, historically attached to a tradition of "good" images, does not want to be a part of ("the piece need not be built", in Lawrence Weiner's famous formulation) – and 5) the specter of cultural amnesia that hovers above this hypertrophic cult of the ever-accelerating, -expanding and -proliferating image world. The forgetting of language that is implied in this vertiginous regime of ocular overload (the more we see, the less we speak; the more we see, the less we remember) is also, inevitably, a forgetting of history, and a forgetting of the many stories that constitute the patchwork of history. Hence (perhaps): storytelling in art.

Zin Taylor certainly is a storyteller, and the narrative impulse (not a mere "turn", this time) is a driving force behind much of his work; many of his artistic projects either involve extensive narration, often told in the artist's own voice, or the publication of these narratives in book form. In a number of cases, these stories have touched upon certain minutiae of recent art history – this does not, however, make Taylor into your typical "referentiality" artist, nor is he overly concerned with the politics of re-enactment – such as Martin Kippenberger's abandoned metro station in the Yukon or Marcel Broodthaers' eagle fixation. In *Put Your Eye In Your Mouth: A Conversational Documentary Recording Martin Kippenberger's Metro-Net Station in Dawson City, Yukon* (the literary character of Taylor's work is also apparent in his love of elaborate titles:

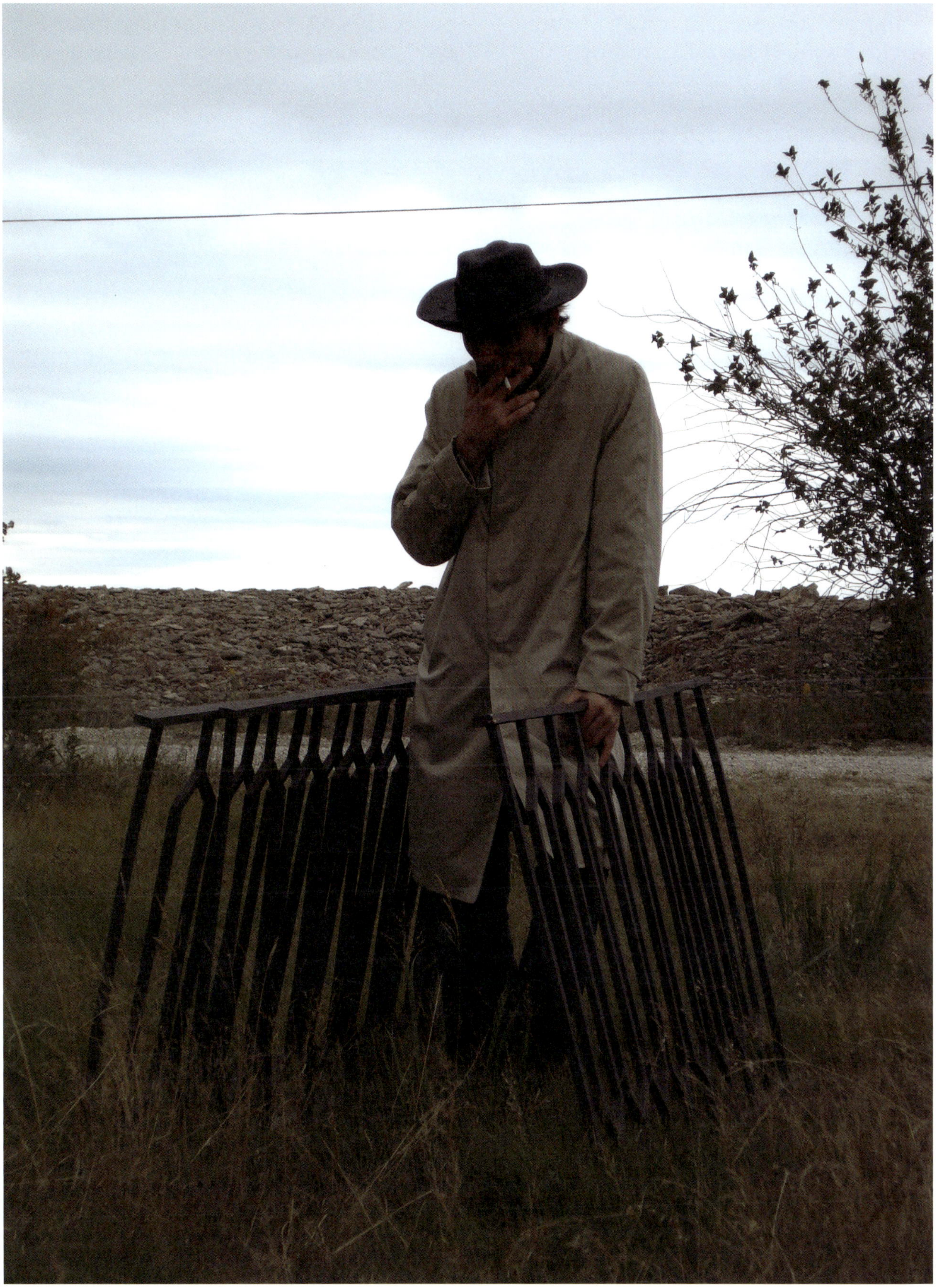

it is hard to imagine any of his works being named Untitled), a work in part inspired by the artist's conversations with the man who paid for and built the eponymous metro station, Taylor set out to uncover what little remains of the Northern Canadian site of Kippenberger's worldwide metro network. The resulting video (and accompanying publication, simply titled *Nook*) is as much an irreverent, quick-fingered fiction as an *On The Road*-style documentary – an obfuscation befitting the notoriously megalomaniacal subject of this homage. Made in 2008, just after Taylor moved to Belgium to take up permanent residence there, *The Crystal Ship* is a video/publication diptych much like the previous work, "a journalistic narrative that approaches the visual working practice of Marcel Broodthaers as a contextual frame to interpret a series of landmarks within an Antwerp neighborhood", as the artist has put it. The work also involves a set of small, unassuming clay sculptures, one depicting an eagle (Broodthaers' totem animal, of course, this one modeled on an actual statue in Antwerp's museum quarter), another a scale model of the façade of the house in Antwerp that was once home to the legendary gallery A379089 (directed, for six months of its all too short-lived existence, by none other than Kasper König), in the garden of which Broodthaers recorded his famous writing-degree-zero performance *La Pluie* (1969) – this garden in turn becoming the site where Taylor would present, performance-like, the various findings of his idiosyncratic research into this (naturally unknown) subterranean local art history.

The speleological metaphor of the artist patiently, if a little manically, burrowing to uncover and unearth truly underground (art) histories is not innocently chosen here, and nowhere has Taylor's interest in a literalized practice of excavation been expressed more clearly as in *The Flute of Sub*, an ensemble of works – true to the D.I.Y. total-work-of-art spirit of Kippenberger and the like, Taylor also designs posters or series of posters to accompany his videos – the central sculptural element of which is a flute made out of plastic and whose irregular, crooked form is modeled after the shape of one nexus in a subterranean system of tunnels the artist happened upon while sojourning in the Scottish Highlands (this piece was included in an exhibition I curated at the Ursula Blickle Stiftung in 2009 titled *The Archaeologists*, for which Taylor also designed the poster). The video, which really functions as an allegorical reflection upon the inscrutable mysteries of "form", recounts the artist's discovery of these mysterious man-made tunnels, while every screening of it has been introduced in the past by an actual flute recital – performed by Taylor himself, needless to say, the flute's material and shape being such that it cannot be played by the uninitiated. As such, the work also exemplifies Taylor's strong reliance on musical culture, often the more obscure ("underground") the better – "psych folk" in *The Flute of Sub*, droning "witch folk" in *White Pearl Sunshine Summoning Charm* (2007), eccentric Jap noise in *The Allegorical Function of Dirt: A Discussion with Aki Tsuyuko's Ongakushitsu* (2005), and abstract grindcore in *The Locust* (2004).

If *The Flute of Sub* essentially revolved around the inscrutable mysteries of "form" while still appearing to be something other, then the question of growth, of the organic, only mildly artist-assisted development of form,

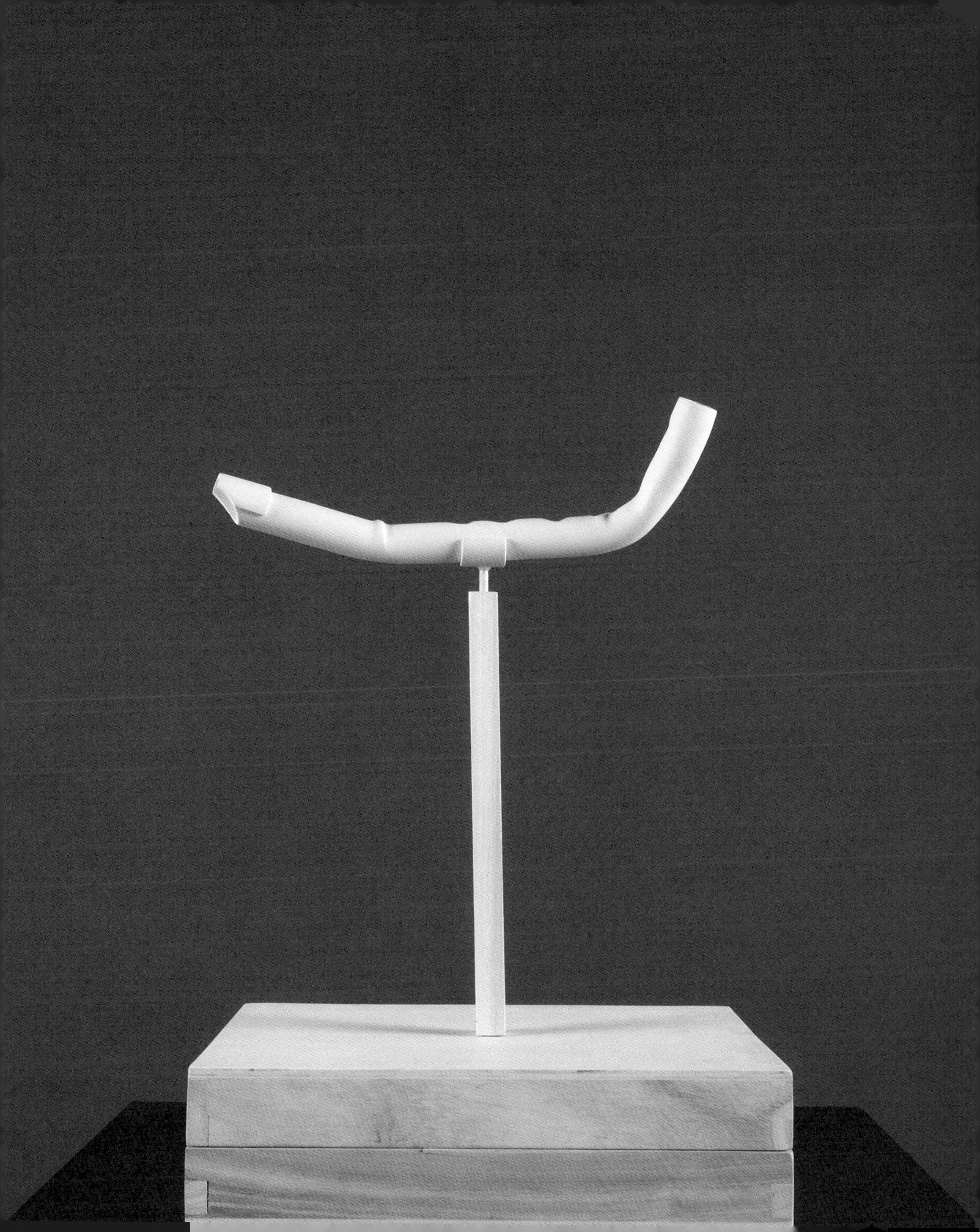

has recently come to occupy center stage in Taylor's work in a much more direct, bare-bones fashion, and works such as *The Bakery of Blok* and the appositely titled *Organisms* (a series of color photographs of kneaded bits of dough) and *Growth* on a Form (a series of drawings of "imagined wood forms that have become overrun with an ooze-like material") signal a definite shift towards a fundamental interrogation of sculpture's basic language, if not of the very assumptions that underlie the enterprise of sculpture and art as such. How do forms come about? Do materials have a will of their own, content to speak through Zin Taylor's hands as long as he's able to give voice to matter's inner thought? In *The Bakery of Blok* (which again consists of a video as well as a series of wooden sculptures, crude replicas of the tools of the baking trade), the art of baking bread is held up as an idiomatic metaphor for the art of giving sensuous shape to thinking – the art of art, in short. Here, we are returning to an origin of sorts – heading for the fundamentals. Indeed, carpentry and the multiplication of breads: where have we heard that story before?

Taylor Made: Zin Taylor and the Story of Form
by Dieter Roelstraete
Originally published in Mousse, no. 27, February-March 2011

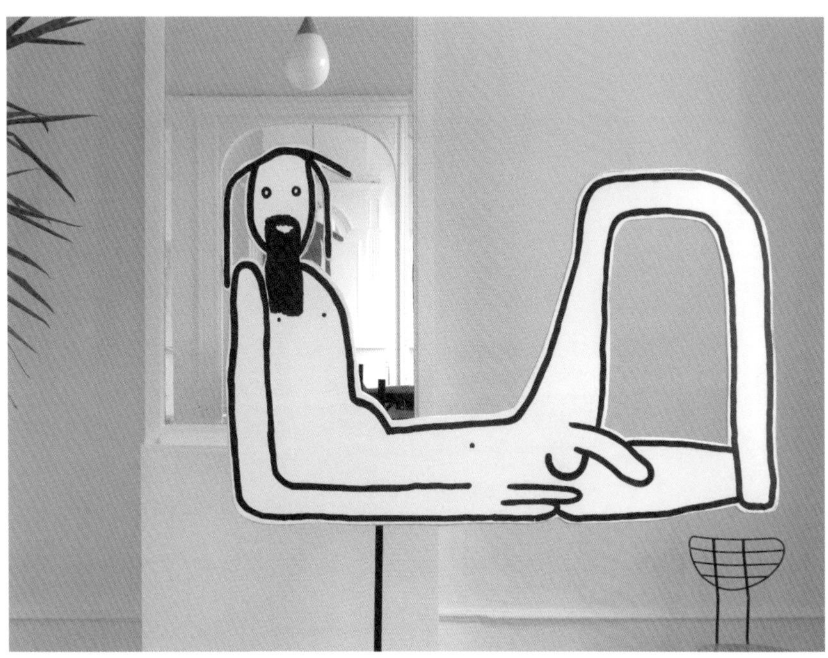

TRANSC

DIETER
ROELSTRAETE

CHICA
AUGUS

RIPTION

ZIN
TAYLOR

GO, IL
T, 2014

DR: Why do you think writing is important?

ZT: I use writing to grow an idea. Coming out of art school, I was looking at writers/artists who could develop an expansive level of content within, and into, a work. Mike Kelley, for example—the texts in his book *Minor Histories*, in particular the one about the Chinese wishing well in Los Angeles, struck me by how effortlessly complex the network of references were. In writing the text Kelley develops a relationship between his ongoing interest in the uncanny as a working/thinking structure, to biomorphic abstraction in the 1940's, and architectural enclosures used for psychological tests involving monkeys, to addressing the amorphous abstract lump of concrete that is the wishing well, a semi-monument intended to represent a cultural community within Los Angeles. I admired the relationship between the writing and the making and how they augment and develop one-another. This back and forth dialogue produces a totality. That's the kind of world I want to be a part of, that's why I write.[...]

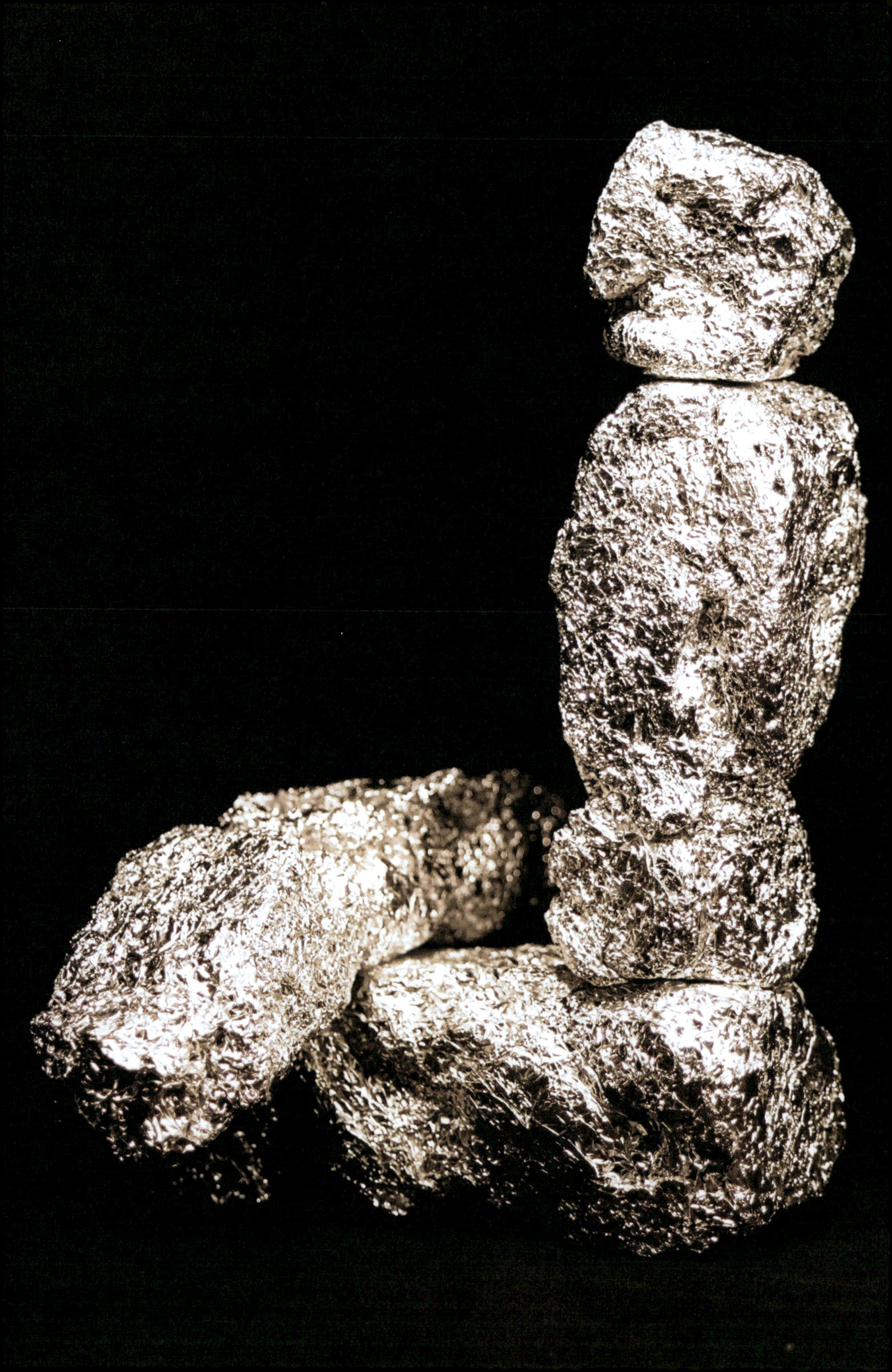

The Crystal Ship was the first time I'd ever had an idea that needed to take the form of a book, and therefore it needed to be written. That realization can be quite frightening when you don't have a lot of confidence in your writing. So, I started by looking at different writing styles to determine how I would communicate this narrative I wanted. I tried to figure out how exactly I would go about creating it. I looked at journalistic structures where the sentences are active and succinct, focusing on qualifying statements rather than ambiguity. I used that approach to assemble speculative thoughts alongside my research. That was in 2008, and this structural approach toward composition has been a continuous routine ever since. [...]

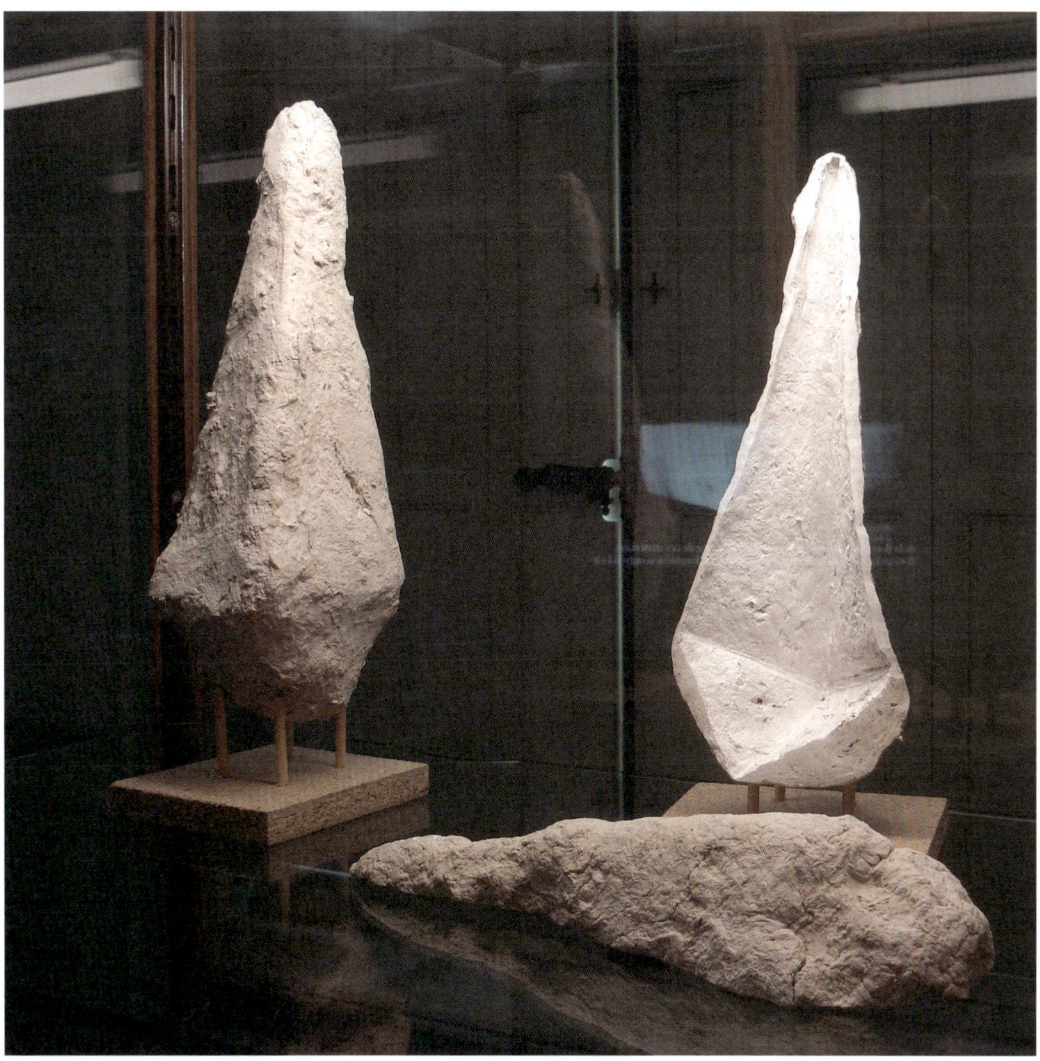

Dear Jacob,

In keeping with the spirit of POST I've designed a letterhead that will deliver (via the postal system) a one-month series of drawings and texts.

Letterhead is an A4 sized piece of paper emblazoned with a design indicating the contents on the page are of an origin related to The Story of Stripes and Dots. This is a narrative series I continue to produce within, in many forms, addressing the role abstraction has in the construction and use of a visual language. Simply stated, a stripe is a dot seen from the side, a dot is a stripe as seen from head-on.

Many aspects of POST at Kunsthal Charlottenborg are reminiscent of what I've read, seen, and understand of 1960's and 1970's conceptual and FLUXUS made art. Serial production, propositional statements, an attempt at dematerialization, projected skepticism reflexively underscored using administrative aesthetics - tools of critique constructed from the environment at hand. Rubber stamps, mail art, made up names.

Central to the exhibition, of course, is that everything must arrive by mail - through and by the traditional postal system. Courier companies are forbidden. The only thing I can imagine being sent through regional post is something personal from one person to another, where what the information is printed on is as important as the information itself. What fits into an envelope? A letter; a form; a special card wishing you well; an artifact collected and passed along with notations attached. There is a traditional aspect to the POST exhibit that is as attractive as listening to Led Zeppelin on a Sunday. Thinking and producing within a specific frame, when thoughts time travel in order to go to work.

For the month of June I'll be sending letters to Kunsthal Charlottenborg. As many as I can, I hope to average at least one a day. I've designed a letterhead with a stripe and a dot. Each page presents an A4 sized proposition related to its self, a story of Stripes and Dots played out on the stage of the page. As these letters arrive I would see them pinned on the wall of the gallery, sequentially in a row, starting from the left. I'll do my best to number the individual pages and give adequate indication as to how casually the page should be affixed to the wall, what height, distance from the next, etc… I've begun composing this piece earlier than needed to account for the time-schedule of a letter traveling through the post. The first gesture will be sent out shortly, I expect arriving a little earlier than expected in Copenhagen. Better early than late. A resemblance to a narrative unfurling in post could be implied, although I'm going for the present-ness of these ideas in space (and the imminent arrival of another), to propel the proposition along.

More soon,

Zin

When I was invited by Kunsthal Charlottenborg for Jacob Fabricius' POST series in 2013, Jacob asked for a series of instructions for what to do with whatever I was going to send through the post. I wound up devising a letterhead featuring stripes and dots as an extension of the series *The Story of Stripes and Dots* that I had been working with for a few years already. Every drawing I sent to them on that letterhead was a suggestion for an additional relationship between a stripe and a dot, where a stripe seen from head-on is a dot, and a dot seen from the side is a stripe.
The text started as a project description, later evolving into this florid narrative where I was able to loop connections together by pulling in references to an administrative aesthetic from the 1960s.[...]

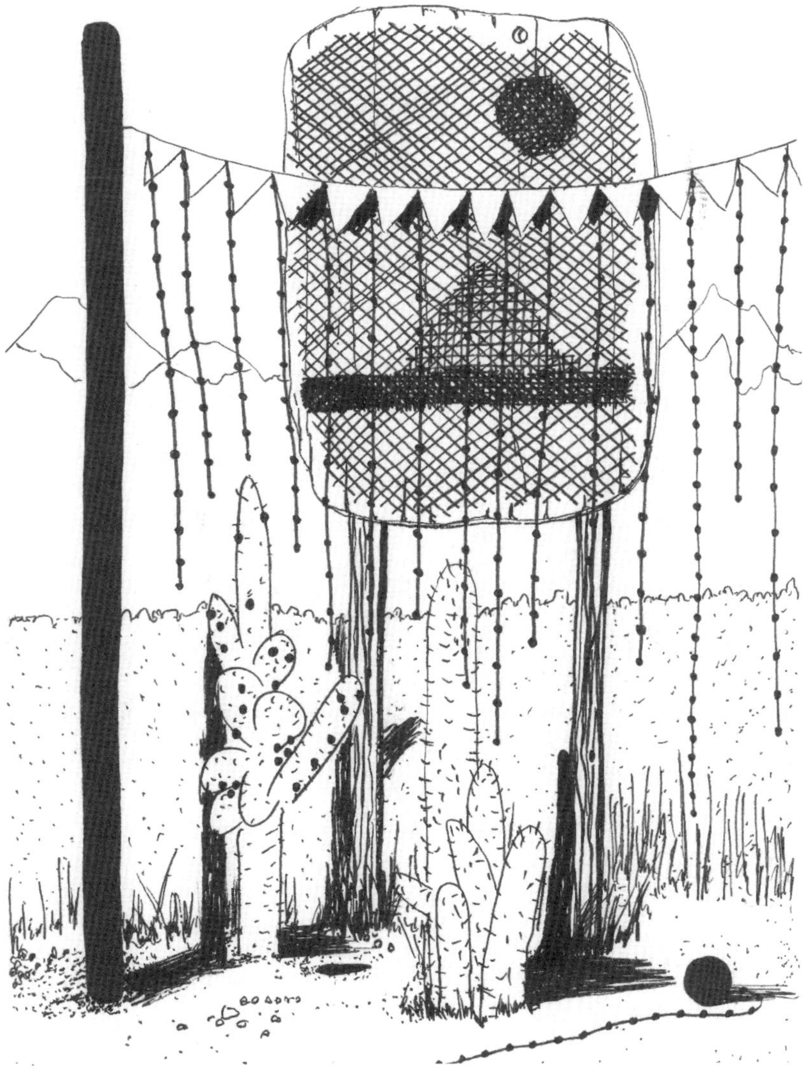

Menu

Spaghetti + Meatballs	10 —
Bitterballen + fries	10 —
Pancakes + Bacon	10 —
Noodle Soup	10 —
Sea Cucumber	10 —
Black Pudding (Sliced)	10 —
Pepper Bacon Burger + pickle	10 —

BANANA SPLIT	10 —
Gulab Jamun	4 / 10 —
Baklava	5 / 10 —

Additionally, through writing, I try to develop titles that allude to something in the metaphorical distance, to build this other dimension of the work. Text can do that. In the last while I've shortened the titles down a lot, becoming very literal with how propositionally crazy some of the ideas can be, such as *The Proposal of a Surface (Lichen Wall)*. Maybe the titles are a little more boring, but they're also a bit more odd, more weirding.

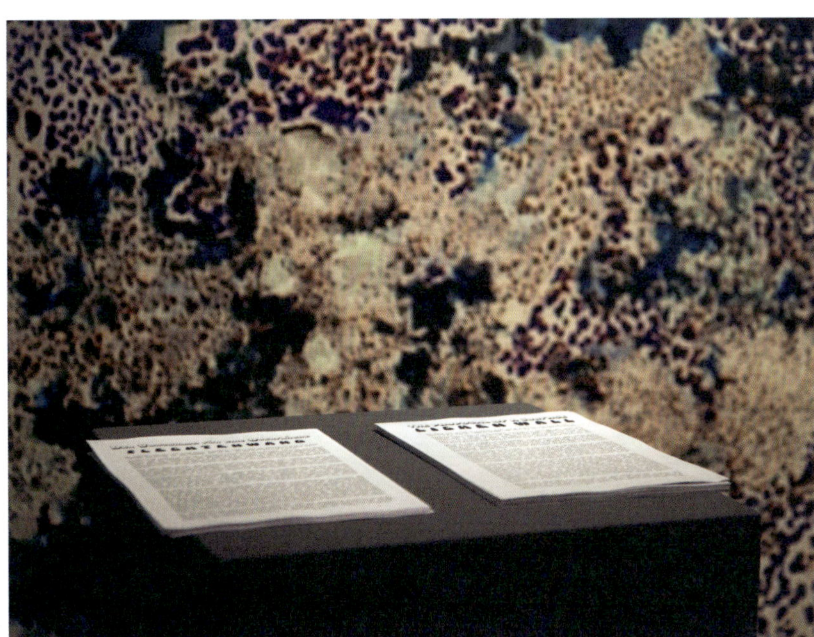

DR: They have this plump there-ness.

SUN
MILK

ZT: *Sun Milk* was used as a portal-phrase to sculpturally translate a bunch of propositions for a Henry van de Velde house in Brussels. The title was used to appropriate and then re-position the homeowner's records into the setting for a sound system. The words "sun milk" were printed on the front of a large speaker I had built, like what you would see in the Kingston sound systems so as to identify the DJ (the author) who was producing those nights. An influential book for me was Bass Culture by Lloyd Bradley. It's a sociological breakdown of reggae and dub that documents how a community produces its own style through activity. Through doing something, things happen, and then they happen again, and again, and they get re-versioned, translated poorly, something gets screwed up...

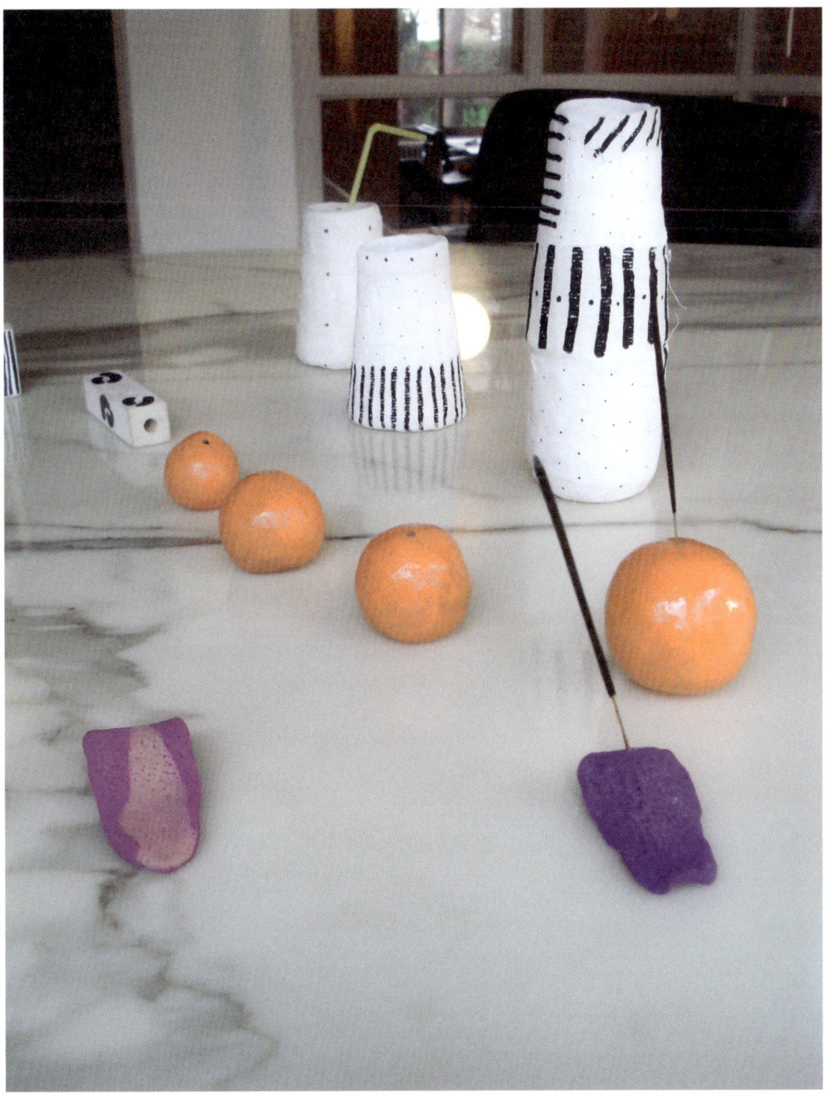

DR: Sped up or slowed down, according to a political climate.

ZT: One chapter discusses colonialism in Jamaica and how Heineken and Red Stripe were politicized drinks. If you drank Heineken you were a colonialist; you should be drinking Red Stripe if you believed in Jamaica. Bradley talks about dub and its relationship to Africa, how the music was related to the spiritualism located within the body, the parts relative to a space. The echo of dub was there to lend the idea that the listener was on the precipice, the edge of a void—the body travels through the void and the sound is the tool that makes that happen. I turned my thoughts about this into ways of looking at material—and by material I mean information. I consider information as material, the same way wood or clay is something that is affected by a usage of it.

DR: And words, and language.

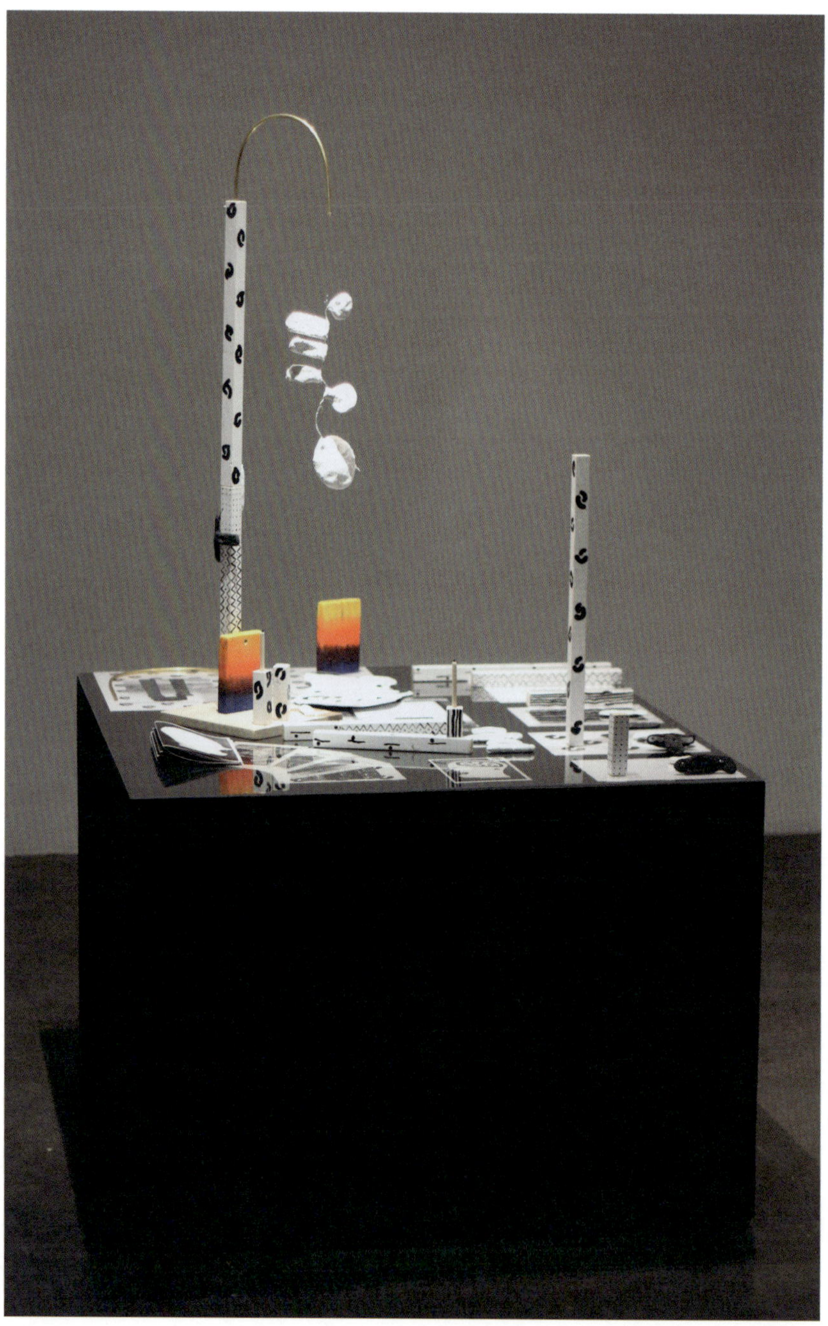

ZT: It's just a bunch of symbols, things that you stack and arrange and compose, and then you have these units that are now talking to each other.

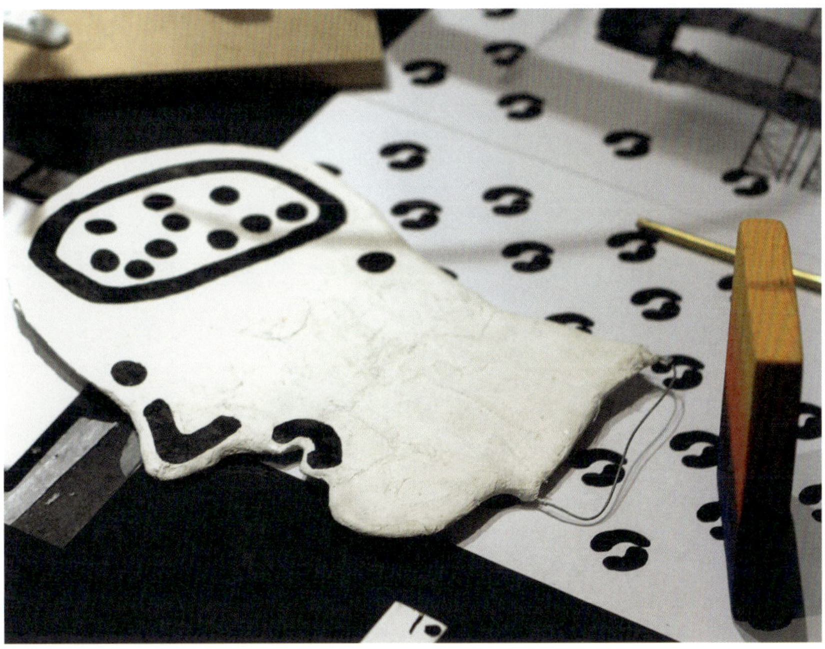

DR: Earlier, we were looking at something and it reminded me of this Melvins' lyric, from the chorus of *Hog Leg* on their 1991 *Eggnog* EP:

**Like Stee Moanin'
Ludlow**

**Rap a tee take a man
and send my own**

Just then my harr harr

**Take a send and tell
it take no dess**

ZT: It was the monologue in the Lichen Voices video that was shot on Fogo Island as part of my residency there. I wrote this monologue after waking up too early one morning, writing for forty-five minutes about everything I could remember ever happening to me while on Fogo Island, and not editing out the mistakes or trying to fix the sentence structure. Basically, I used automatic writing as a technique to create a certain ambiance for a narrative to unravel within.

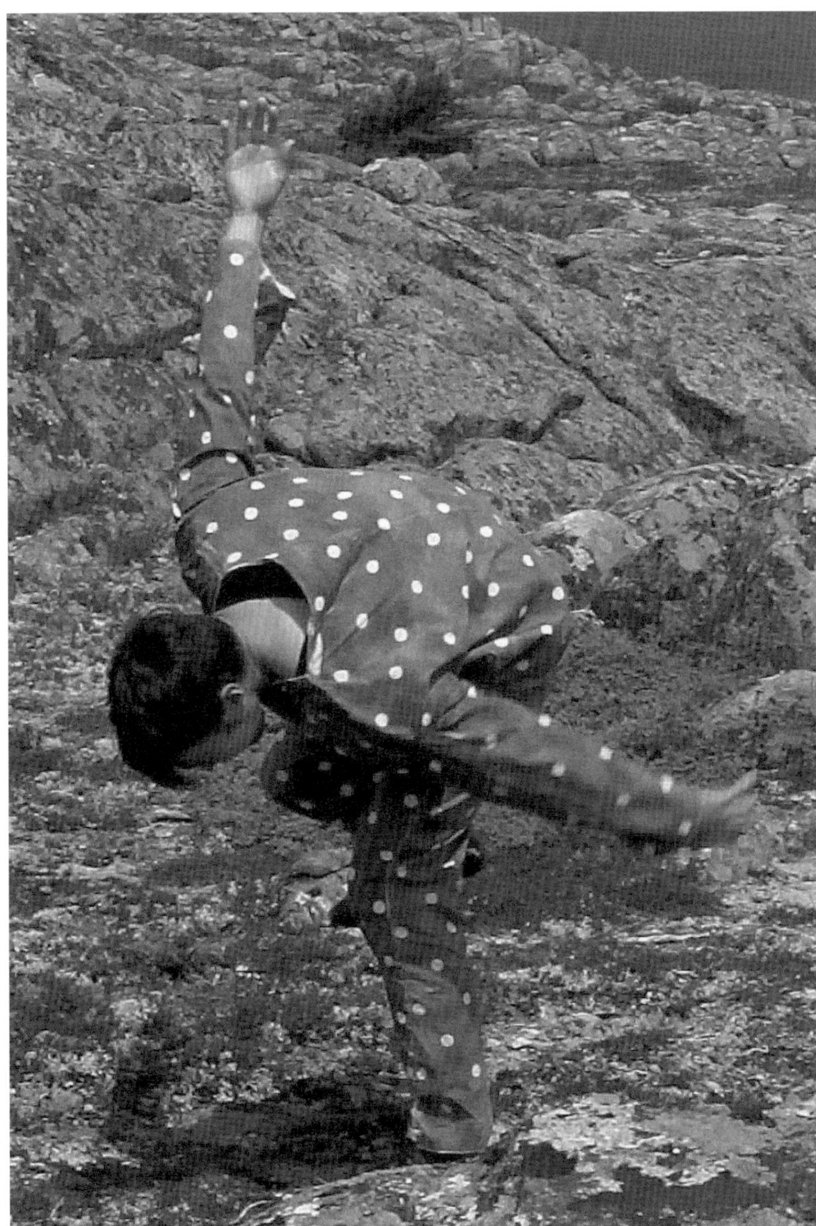

DR: What struck me about the writing, in thinking about writing and meaning, is that it's difficult to string words together in such a way that they don't make any sense at all. Of course it's very easy to make concrete poetry. In concrete poetry, you cut up words and toss them around and you make a collage or something based on aleatory combinations. I work with words, my livelihood is basically the stringing together of words. I can, as a writer, be quite jealous of people who can use language in that sculptural way, in that way of sound. The thing with language is that it's words on a page, but it's also how things sound. English is a really great language for that. It's very sonorous. It has so many more words than many other languages. It's super rich. It's modular, you don't deflect. Units. Verbs are the magic shit. I love adjectives, and adverbs. I like qualifiers. Even though I should like nouns more, but I can't help it. So talking about writing—*The Fog*...

ZT: *Palms of the Fog*, which was initially called *Parrot Soup*.[...]

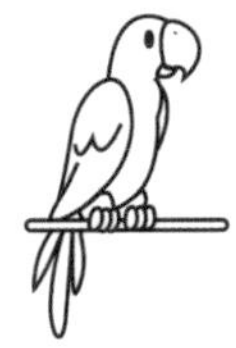

Parrot Soup

Wild Parrots have infested the park by where I live. A company of twenty moved in, and never left. Parrots are incredibly loud and bossy – like a gang of random thoughts loitering in the public space. They spot the ground and trees with their color, and fill the air with their speech. I imagine these birds, these organic recorders of other people's sounds, collecting fragments of thought from the people passing by. When the Parrots take flight, their voices fill the air with the amalgamized chatter they have collected - overheard ideas and wonky propositions, repeated elsewhere for the benefit of others.

I stroll with one of these birds, the colored body tucked beneath my arm, re-telling ideas I've had about this and that, making them mean a little more. Models and metaphors are explained in detail. I tell accounts of one thing so I can explain another. Thoughts gathered into a story after being loosened. Surfaced in a way that only a good walk can bring about.

As the parrot takes flight, the stories become part of the air. This bird floats through the trees, talking as it goes. Vocalized propositions filling the atmosphere, residues of speech and thought settling onto the landscape below. Ideas about one thing are collected into forms of another.

Parrot Soup is the telling of stories, where thoughts about the big are relayed through the small

Parrot Soup is thoughts collected on the surface of a panel

Parrot Soup is a mobile - 64 eyeballs, a color spectrum, a form of black, and one of pattern

Parrot Soup is language in space

Supportico Lopez + Zin Taylor + March 1 – April 13

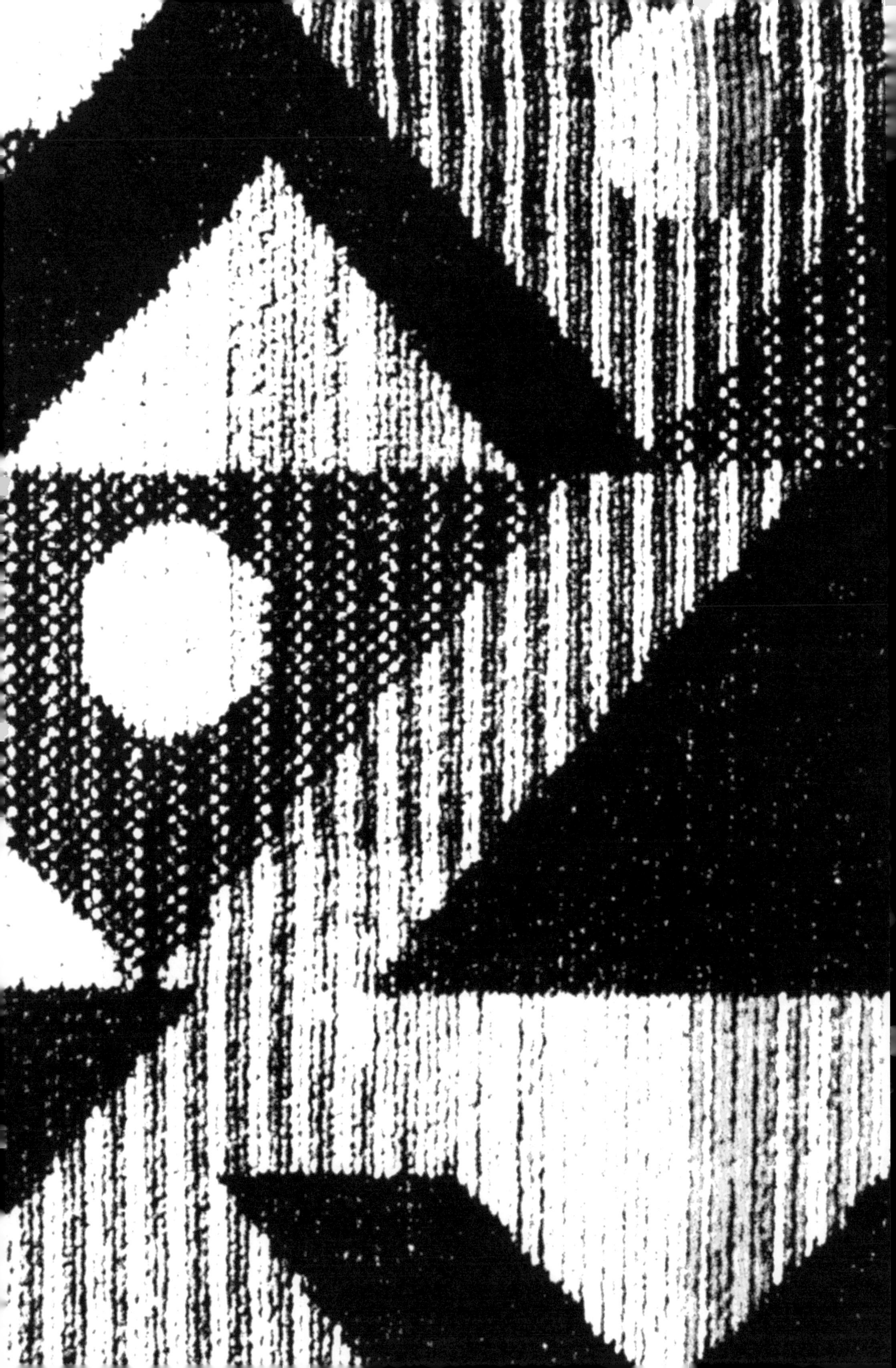

The title *Parrot Soup* came from the press release I wrote for a show at Supportico Lopez in Berlin in 2013. I would go running in this park by my house in Brussels that's filled with squawking, wild, green parrots. There are hundreds of them, and they are everywhere. I started thinking about a parrot. What is a parrot? It's like a bad recorder. It samples a bit, and then repeats it. Those parrots fly around the park, eavesdropping, picking up pieces of stories, stringing them together, and repeating them elsewhere. This was a way to talk about this mélange of information that I had strung together to build the text. For the book, I used my interests in music and music culture to understand something greater and more complex. Issues around post-colonialism, feminism, etc., are all addressed in the book, accompanied by photos I took of palm trees covered in fog.

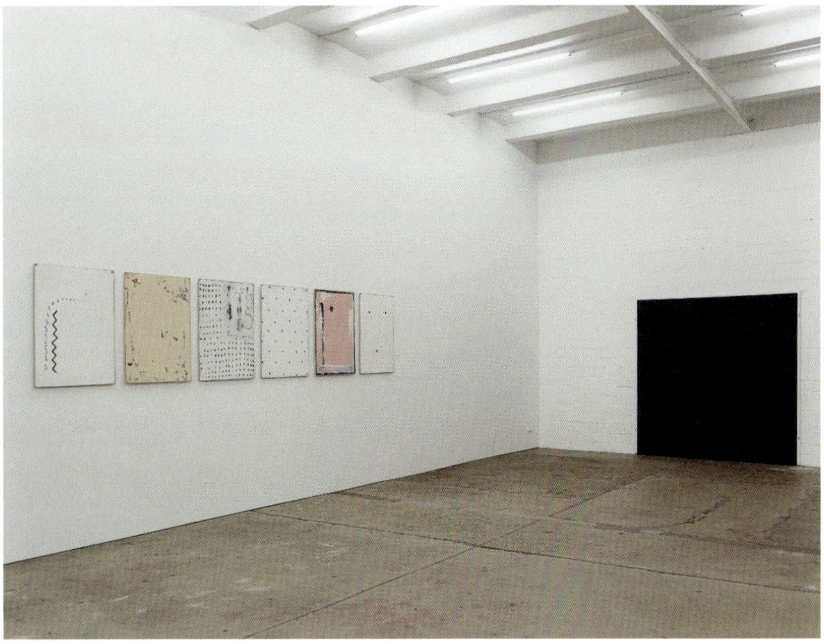

DR: What's with the palm trees though?

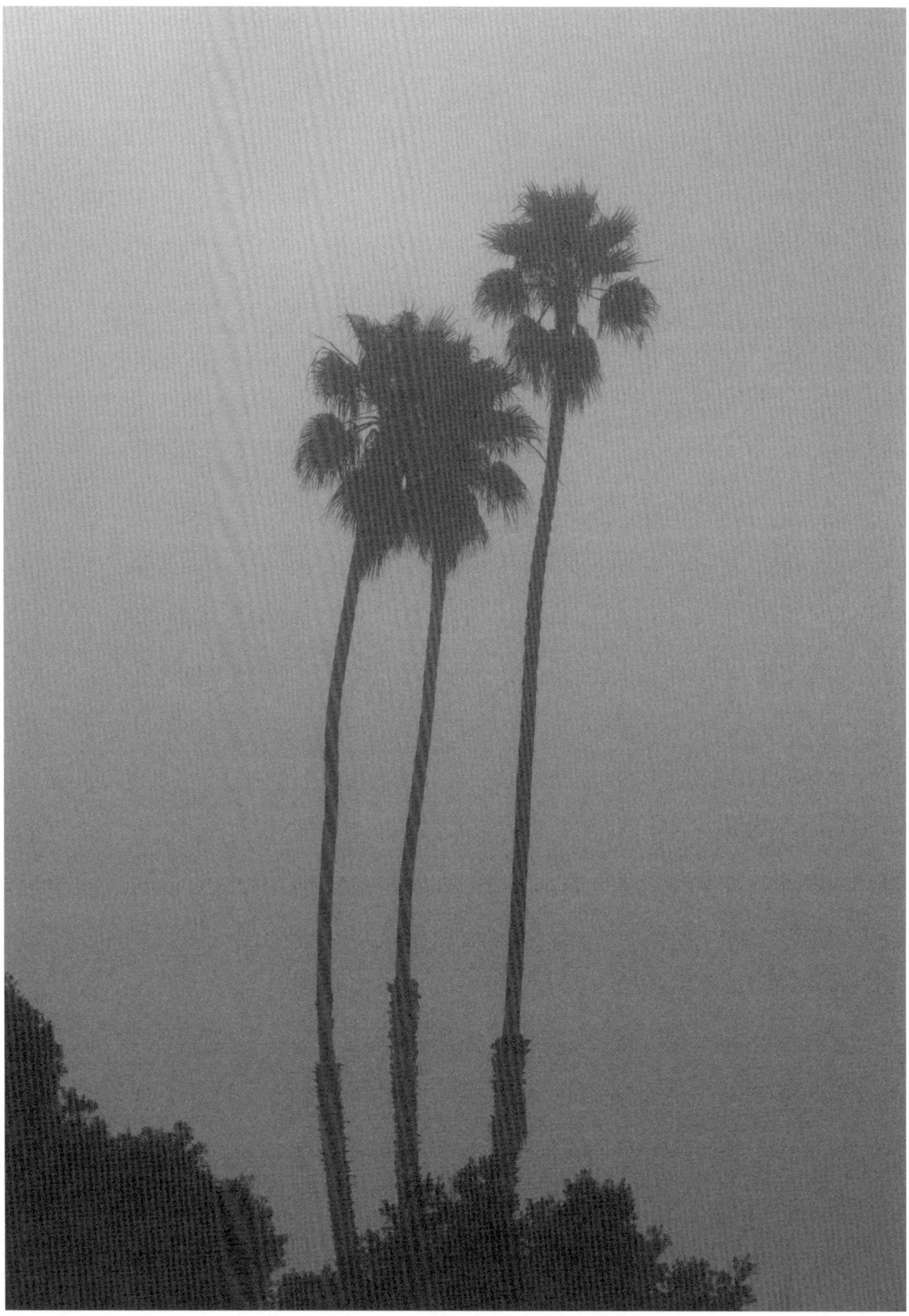

ZT: I was in Santa Barbara, California. I woke up in the morning, and a deep fog had rolled in from the ocean. The palms there are beautiful—they are six, seven, eight stories tall. I had my camera and decided to walk around and take photographs of them. It looked like some other world, like Nam in the '60s, when the shit's going down. It looked incredibly special, and so I took all these photographs because I thought it was a good thing to do. The fog was a kind of phenomenon—no big thoughts there. I remember showing them to someone, and he said yeah, whatever, palm tree photos... But you take these pictures in order to have this material, to think on it later. That's part of the process. A palm tree is symbolically a survival emblem. If you are stuck with a palm on an island, it produces nearly everything you need to survive until someone hopefully comes to save you. I saw each of these trees as a subject that was just *there*, and what changes is the air. Maybe the tree absorbs some of the stories that are going on, and that assists in the growing, adding another ring or length. I imagined the fog to be breath in the air, as a result of talking, obscuring these forms with narrative haze as they grow. Fog equaled narrative. I saw the text as a way of progressing beyond music connoisseurship while turning it into some kind of model.[...]

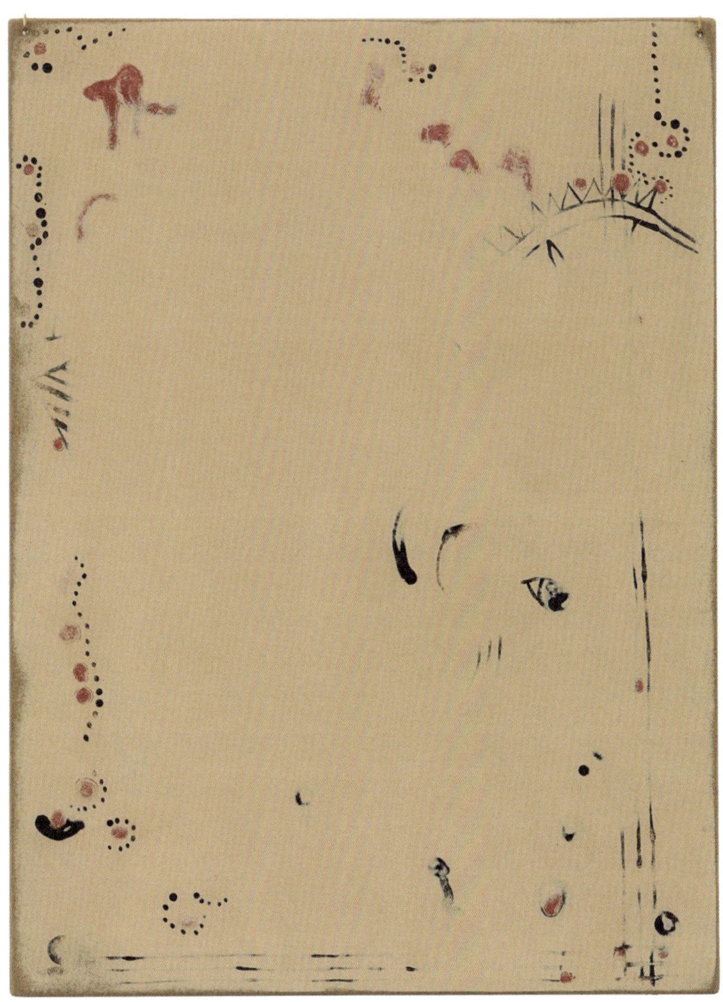

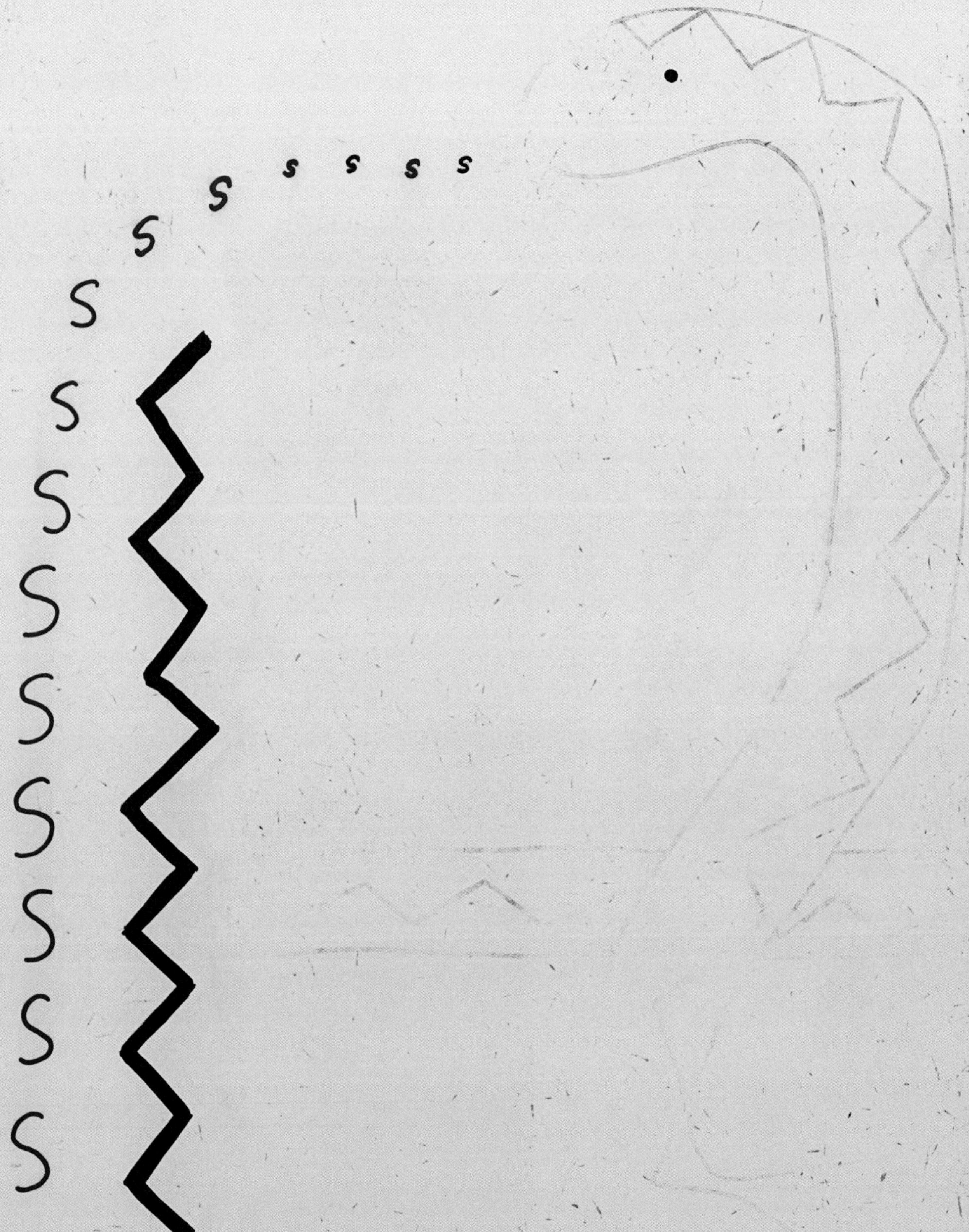
s s s s s s S S S S S S S S S

That is what *Palms of the Fog* attempts to do. Every one of those texts is a model that looks to the immediate to explain the more abstract.

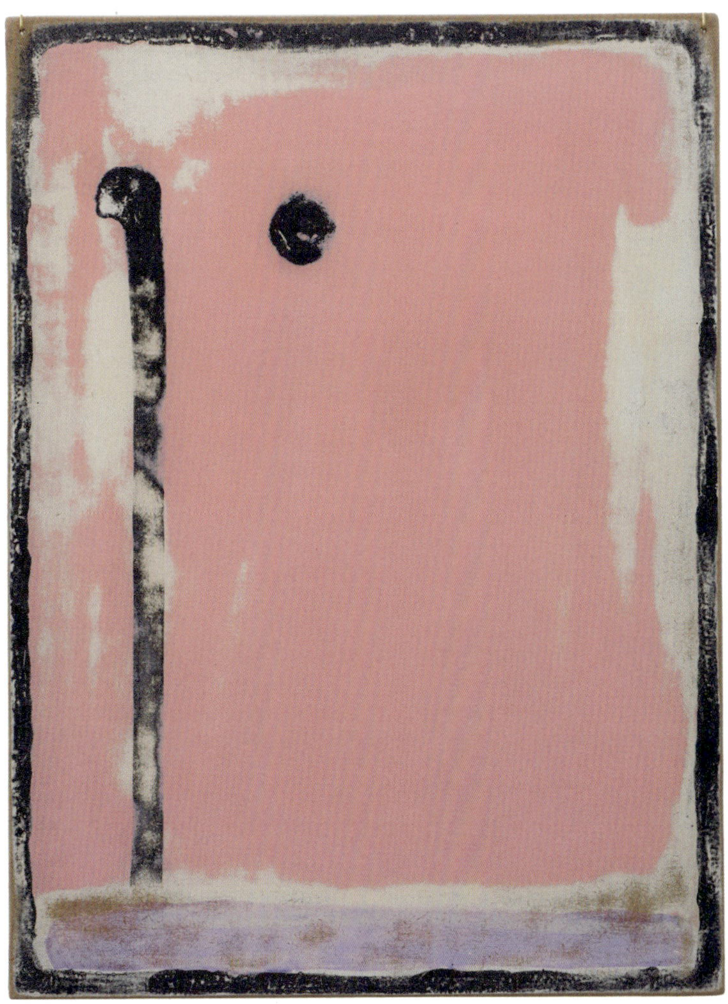

DR: Let's talk about snakes. Snaking as in the verb, to snake around, sneak/snake—it's an anagram. It's not your fetish animal, but something about them exists in your work. Can you talk a little about that? Snakes, zigzags, lines...

ZT: A snake is a zigzag. The path it forms takes way longer to travel than just moving linearly from point A to point B. Then there's the hiss of the snake, the sssssssss. Linking those ideas together creates a visual ideogram where the letter of the sound is also the shape that is made when a snake moves. The way it moves between those two poles of A and B is a zigzag. The movement is always back and forth, never straight. So this organism, if you were to imagine that movement, is a stand-in for dialogue, a stand-in for a way of talking around something, or for talking about a subject with someone—a visual way of representing discourse between two points. A snake is a line that's also a dot when you look straight at it.

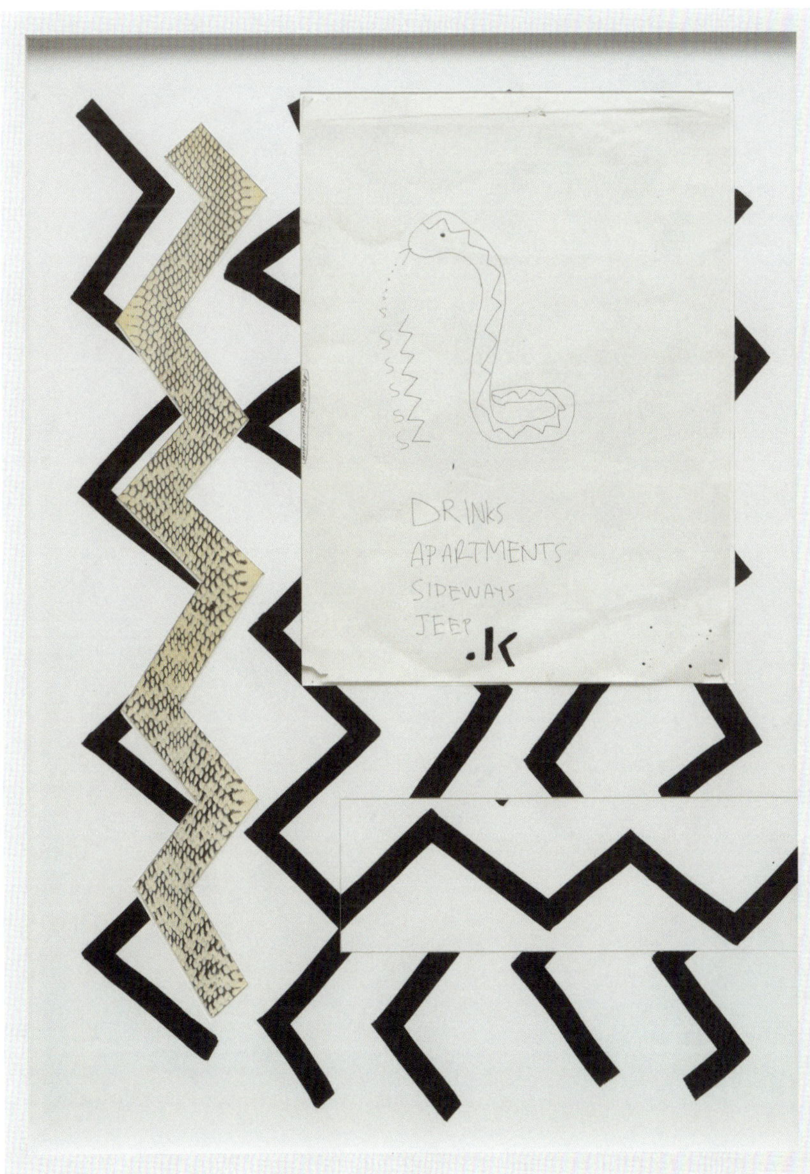

DR: For you, it's primarily about shapes and forms, because snakes come with cultural histories and associations. Although, sometimes a snake is just a snake.

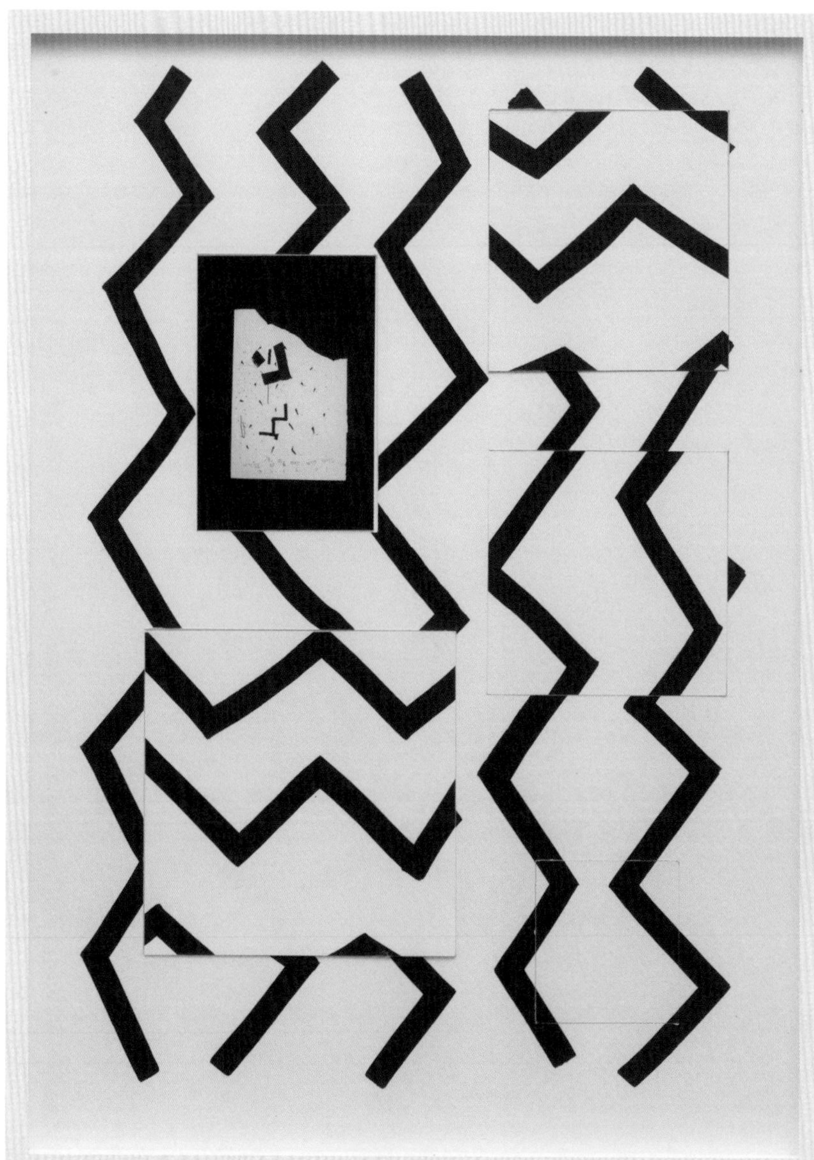

ZT: At times I'm wilfully ignorant about associative meanings, although always in order to talk about something differently. Sometimes you don't need all the information, you just need enough to start. This lends an opportunity to talk about that subject differently, as opposed to re-treading what everyone else already knows. The part of talking about a snake is that when you say "snake" people know what that is. Familiarity becomes a tool for communication. So you can also suggest difference for that thing, and that difference is the part that is much more interesting.

When I was in southern Italy I noticed that many of the pharmacies there had incorporated an elaborate snake as part of their emblem. Later in the day, when visiting a small mountain town, I found graffiti squiggles on several doors, all of which looked a lot like snakes. A certain part of my mind thought that this is could be an unsanctioned pharmacy—in other words, is this where drug dealers live?

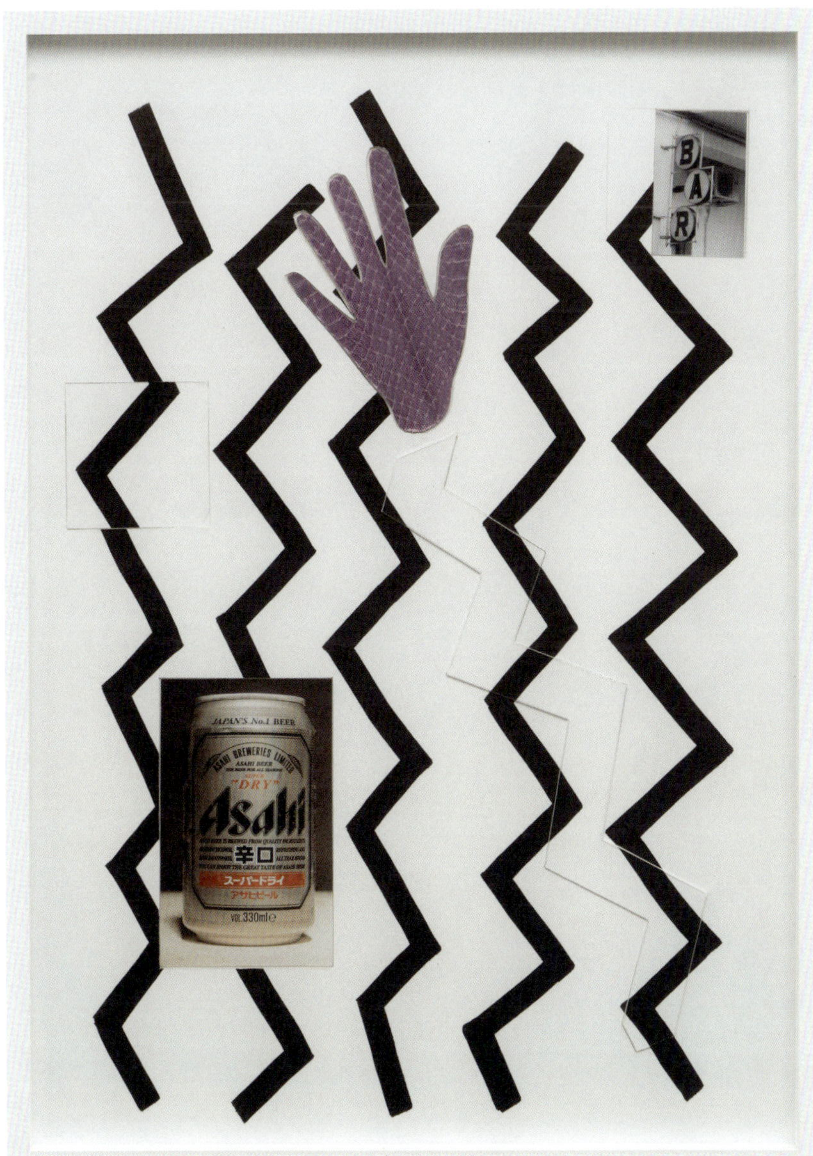

DR: Did you knock on the doors?

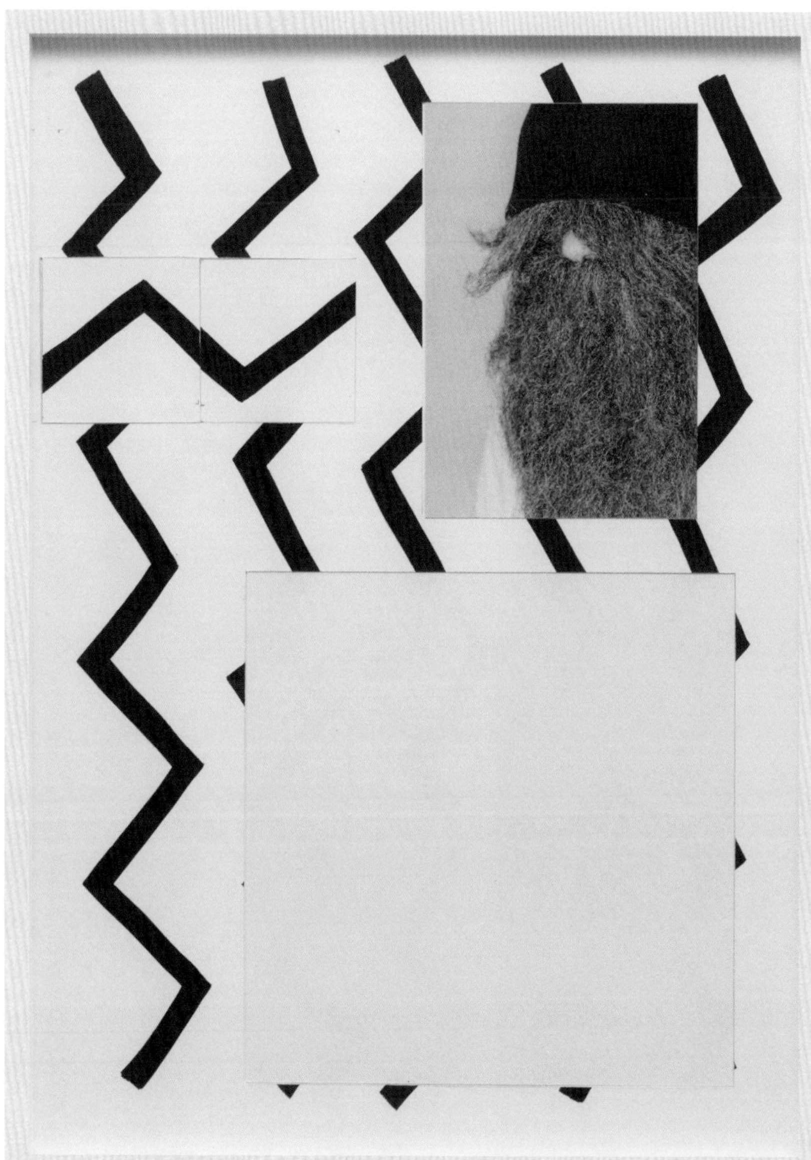

ZT: I was way too nervous for that. I photographed them and kept on walking. This was something that when seen triggers a thought associating toward something else.

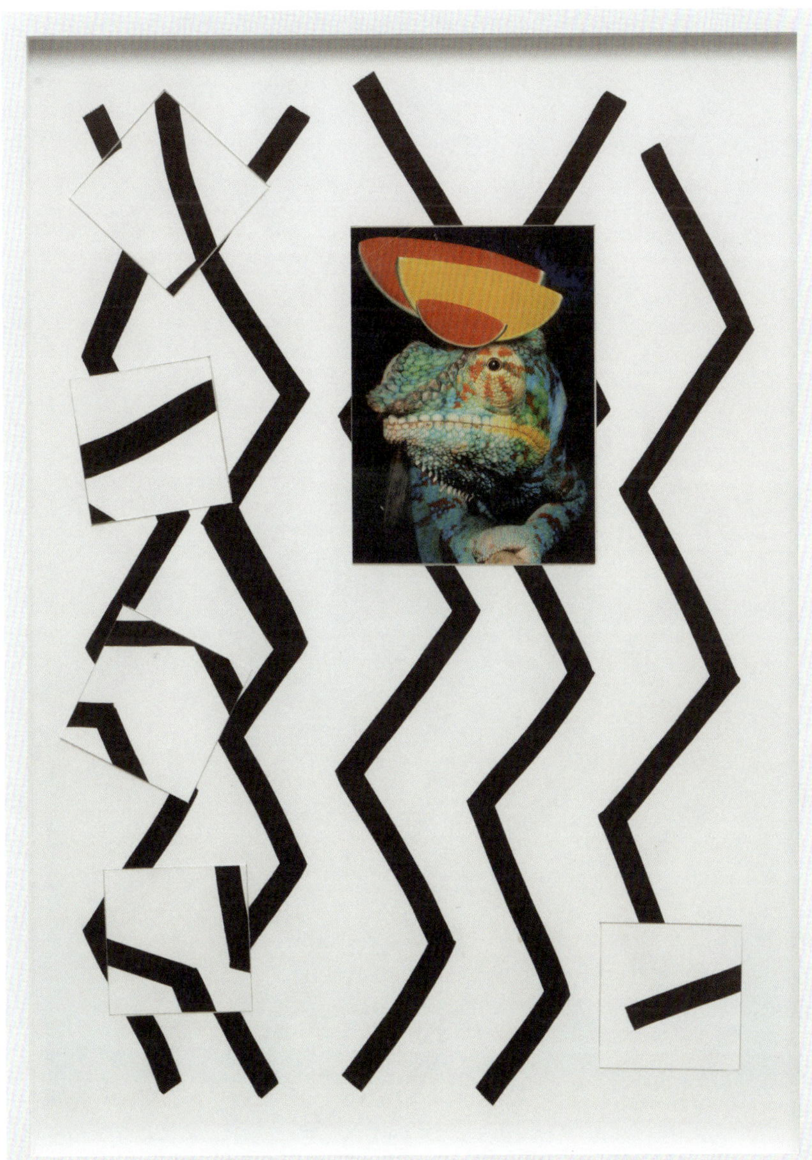

DR: A mark made.

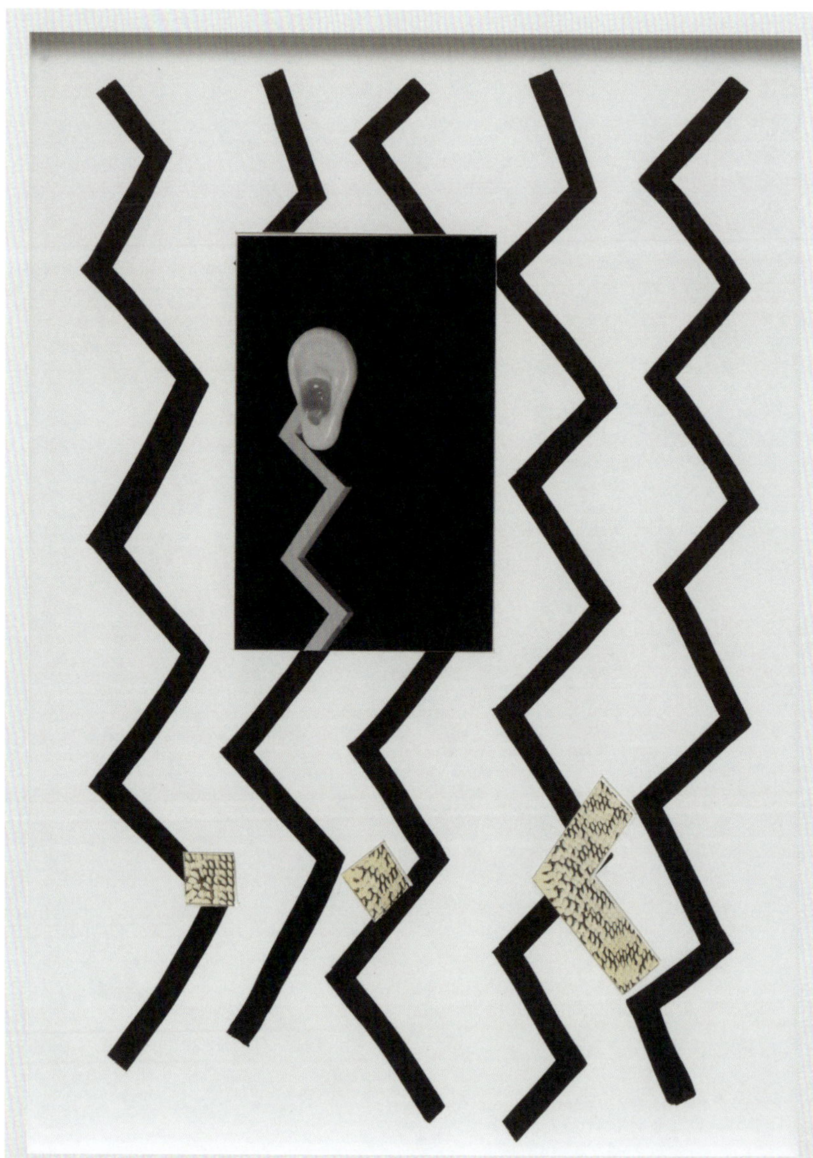

ZT: A mark made as the signifier of an alternate economy, drug dealer versus pharmacy. What's the difference? Historically, the craziest drugs were commonly prescribed, most of which are now illegal.

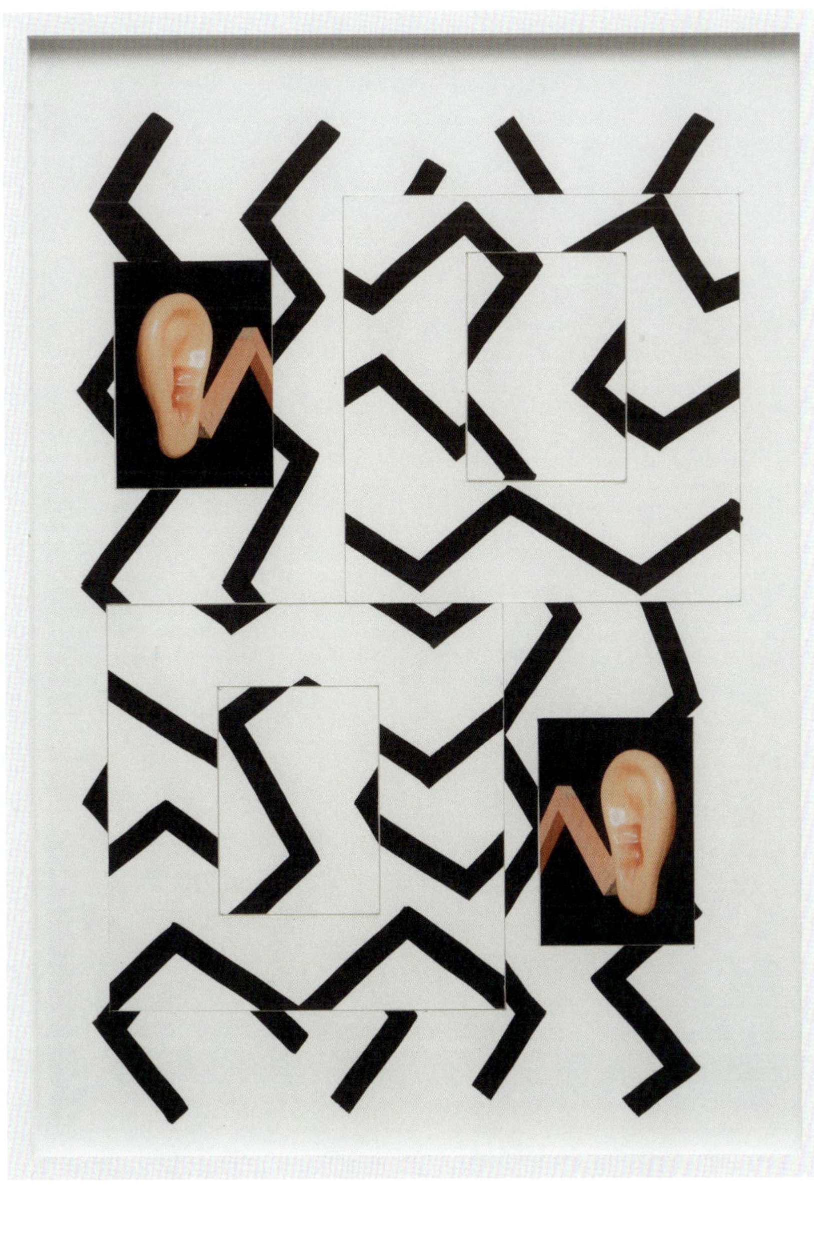

DR: Freud's first published article was on the medical uses of cocaine.

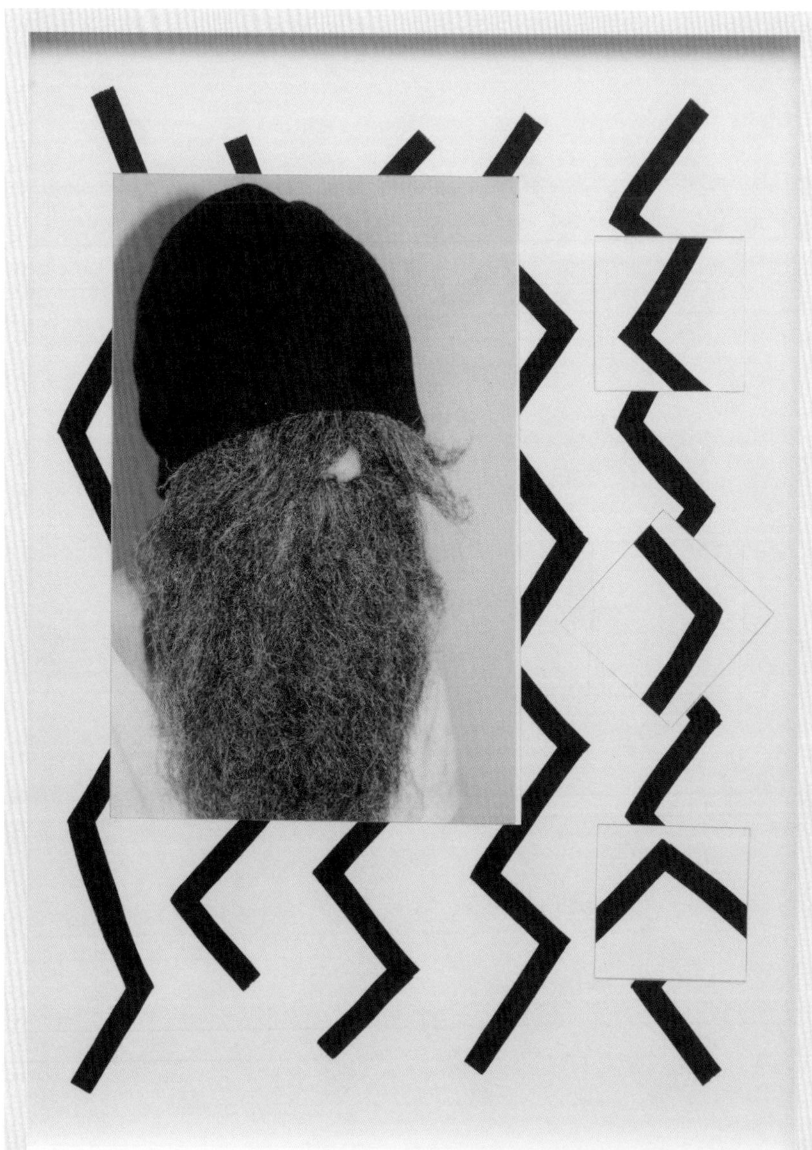

ZT: Which he probably got from a sanctioned snake dealer. Then you have snake oil, a metaphor for deception.

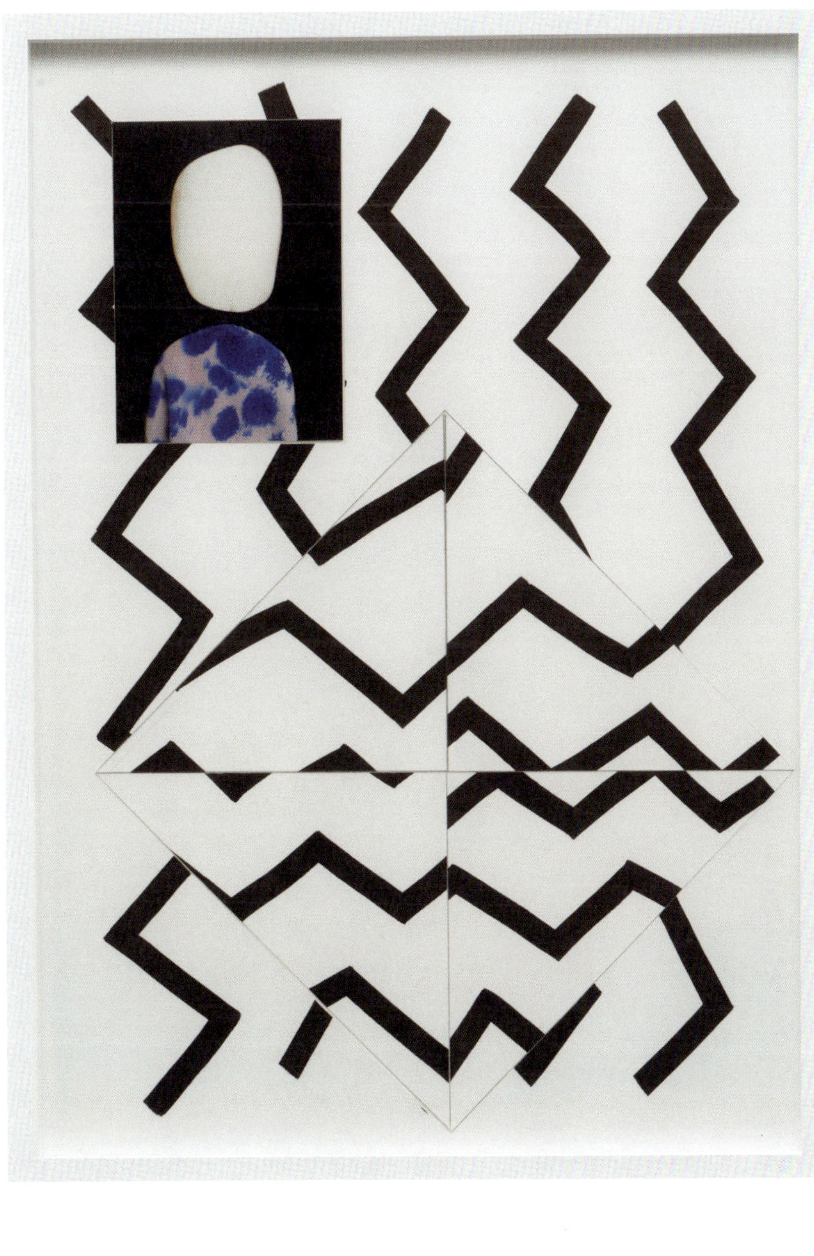

DR: Earlier today we went for lunch at Valois (a landmark diner in South Chicago), and you said something that I'm curious about: you like food shows on television. Maybe it's that you watch those things for entertainment's sake, to relax. But I feel like there is something about your work that is a little bit gastronomical. *The Bakery of Blok*, for instance, along with the other works you've made with dough... a lot of your more recent work is a departure from this, but there is something about it that reminds me of digestion.

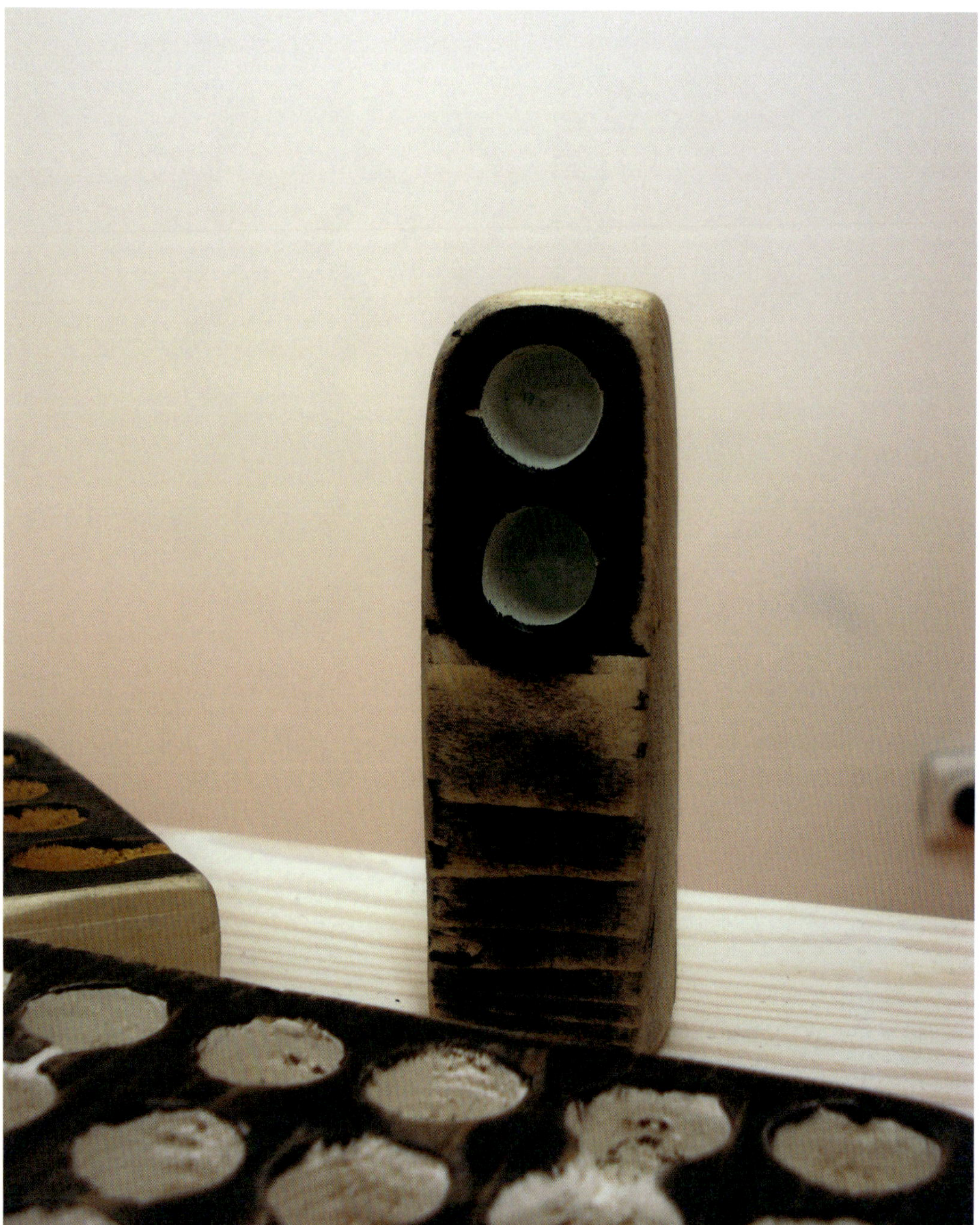

ZT: I see a show about cooking as using one thing to navigate another. You always need to eat, just as you always need to brush your teeth, no matter where you are in the world. These common chores have to be done like a routine, that's a reality. They also change, they have this ability to represent the difference that's present in an environment—you get to access a story. Formally, if we look at a recipe, it's a dish that comes from something; it's a narrative script for a series of ingredients: units going into a kind of statement, coming out as a flavour. You can talk about a time and place, of people cooking and baking, and then you can look at how that changes over time, through the centuries, or, how it doesn't. [...]

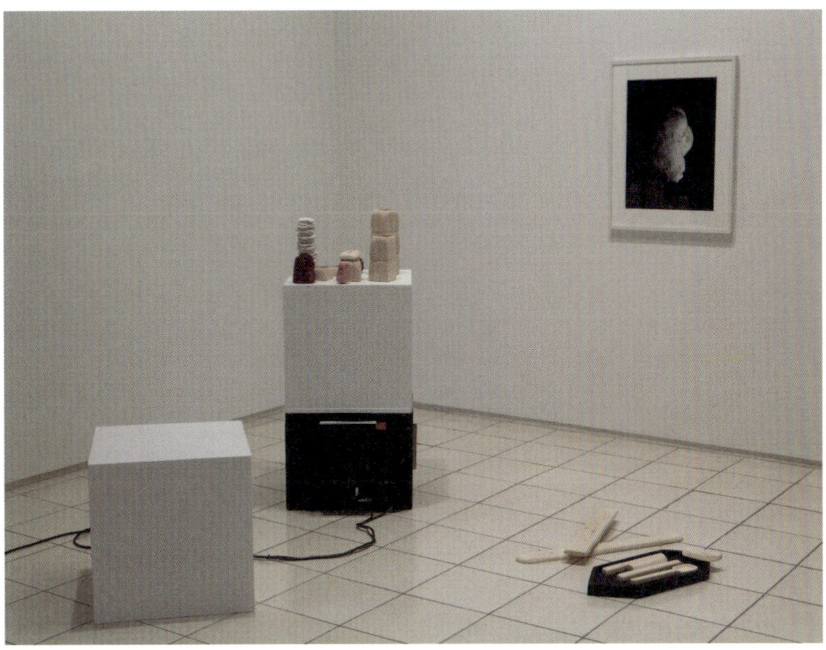

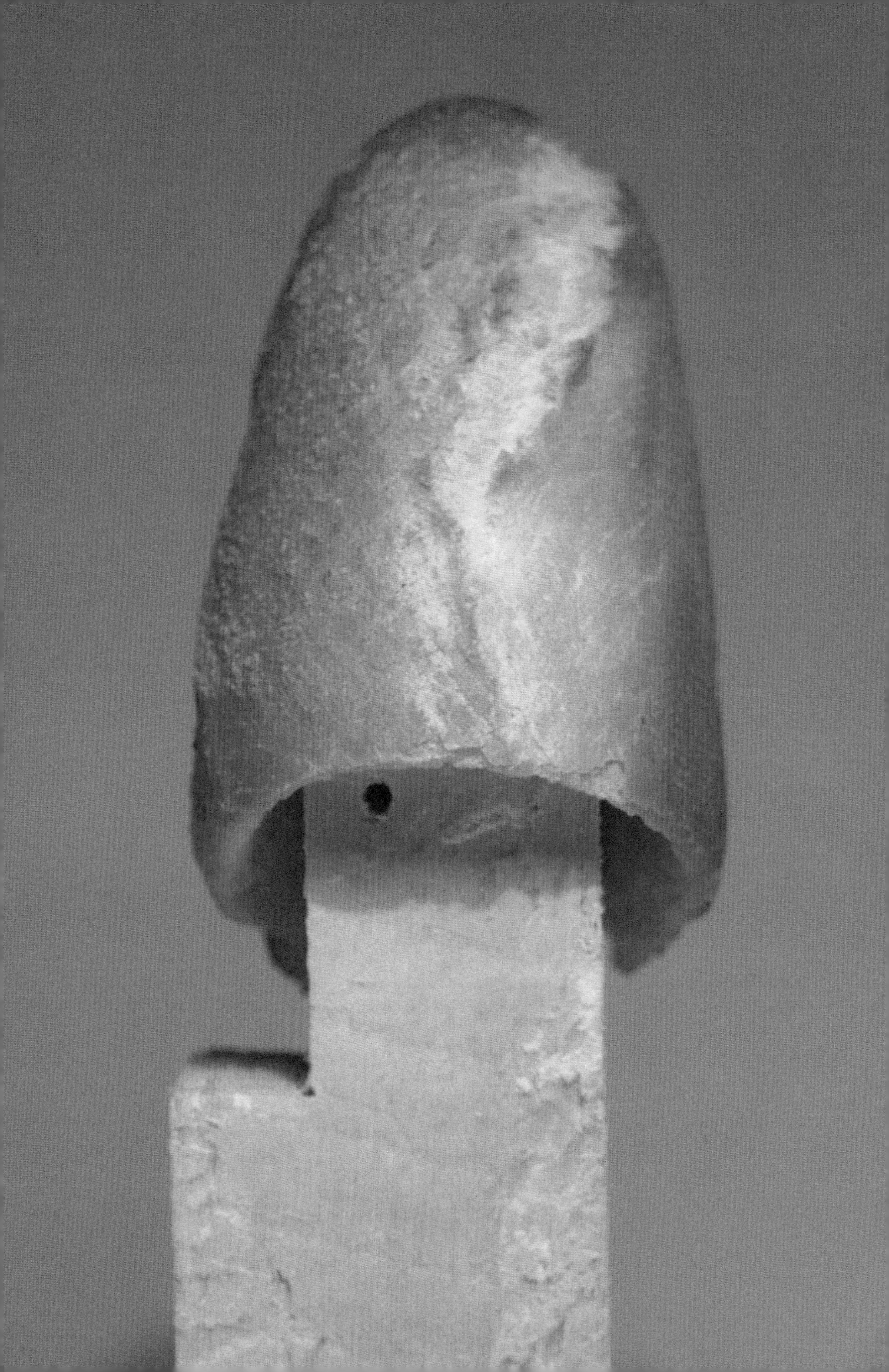

The Bakery of Blok came out of a similar approach. There was a formal background of the unit, the standardized unit of a French loaf, the prescribed amount of ingredients that went into making one. I think it was the Napoleonic era that introduced a set standard for all the bakeries in France. Part of this was an argument for the people, that everyone could have access to this unit of nutrition. As a result, bakeries represented a little moment within a community where people came together, picked up their units, and went back to their lives—there was an intersection between an object and a person.

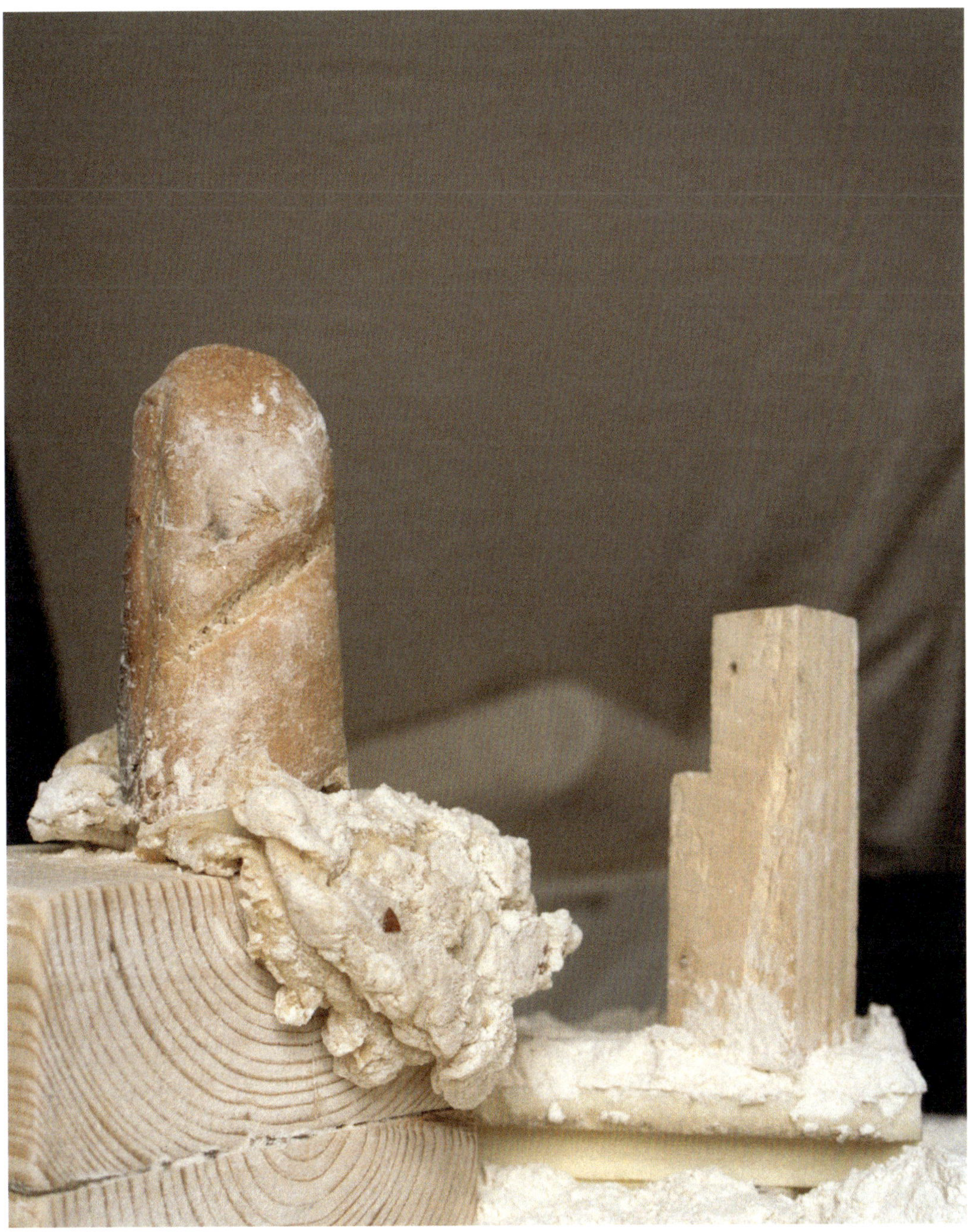

DR: There is something in your work, or what you do, that seems to revel in a certain kind of rudimentary primitivism. There is something quite crude about the things you make in a way, they aren't glossy.

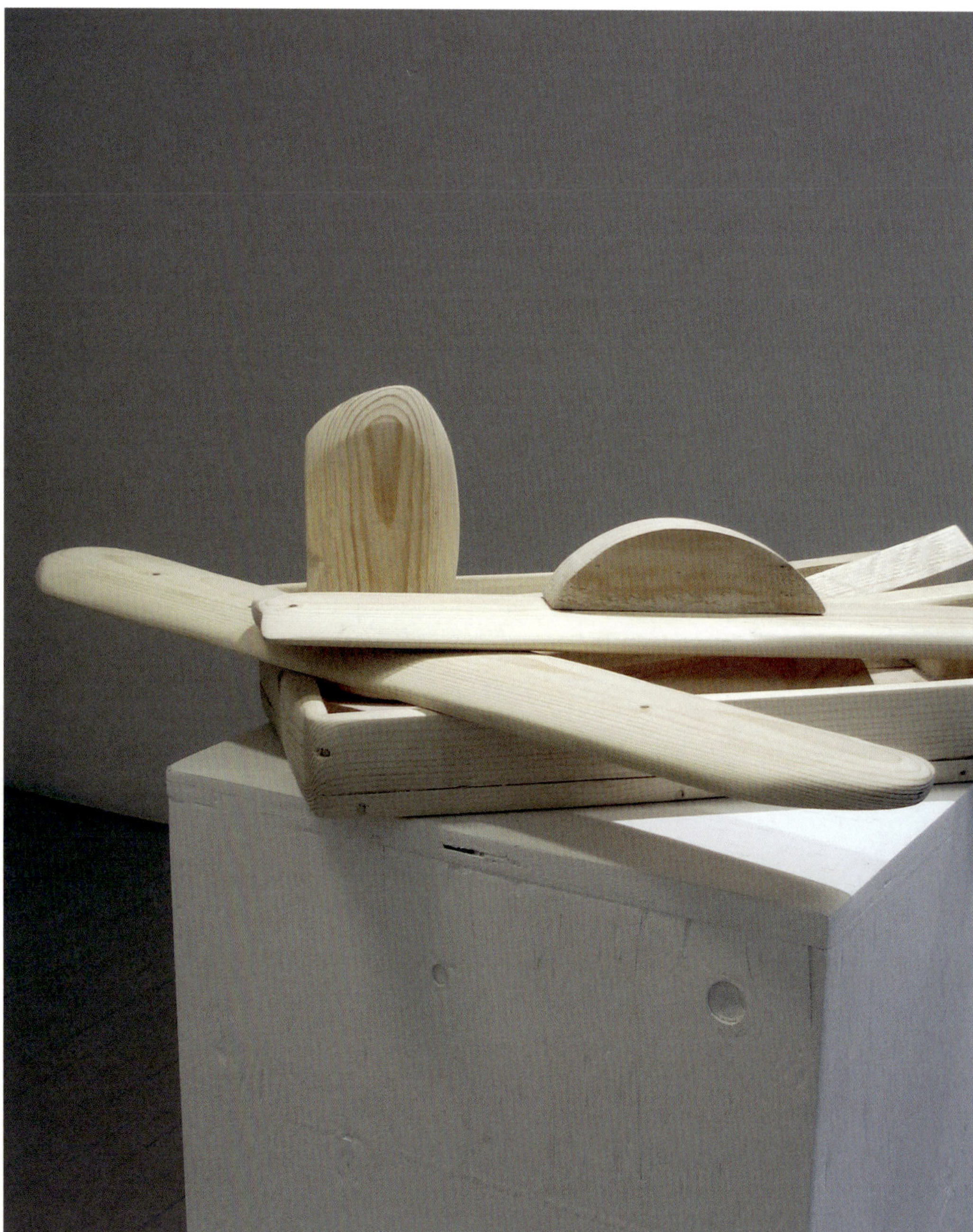

ZT: As a way of communicating that anyone can do this, I try to keep it simple. Maybe that addresses the crudeness you observe. It's why I avoid fabrication and what you identified as the "glossy." I have an interest in those vernacular forms, those things that talk about people doing things. It's a way of working and a way of looking at information as a kind of material to make with. Like food on a plate—how are you going to arrange that sustenance? The thing about food is that potentially, with a little practice, anyone can grow it. Or if that fails, you can go to a grocery store, which can be seen as a giant library of material where little bits of information are selected to construct something that you can now use for your unit/body, for your form. It helps fuel the form in order to produce something else.

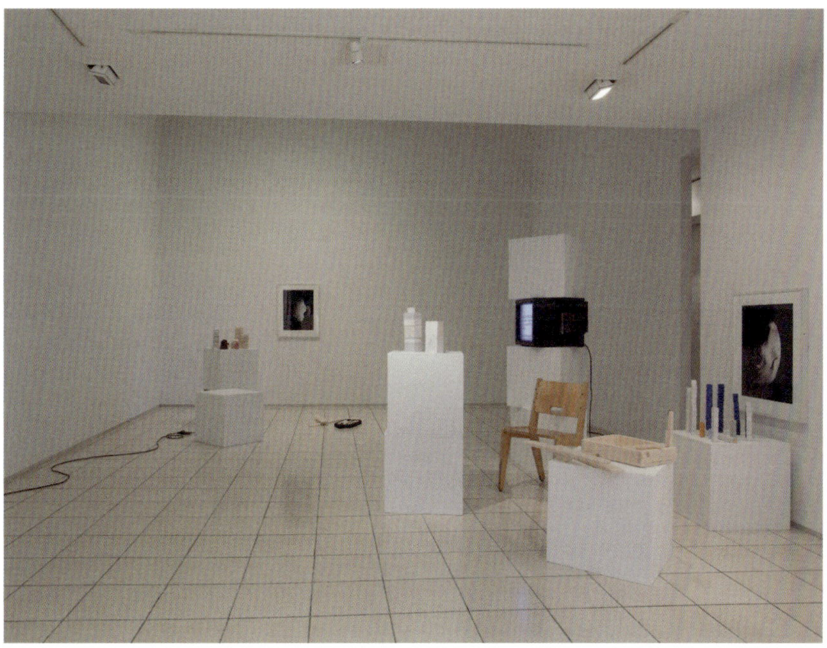

DR: You said something about fabrication. You do things yourself, you want to know how things work. You like making it yourself. However, scale is important in your work. Some things are bigger than people, although not much, and there is an anthropomorphic dimension to what you do, life-size as in people-size.

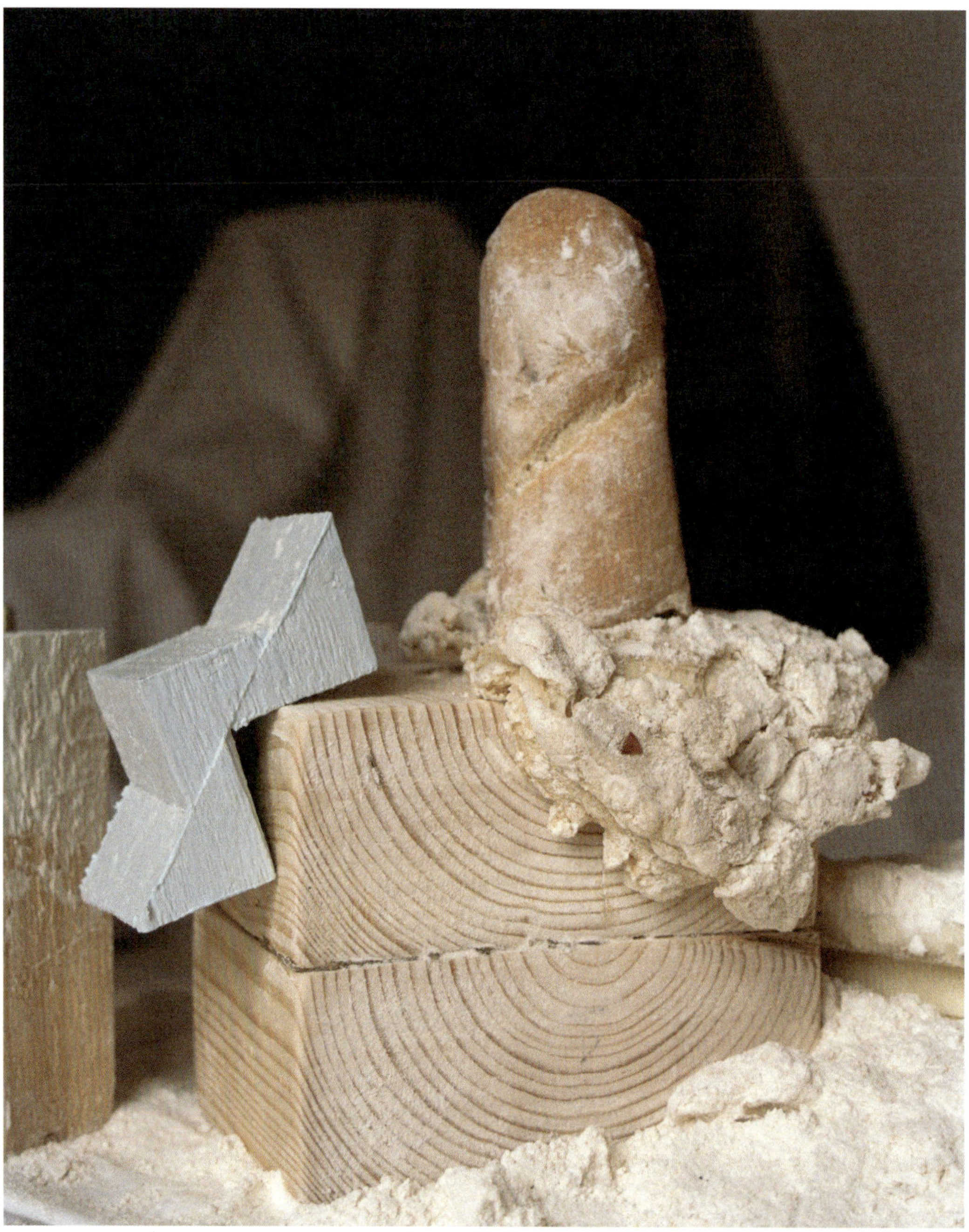

ZT: The anthropomorphic scale is about locating you (the viewer) into an active position with another form, where the form is a thought, but on equal scale. It's the one-to-one thing. I associate miniaturization or enlargement with bad fiction, a version of forced theatricality. For example, when I make a sculpture of a knife, it's a life-size knife. The form is trying to be that word "knife." With *The Bakery of Blok*, when I made the baking instruments, these were meant to be used; the weights, tools and containers could be all be employed, and were employed, for the process of baking bread. [...]

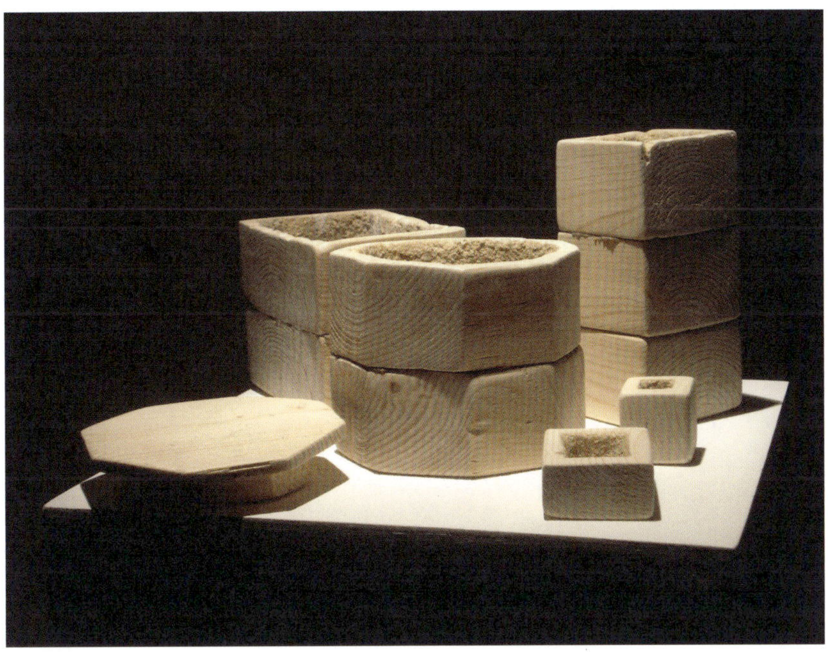

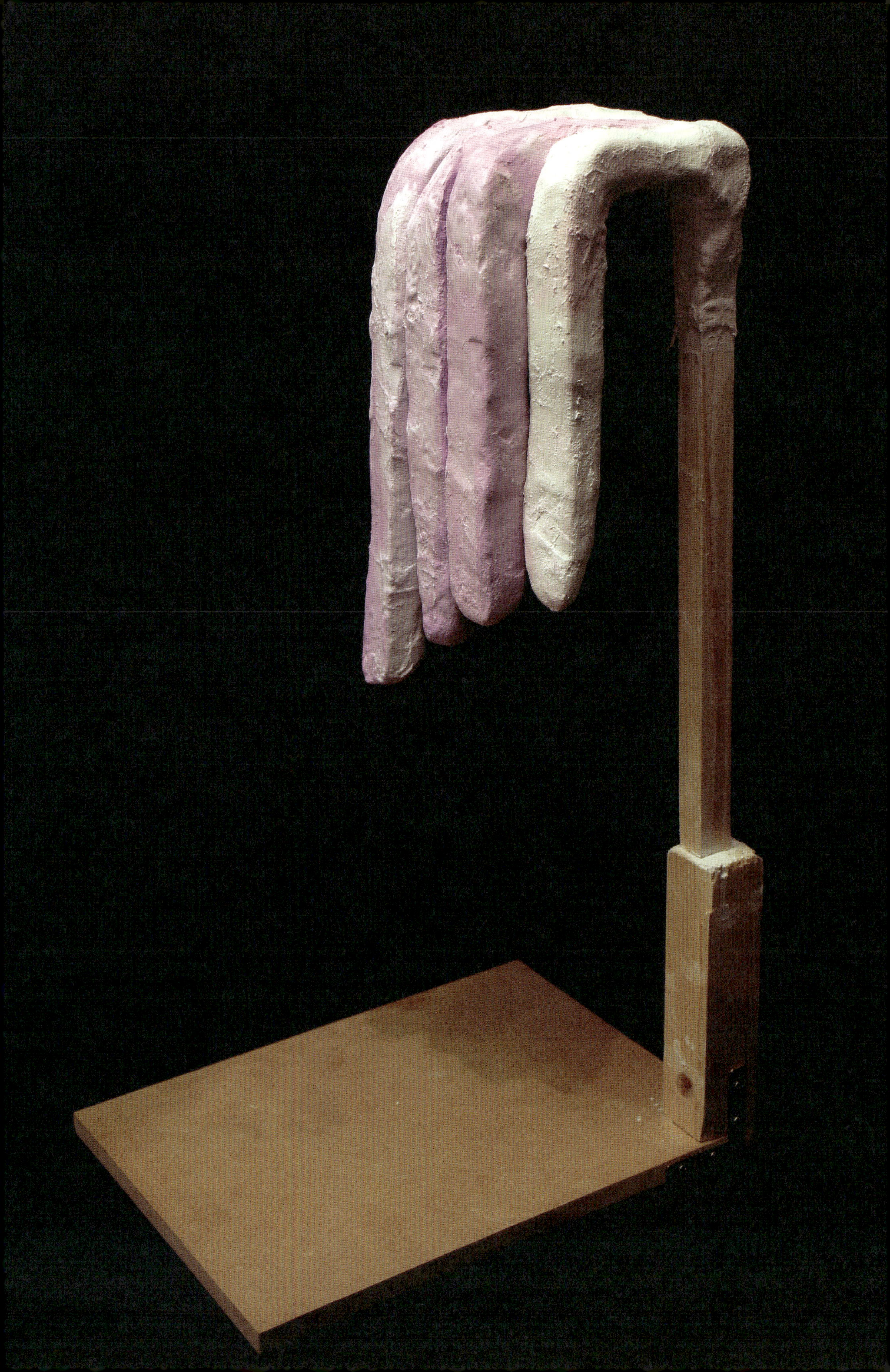

With *The Flute of Sub*, the flute had to be scaled appropriately because it had to be played. This impulse of the one-to-one is part of creating these moments that intersect a reality with a proposed narrative difference. It's too easy to blow something up super huge and have that make an effect.

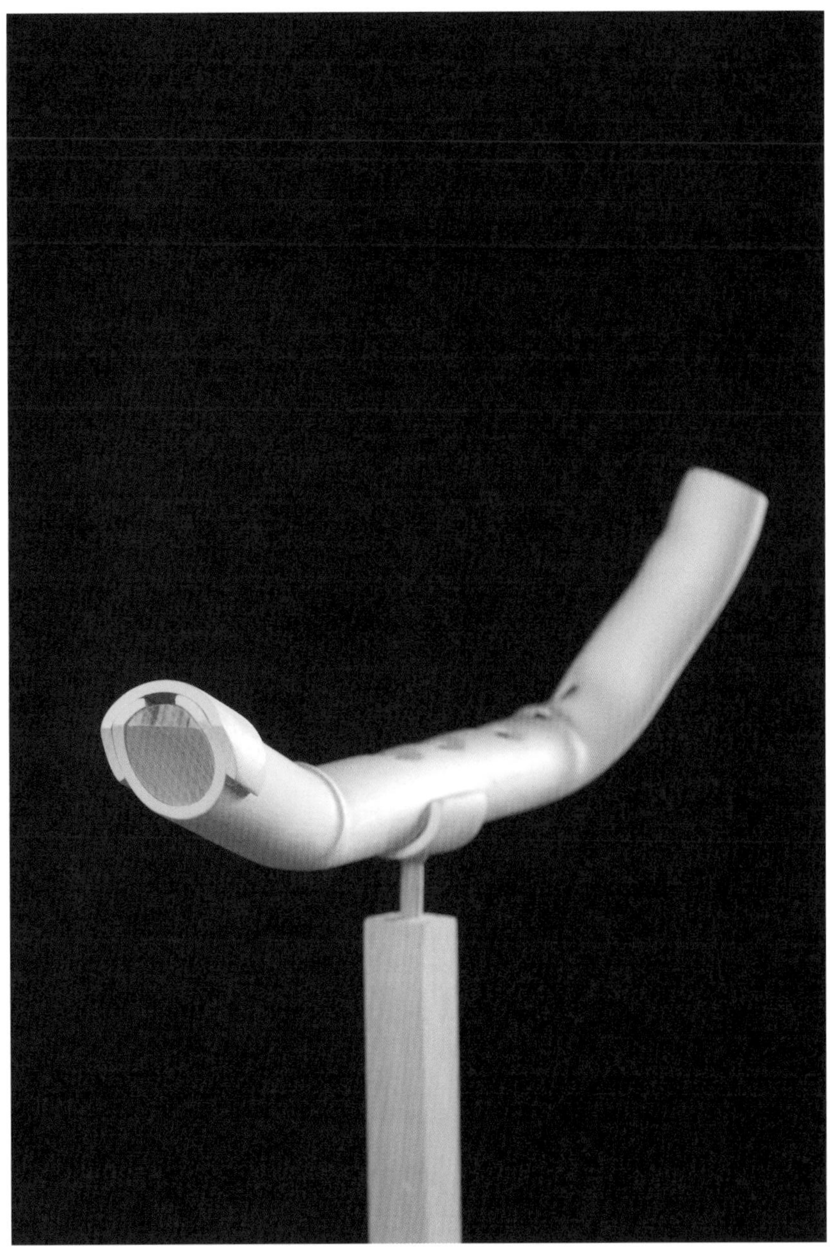

DR: Or make it tiny and precious.

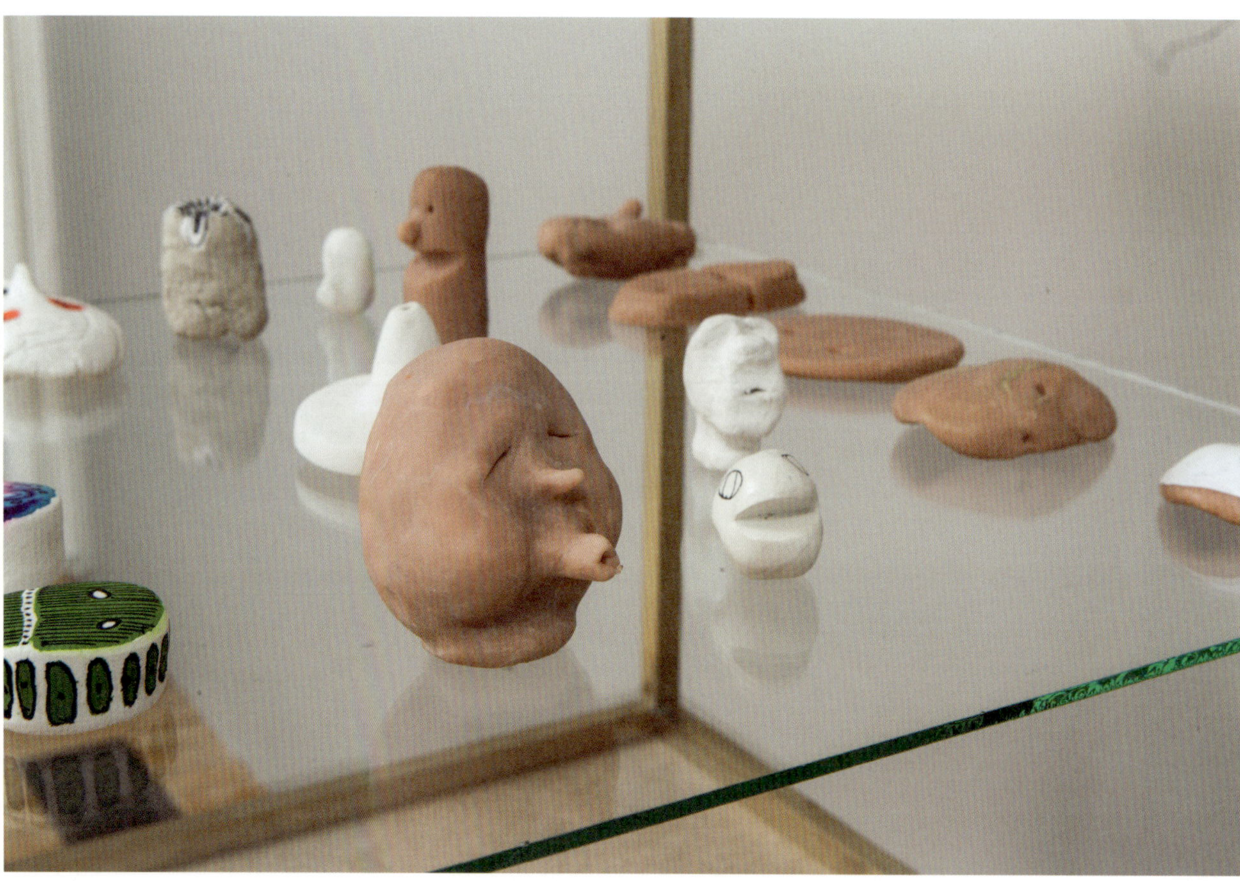

ZT: It's too "spectacle"; I would rather have it just exist.

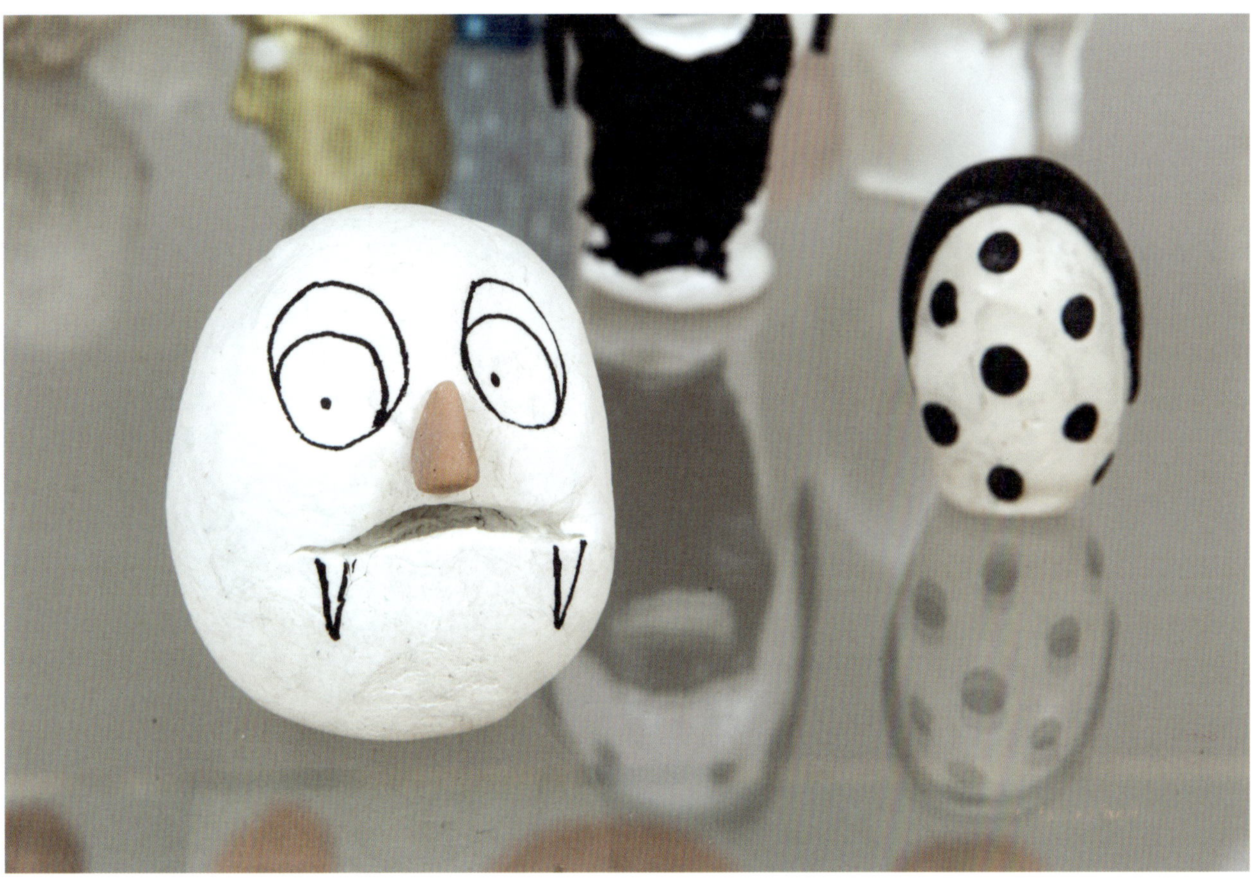

DR: So use value is something big for you?

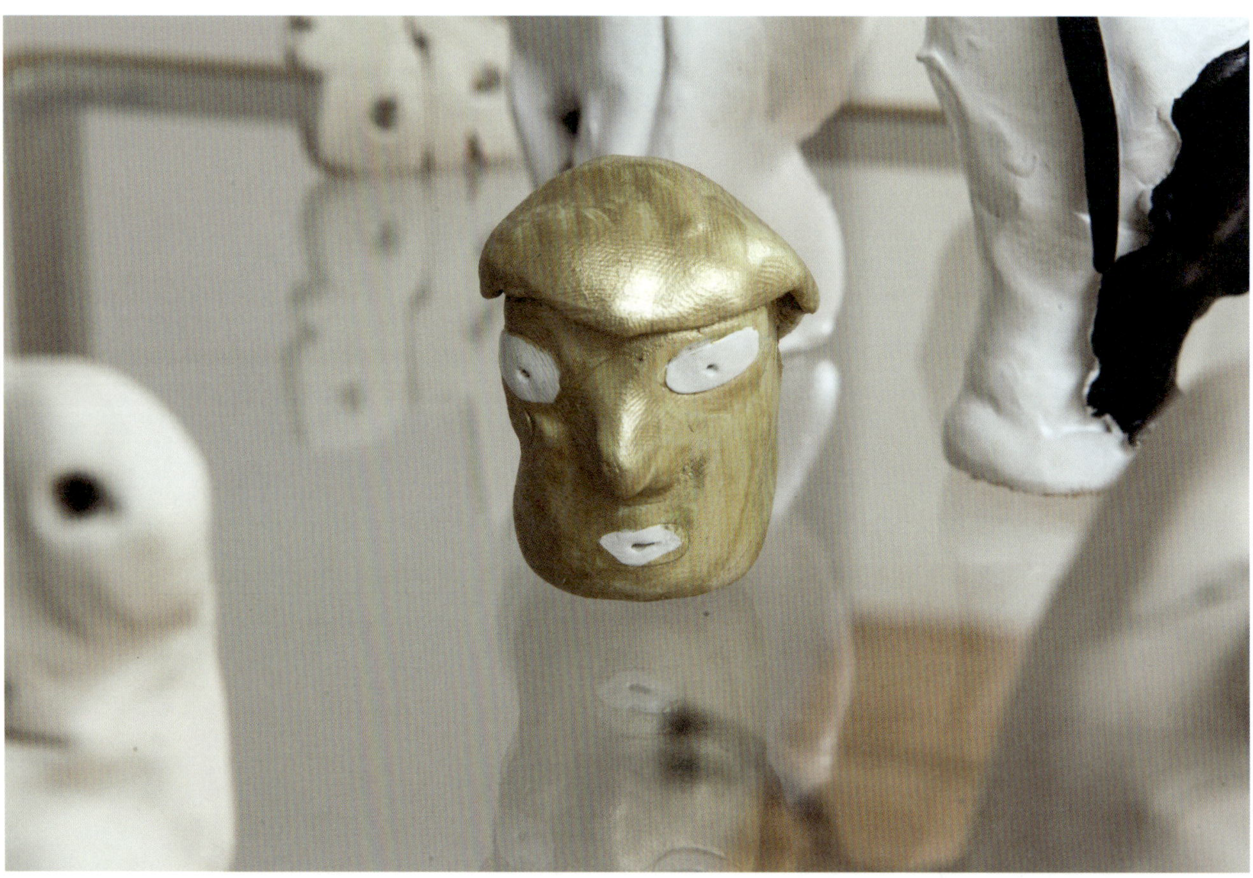

ZT: Indeed, some sort of latent working class thing. That's why I do books, small books that are cheap, that people can buy for a few euros.

Fluxus was renowned for their approach to the multiple, it came out of a real movement to make art affordable and accessible. Popular forms of production were used particularly because anyone could access them. Xerox-printed zines in the '80s and '90s was how subcultures reproduced themselves, just by using a serial production machine. You could do a zine for twenty dollars and make fifty copies at Kinkos, you could put that idea out there, that was your manifesto, that was your thing. But if you have to come up with 10,000 dollars to print that manifesto, it's going to be a different kind of manifesto from a different kind of person because, economically, not everyone can do that.

I used to shoot video a lot, I print photos using walk-in photo labs—I like the simple stuff. This crudeness you talk of is part of that. Waking up and making an idea with what is readily available, so that the material is reflexive to what your brain wants to develop. Those Donald Judd boxes, the really early ones made from plywood, are way more fun to look at than his later work because they seem like ideas that appeared from the environment, as if he had an idea and then went out and made it that afternoon. When Judd's boxes get fabricated in metal and plexi, the formal presence of the object/concept travels toward a different realm, away from that idea-area of the initial proposition.

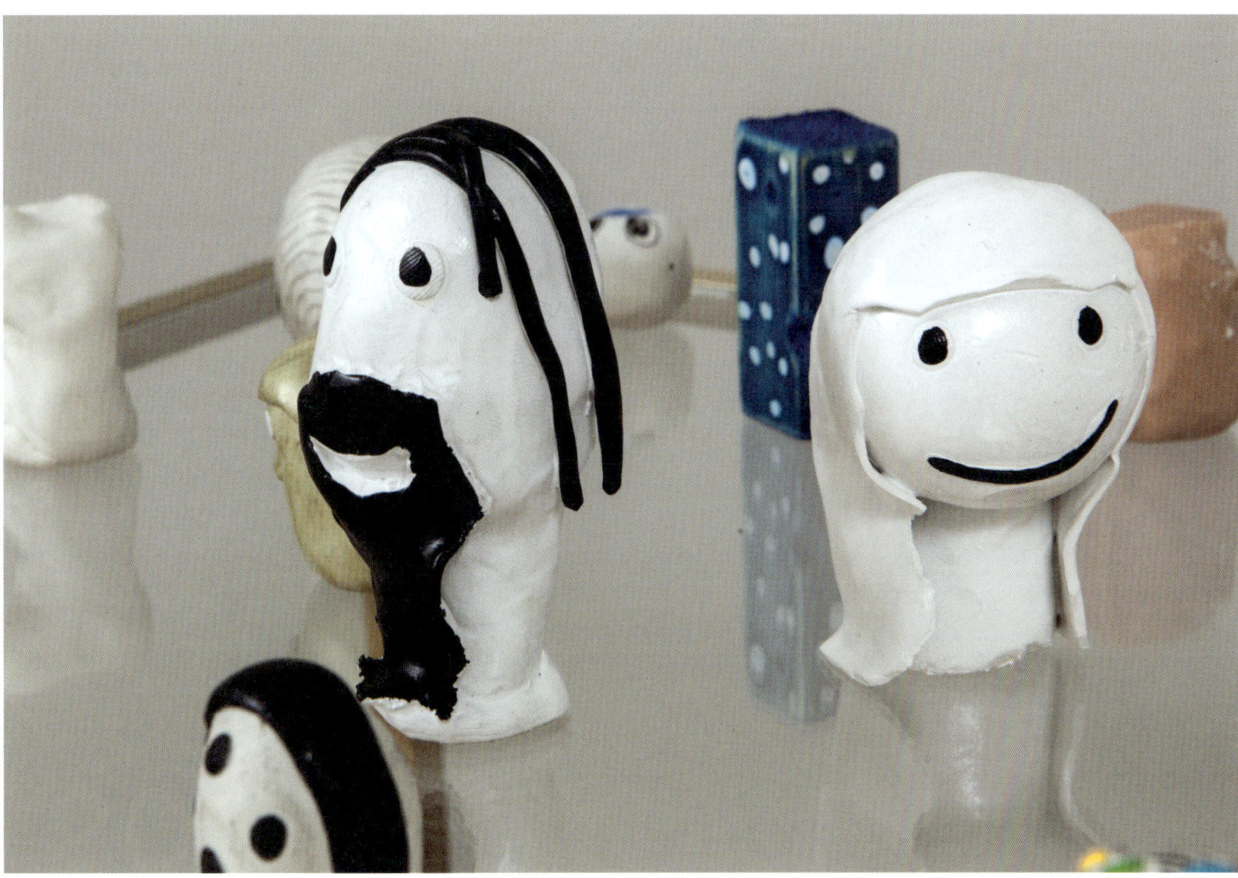

DR: I never really thought about that particular economic dimension of your work, and that being the grounding for your investment in these slightly poor materials.

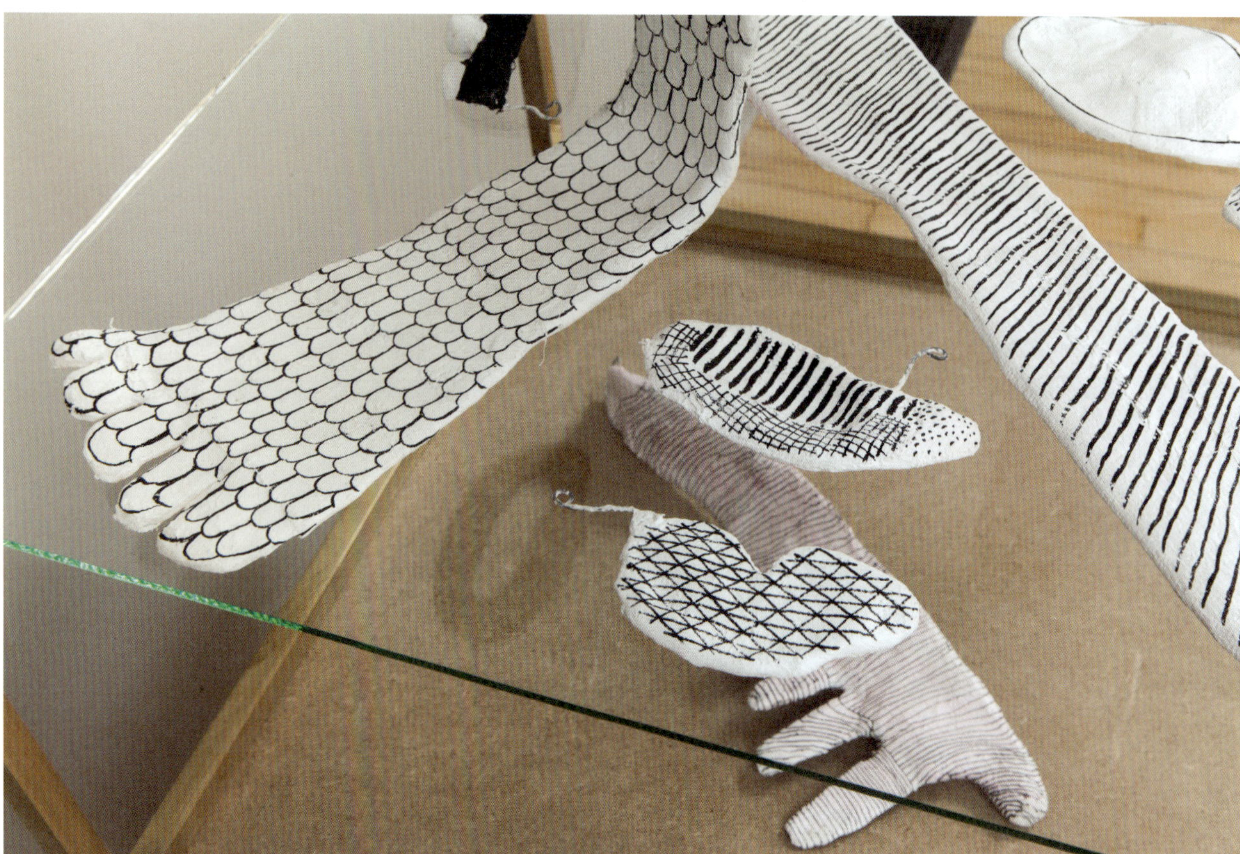

ZT: It's the fact that I could go to a hardware store and pick up a unit, an always standardized unit of material, and make something out of it. The same material is augmented through authorial use to introduce a dialogue. If I use plywood to make a box, the same kind of plywood Judd used, my intent comes out differently, it influences that form. That's the part that every individual can have complete control over, that's the vernacular. When getting into fabrication you're using someone else's language to produce your own idea.

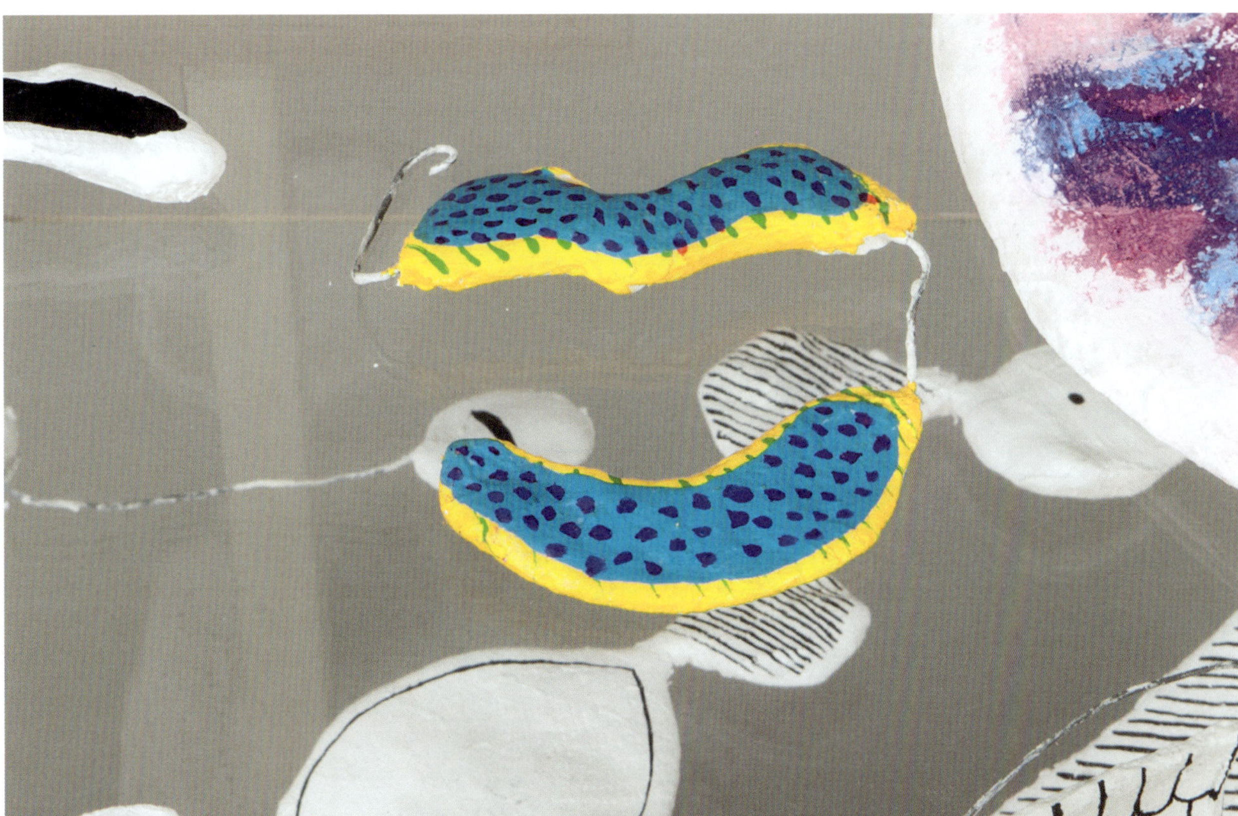

DR: That can be part of the idea, or the point of the work. If fracture, production, making something, expressing, articulating, if all those things are essential to the artistic project, then it becomes an issue. With *The Bakery of Blok*, *The Story of Stripes and Dots*, *Palms of the Fog*, are you making one work? Are you writing different chapters of one book? [...]

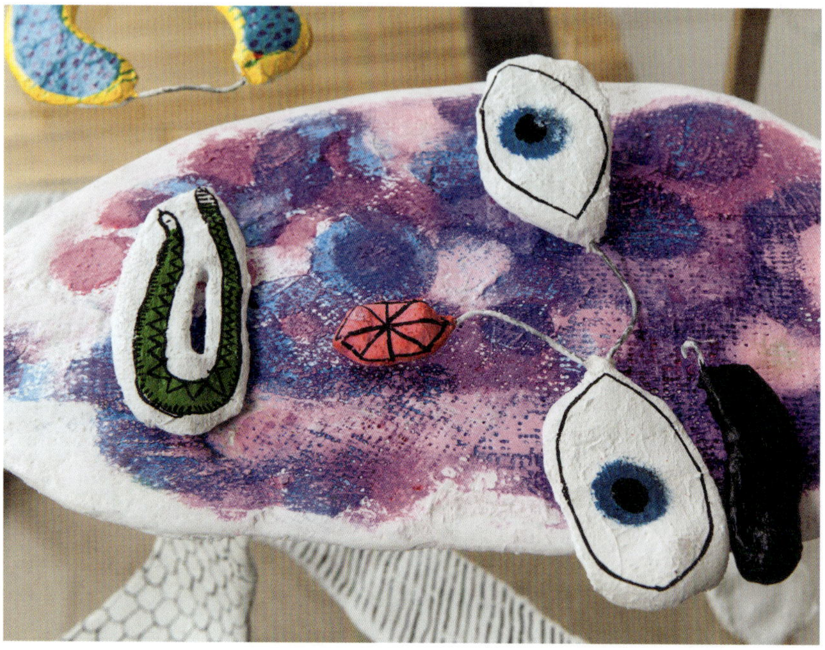

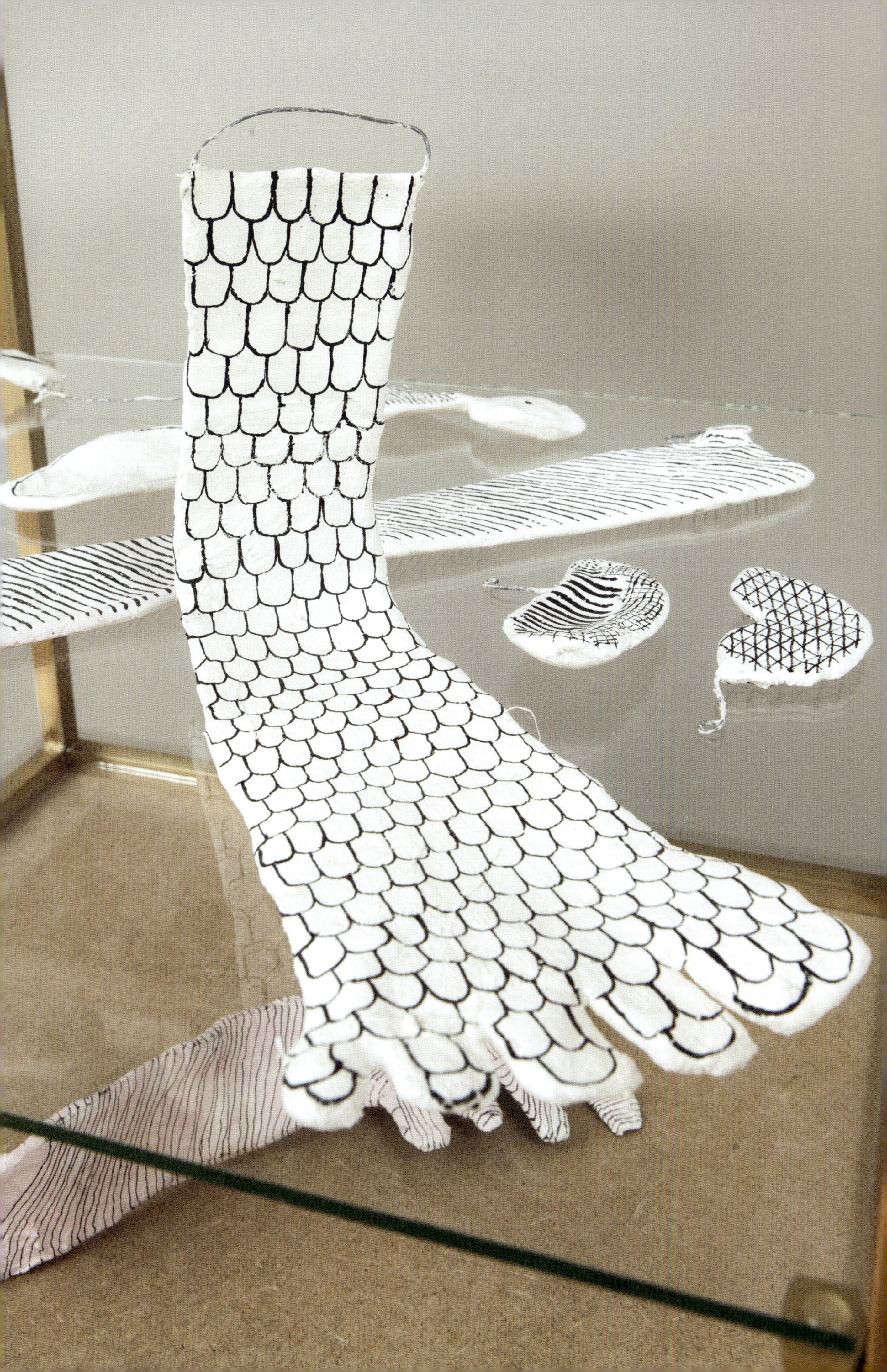

For a number of years now your research has really centred on one thing. I'm curious about how a project is born, how a show is born, because it looks to me like you don't really think in terms of one work. To me, it looks like you think in terms of a body of work, an ensemble, like a family. [...]

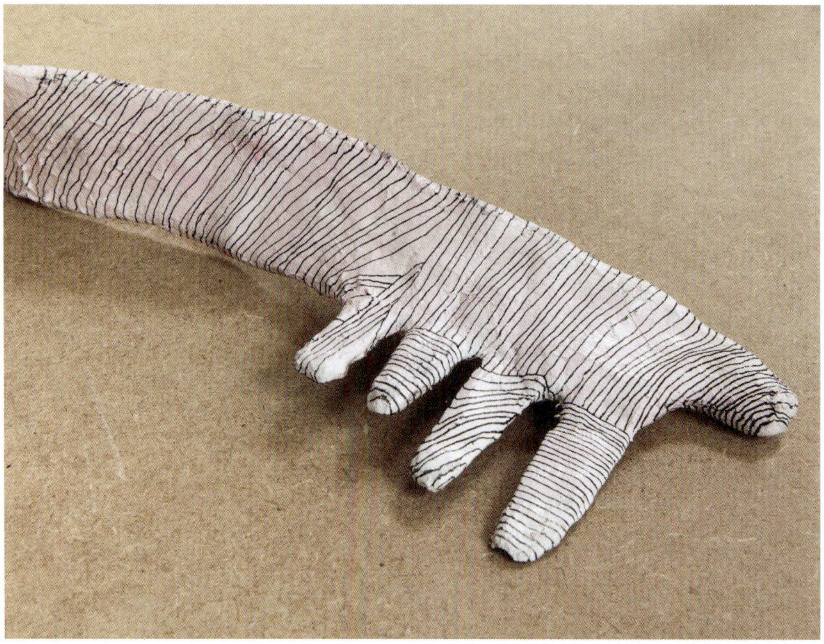

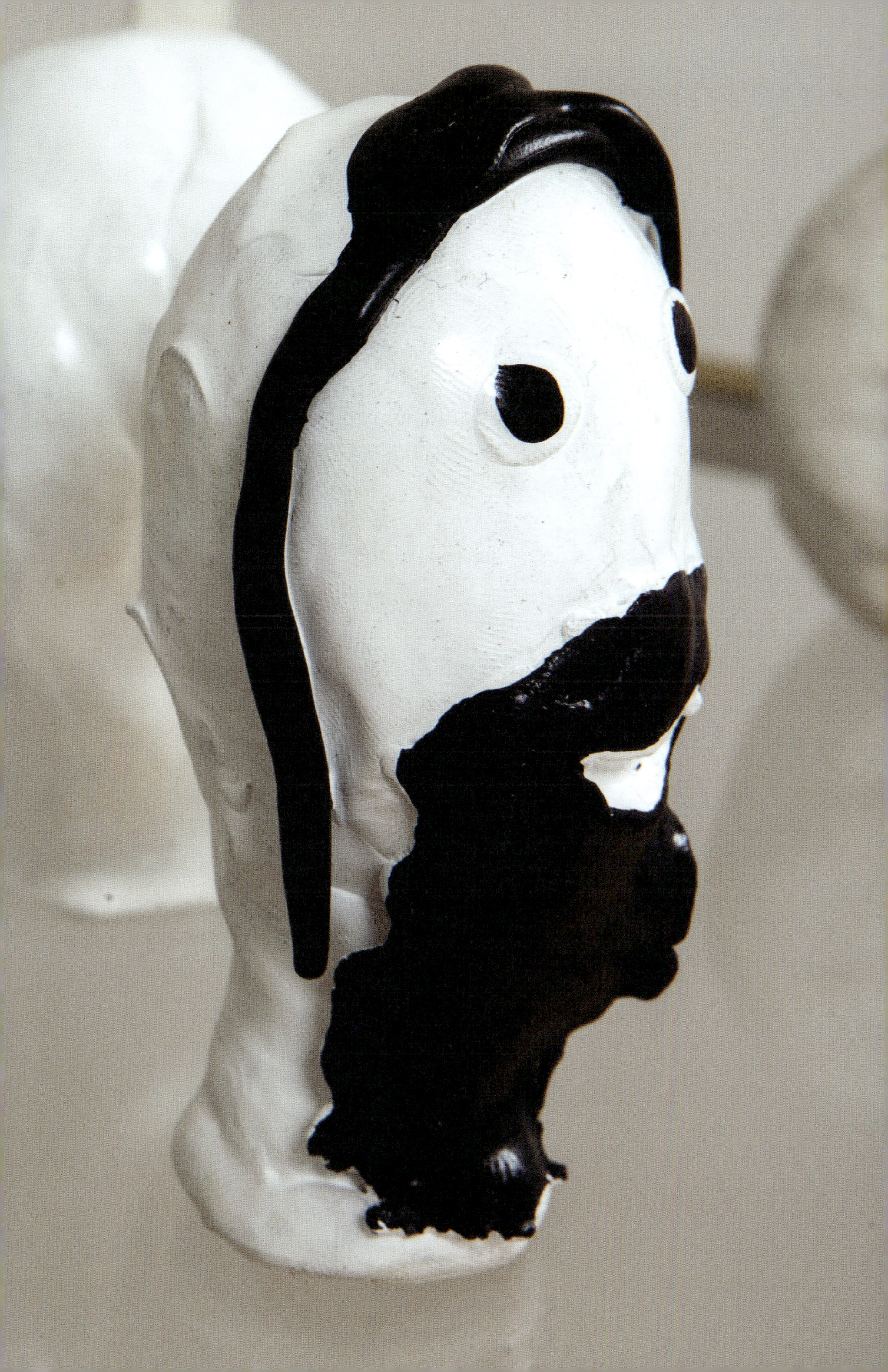

They exist in groups, series, but like a little universe. All of those little universes that I know, they all seem to circle around this one question, and so I wonder how something starts. How do you begin?

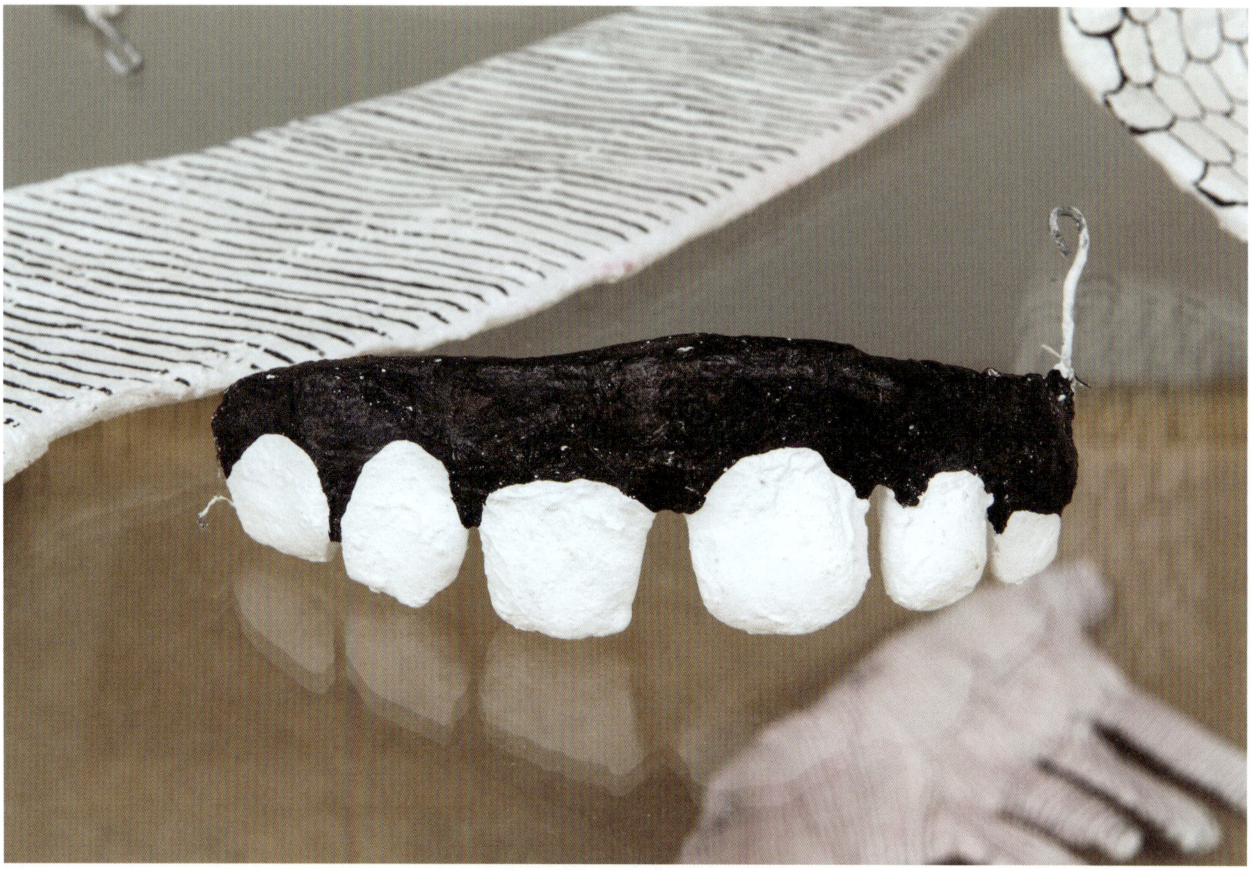

ZT: I start with my thoughts about a subject. I find a subject and I think about it. A lot of the works I make come out of things I've been thinking about for years.

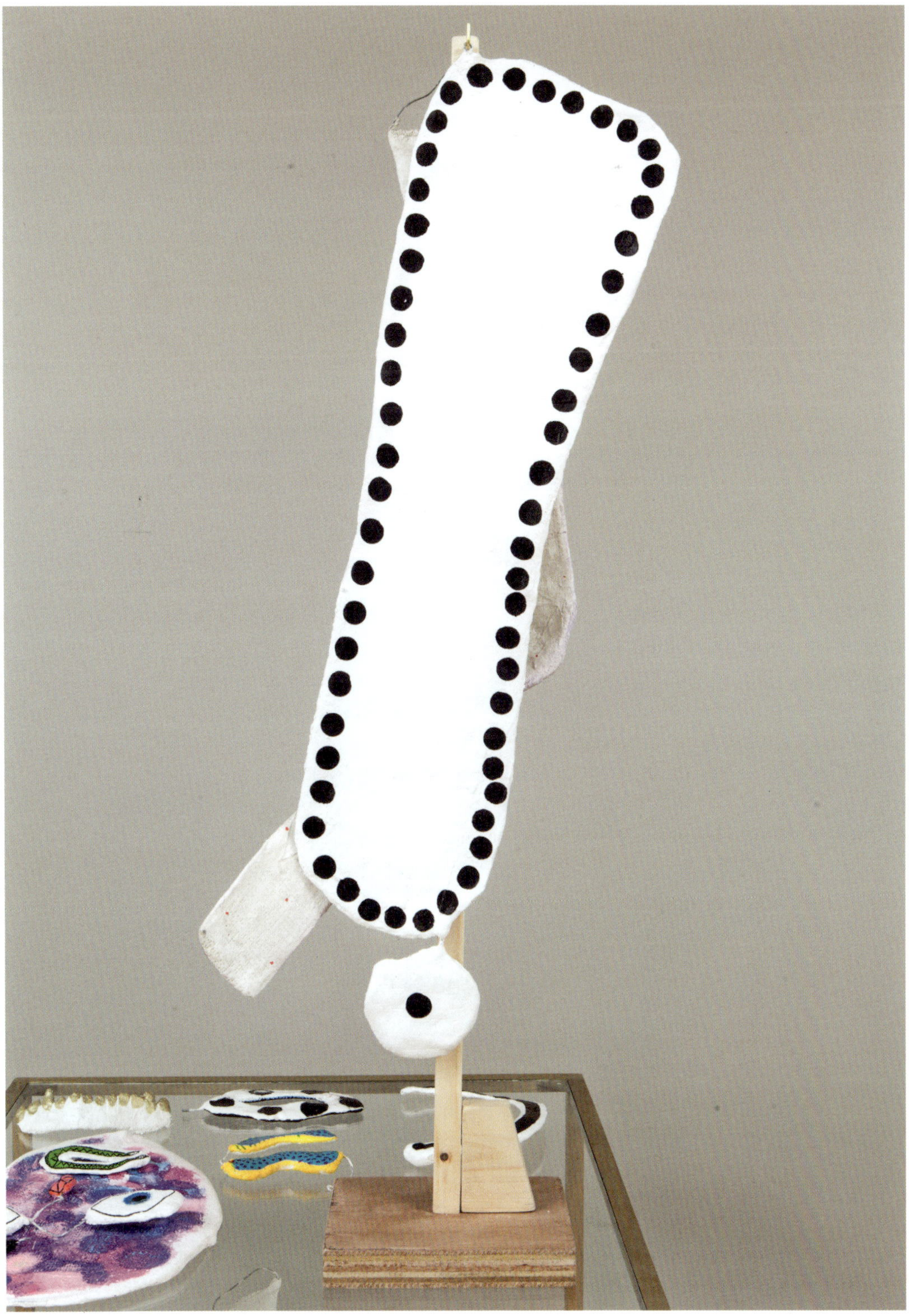

DR: They incubate.

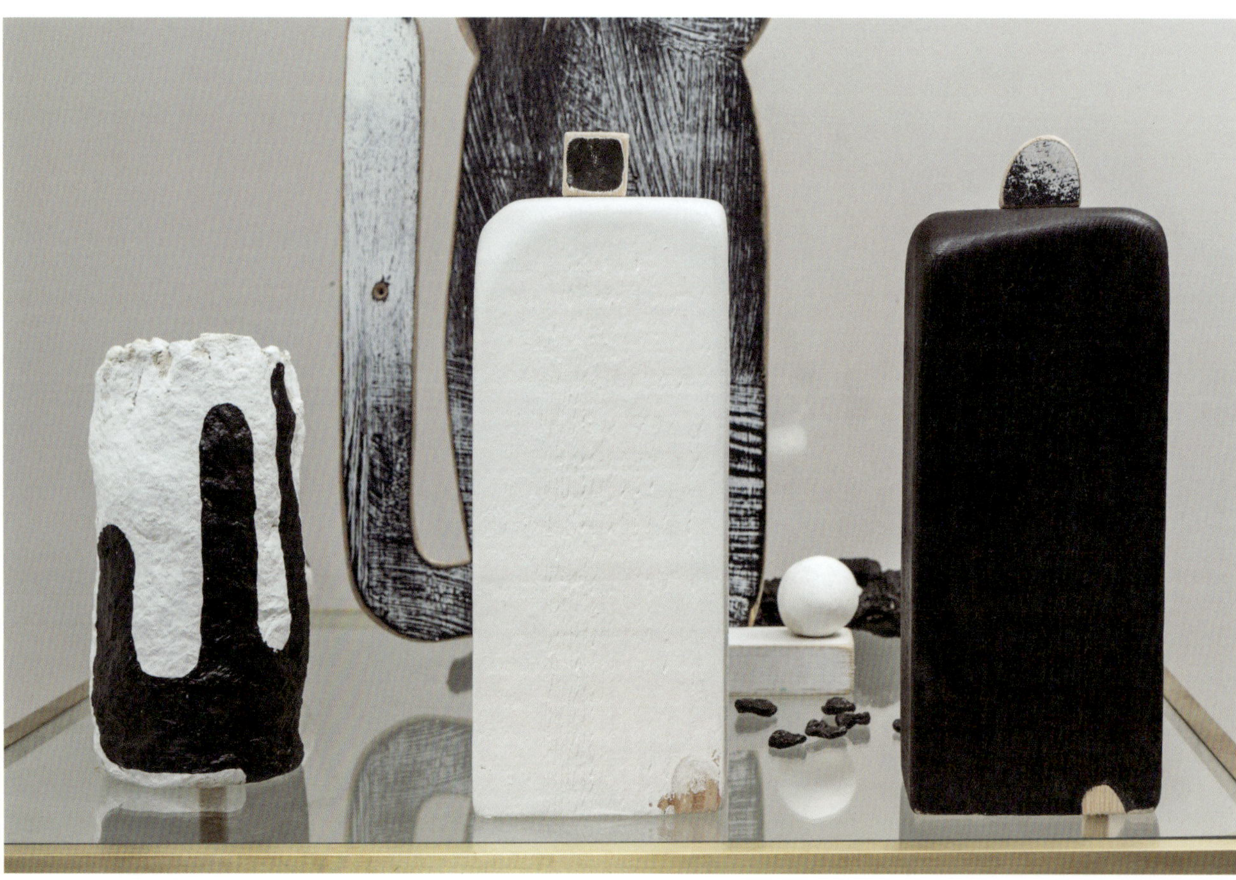

ZT: Thoughts run into others that I have during that time, slowly helping to edit themselves. I look at what needs to happen differently in order to move an idea forward, and then I make that. This process sets up an initial approach to looking at information. Because you're right, it is a kind of universe, a dictionary that I am trying to author. Which is why you can say that I talk about bread, or snakes, or zigzags, or stripes and dots, or an underground tunnel—these are all subjects that could be found within a dictionary or encyclopedia.

9 fingers of Malakoff

Things I observe above the ground are the result of a logic hidden below the ground.

This narrative is set within the French village of Malakoff, during a June afternoon, on a Sunday, in the year 2010. Departing Paris I arrived in Malakoff by Metro Subway. The station of Varenne can be found along this route, the stop garishly advertising access to the Musée Rodin; indicated monumentally by copies of the artist's sculpture arranged upon the Metro platform. I will visit this later.

Malakoff is a Parisian suburb 4.5 kilometers from the centre of Paris. In this village there is an art centre, La Maison des arts de Malakoff. The building is located within a sheltered garden that is accessible to visitors. Within this garden is a reflecting pool. The shape of the pool is a large teardrop, intersected from the front by a lazy circle that refuses to close; a geometric collision that houses a peculiar series of forms. At the rear of this pool are nine marble fingers, rectangularly cut, and placed within a diagonal grid of three by three.

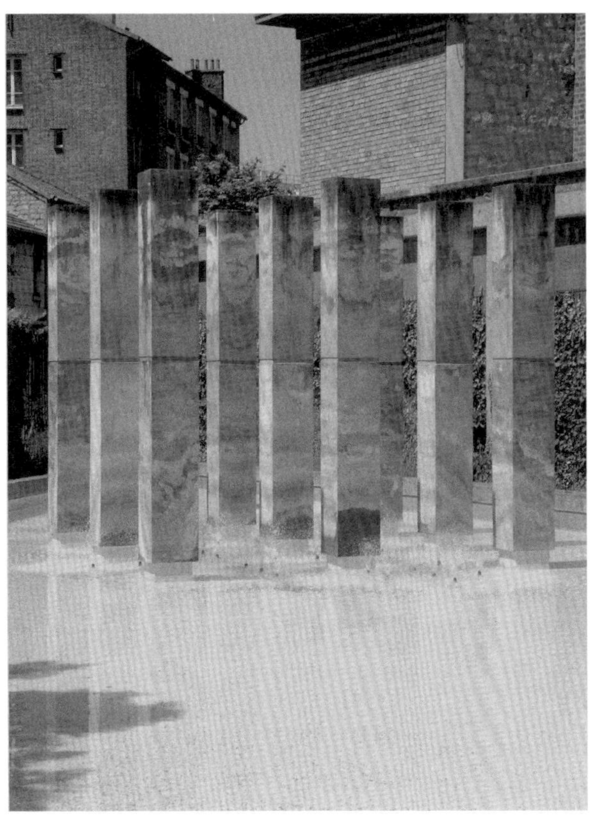

DR: But it's a dictionary of something, no? Of what? All of the things that you have just now said— snakes, tunnels, bread, stripes and dots—all of them cluster around one notion, or one overarching concern. So in that sense it is a dictionary, or an encyclopedia, of something, because it's not an encyclopedia of everything. The central concern seems to be the miracle of formation, of emergence, of shapes and forms and how things come into being, physically. For example, "units" is a word that you use so often.

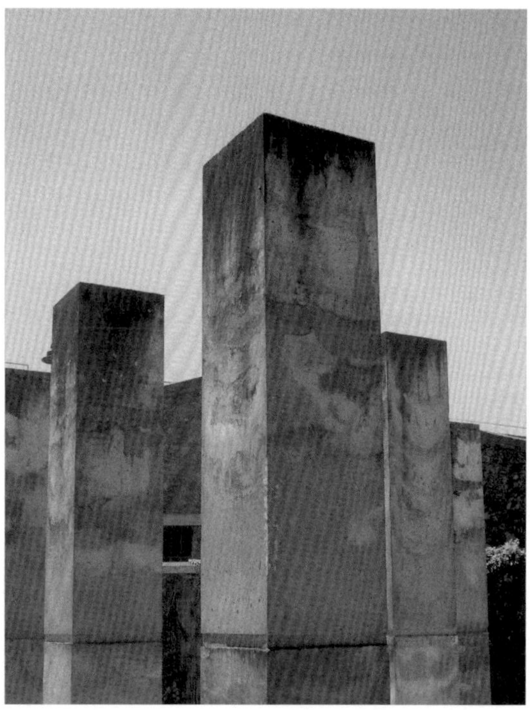

Each finger is made of two identically proportioned segments measuring180 cm tall, with four equal sides of 60 cm each. Green lichen tops each segment, a photosynthetic fade recording each form's presence in this location. At the rear of the pool is a hatch, a suggestive portal indicating an undergroun habitat hidden from sight.

As a visitor I cannot enter this portal.

Opening the hatch I descend beneath the pool. The two segments of marble above the ground are re-confirmed by a third segment below. A complete finger, a digit, one of nine, is presented.

Marble in its natural state presents a visual similarity to a Reservoir of Conversation. Watching the blend and fade of the material I imagine a liquid pool of pink and white communicating through color and tone as it flows underneath a layer of rock. Evolving through time, a series of fluid relationships embedded beneath the surface solidify when met by the air. The process of mining extracts sections of this evolved conversation for use elsewhere. Separated into units of value according to an external economy, the once fluid subject of the marble's form is edited into objects akin to obscure gestural statements. Flooring, counter tops, rolling pins, and public sculpture are examples of marble's economy of use.

The nine marble fingers at Malakoff are from a related quarry. While existing individually these forms reference a collaborative origin through striations of pink and white. Similar to a mythological Hydra, the individual lengths share a common origin while acting of independent accord. Agreement and collaboration met with obtuse discord, collectively observed across the colored veins of this material. The third segment of this marble digit projects the origin of a hand. A nine fingered giant buried deep within this Parisian suburb.

Nestled in the palm, I look upon these nine fingers. Three identical units, four sides of 60 centimeters in width and 180 centimeters tall, create a form I now think of as a digit: a unit of measurement derived from an organic reference.

Throughout time communities have introduced units of measurement to accurately record value. Communal standardization of weight, length, and time ensured abstract representation moved from an individual's logic towards collective agreement. Buildings could be erected through divisions of labor, goods traded accurately, and monetary value preserved and controlled once standards for value were implemented.

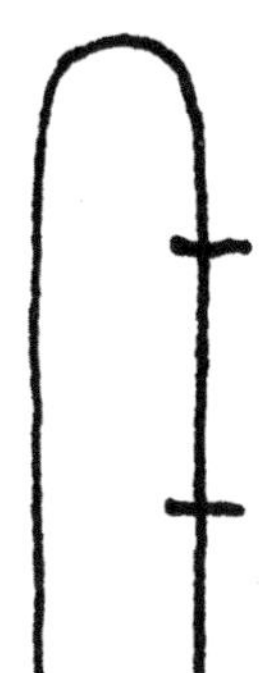

Ancient rules of measurement originating in the Indus Valley dating from the 4th and 3rd millennia BC develop standardized measurements within the body and the environment. Time was recorded using the sun, moon, and stars. Lengths were measured using the forearm, hand and finger. Measurements correlating to the finger register as 1 3/8 inches, or 3.4925 centimeters. Residents of the Indus Valley found the measurement of 1 3/8" to be incrementally distributed over the human body. A finger's segment represented an Inch, then referred to as an Angula. A unit of measure 24 Angula's (33 inches long) is called a Hasta, Kishku or Muzam. Calculated weight was controlled using elements from the environment. The carob seed was popularity used because of its consistent weight and size, its "unitness". The measurement of the carob evolved into that of the carat. The carat is now used exclusively to calculate weight for gemstones and pearls.

ZT: You can put a unit in your pocket—a unit of time, of information, of abstraction. This could be about making the incomprehensible, comprehensible, in order for it to be worked with on a human scale. Part of my anxiety is that, maybe, the work really isn't about anything.

Civilizations emerged through time to introduce differing standards for measurement. The larger and more influential a ruling nation was, the more widespread that system of measurement was used. New rules of measurement were adopted echoing the influence of an individual ruler. The language of a daily economy was determined by this individual's influence then imbedded within architecture, time, and trade. Popular mythology relates the creation of units for measurement such as the inch, foot, and yard to that of an Emperor or King's thumb, foot, and arm.

Contemporaneously, a movement away from the individual towards the thoroughly abstract concept of The Institution is signified with the introduction of standardized measurements to replace those established by a ruling class. A foot one year, was not a foot the next. Now, a foot is just a foot. These organic analogs for measurement describe the practice of Anthropic units: a process of procuring measurement using the human body as the index. The use of the hand during Medieval-times was a popular reduction of unitary reference. One finger length was the width of a palm. A hand was slightly larger.

Auguste Rodin (1840-1917) was, amongst other things, a collector of hands. He had drawers of them. Cast hands, sculpted hands. The last work made before his death was a cast of his own two appendages.

Rodin, describing his sculpture as "Form giving rise to the idea" developed an idiosyncratic approach to constructing sculptural narrative through the assemblage of human body parts. Called Marcottage, Rodin and his assistants would cast numerous gestures of hands, feet, arms, torsos, etc... to be interchangeably layered for the building of figurative monument. A hand for one sculpture would be recycled into that of another. Rodin's unitizing of representational form to construct his sculptures, to arrange his narratives, acknowledges a self-established system of trade used internally to address the construction of narrative utilizing an individual vocabulary of form. Rodin's atelier shelves contained multiple versions of every body part and were arranged according to type. Finished sculptures were cast and then dissected to capture the gestures these contained for addition to his library. The more Rodin made, the more he had to draw upon. Gestures attributed to specific narratives were isolated. This approach developed a cosmology of Rodinian language with which to address a subject. His thoughts about a subject were conveyed using a material alphabet of his own design. Not only did "Form give rise to the idea", it conveniently supplied the alphabet to spell it out.

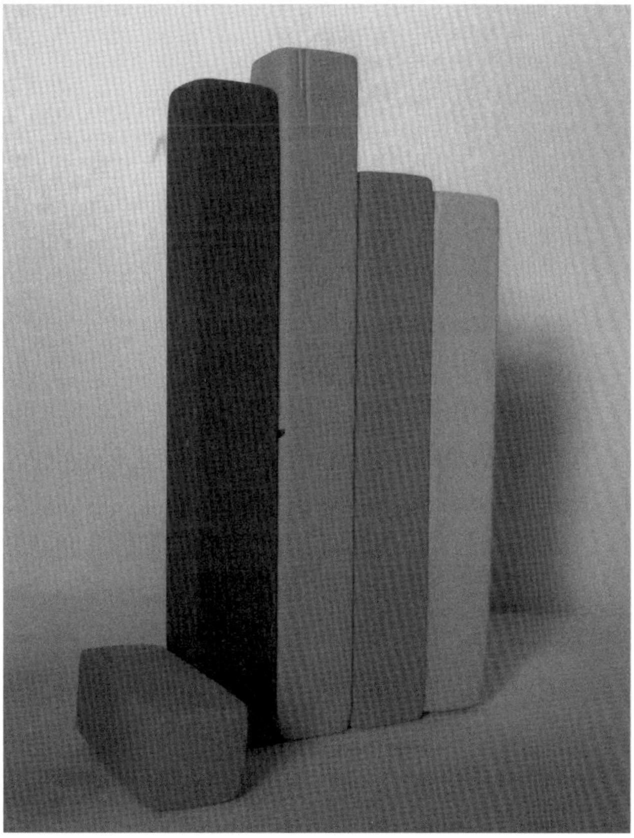

Returning to my seat on the Paris Metro, I'm arriving at the station of Varenne.

The platform of this metro station is flanked on either side by tracks of opposing direction. Amongst advertisements for consumer products there are placed signs of Rodin's cosmology of representation achieved through an acknowledgement of narrative within a material. Standing within this middle zone I am confronted with two, and three, meter tall versions of Rodin's language, an object advertising an ideology located elsewhere. I'm looking at The Thinker. The sculptures are displayed alongside advertisements for consumer products and services. Signs are located at a point of transition when a passenger decides where the next destination would, or could, be: the museum, the grocery store, a service on the internet, etc... The station is a place of transfer where mental paths are made. Each of these signs, Rodin's and the others, announce a narrative option present at the site. The meaning of each sign unfolds when it is chosen. I choose the museum. I'll do the internet later.

DR: Well, I'm trying to avoid the word "about," which is difficult because you're largely from the western tradition, which is based upon the question of what is it about? Or what are you saying? Or what does it mean? With Rubens, for instance, his paintings were about something. They had meaning, but it's difficult, and somewhat of an insult to an artwork to demand that it says what it's about, it's silly. It's a bit of a shortcoming that I have as a curator, that I have difficulty wrapping my head around work that refuses to be about something. I just can't think like that. It has something to do with the fact that I don't really read a lot of fiction. I read non-fiction, art history. More importantly, I don't write fiction. I write non-fiction, and non-fiction means words about something in a real world, that something happened. I can't really invent, but you do though... you invent, no?

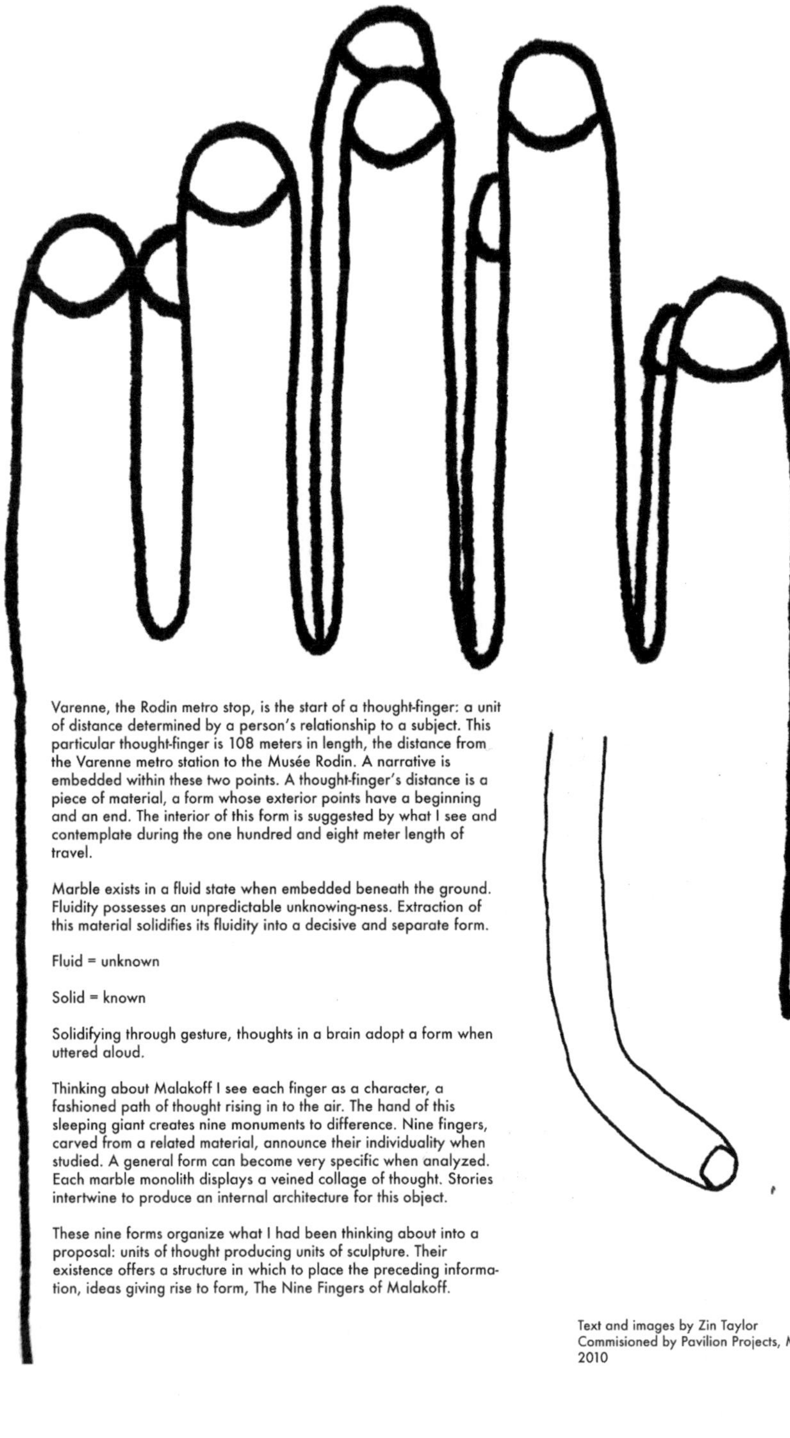

Varenne, the Rodin metro stop, is the start of a thought-finger: a unit of distance determined by a person's relationship to a subject. This particular thought-finger is 108 meters in length, the distance from the Varenne metro station to the Musée Rodin. A narrative is embedded within these two points. A thought-finger's distance is a piece of material, a form whose exterior points have a beginning and an end. The interior of this form is suggested by what I see and contemplate during the one hundred and eight meter length of travel.

Marble exists in a fluid state when embedded beneath the ground. Fluidity possesses an unpredictable unknowing-ness. Extraction of this material solidifies its fluidity into a decisive and separate form.

Fluid = unknown

Solid = known

Solidifying through gesture, thoughts in a brain adopt a form when uttered aloud.

Thinking about Malakoff I see each finger as a character, a fashioned path of thought rising in to the air. The hand of this sleeping giant creates nine monuments to difference. Nine fingers, carved from a related material, announce their individuality when studied. A general form can become very specific when analyzed. Each marble monolith displays a veined collage of thought. Stories intertwine to produce an internal architecture for this object.

These nine forms organize what I had been thinking about into a proposal: units of thought producing units of sculpture. Their existence offers a structure in which to place the preceding information, ideas giving rise to form, The Nine Fingers of Malakoff.

Text and images by Zin Taylor
Commisioned by Pavilion Projects, Montreal
2010

ZT: Maybe that's why I'm reading so much Norman Mailer now, because this is a guy that writes fiction by using facts. The text is clearly fiction, yet not. I find it rather strange. He wrote a book that was commissioned by NASA, a series of stories about outer space (a place where very few people will actually get to visit). I make things up using cues given by the things that surround me. I treat information as material units that enable abstraction. [...]

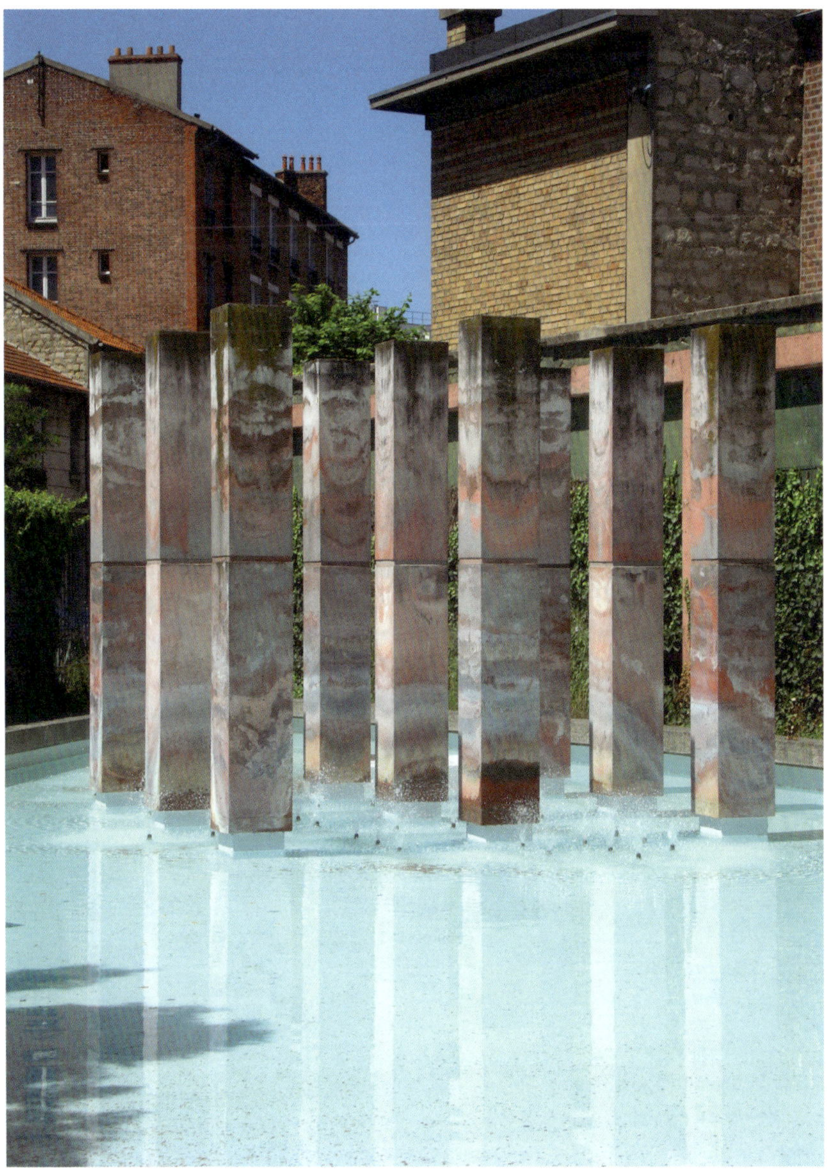

PALMS OF THE FOG

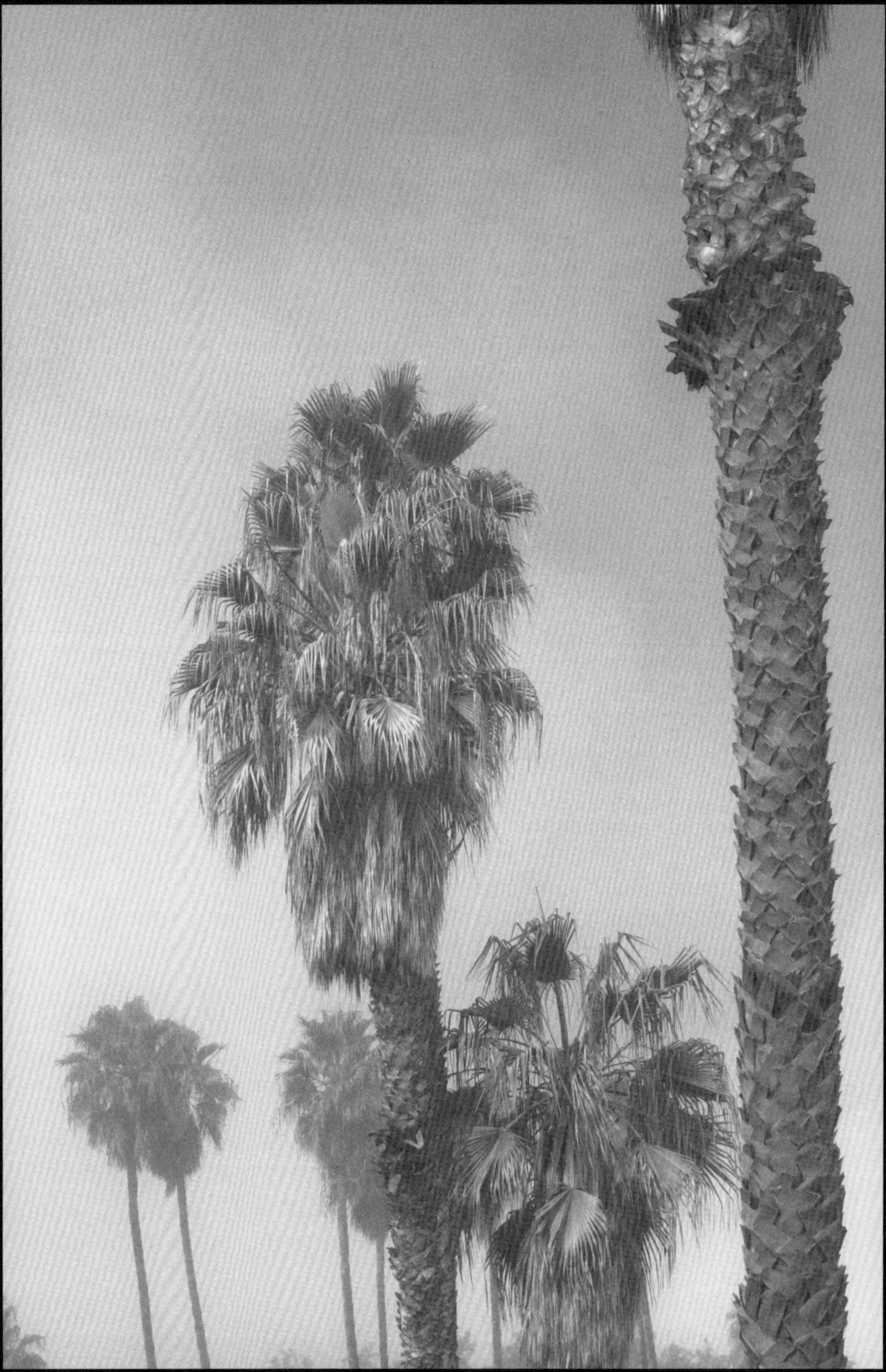

ZIN TAYLOR

The texts in *Palms of the Fog* book, for example, come from thinking about music, by looking at forms of music, music scenes, and how they can be used to think about something else. For example, I think a more succinct understanding of Feminism can be achieved by looking at Riot grrrl music and culture than in reading texts about it. At the time, in the early 1990s, this was an ideology that was made into a sound, one that was played by people, listened to by an audience, and that took up space and was discussed. [...]

Foreword

Here we are, we've arrived on an island jungled with palm trees. Soaring thin trunks, crowned with extended leaves, sway in response to the traveling winds. A deep fog in the jungle, separates these skyward forms into isolated monuments, growing; their slow silhouettes obscured by the fog.

Traveling through the palms, we've encountered moments that have turned the ethereal misty material of memory surrounding us into spoken accounts of narrative subjectivity. Fog is breath made thick; a series of thoughts and memories on the way to being collected into something more solid and present. The almost-somethingness of this ethereal expulsion is everywhere—an island of trees obscured by a million thoughts composed of hazy halfway points.

I collect this material into a composition, condensing the fog into a statement, and the result affords a clear view of a single palm. The trees on this island feed on the fog, the moisture giving life when absorbed through the trunk and leaves, and downward through the ground. The stories I tell float alongside, surrounding these semi-static arboraceous forms.

V

It evolved, it had a look, it had a feel, and this enabled the politics to be extremely well-communicated. There was an audience for an idea. You can't separate Feminism from Riot grrrl music, and that music has gone on to influence so many people since then. The incorporation of politics into music and subculture is different from what went on in the '60s. The music then was political, it was resistance, but I don't know if it was really political in that theoretical way. Certainly not in the same way that Feminism was deployed by teenagers in the '90s. As a teenager you could learn Feminism through music, which is kind of incredible. The music was able to do that, and for me that was one form used to communicate another form. As in, what's the most applicable route? How do you administer an idea, keep it going in such a way that it can generate other ideas and forms? So this question of what's the work about? I don't know, that's so...

ence could understand using a kind of language that is very immediate. Sound is introduced young in life. The comprehension of music comes shortly after. When watching a band play, you don't sit down and read, you stand up and listen, and then you think.

Receiving this album was a literal invitation into a discussion of politics and aesthetics that I was not part of, and could not be part of, because of my gender. It was familiar though. It made sense. A person would be quite ignorant not to see inequality projected towards women, or any sort of person not straight-aligned with the cliché of belonging. I could empathize though. I could project a link. I would never be inside, but I could be beside it, next door, listening in. At the very least I could act as if I belonged. I figured everyone had a choice—this understanding would affect my language, actions, and thoughts. Giving additional tools of critique to address what was going on around me. The "life" that was going on around me.

The sound of an extremely articulated difference was encouraging in order to see how far this politic can extend into life. What were the rules? Riot Grrrl performances, the shows, were famous for being all women (womyn) affairs. No guys al-

16

lowed. This hurt a little to hear, as I always wanted to attend. I understand though.

Magazines like *Raygun*, the design miracle that it was (famous for printing navy blue text on black backgrounds) would eventually flesh out the characters and scenes occurring and reacting at this moment in time. This era was post-Nirvana, pre-internet. One's knowledge was collectively linked to the people they knew, these were the sources that could be accessed. Zine culture was incredibly important—a kind of analog blog communicating and documenting different points of thought. Points of thought that would manifest into fashion and music—these were the subcultures. Ironically, at this point, the image of a subculture was typically black and white, and printed in a standard size—8.5 x 11 inch paper that had been folded in half and stapled twice. It really was a kind of formula.

An abandoned photocopier was such a gift.

My friend and I (the one who gave me the Bikini Kill album) had access to one. With this lone item, in an unmonitored area on the second floor of our High school, we began a publishing operation. Over the course of eighteen months of High

17

DR: It's so impolite...

school I produced seven issues of a zine I called
2B *Gimped.* I'm not sure why I picked this title, I'm not sure I would pick it again. *Gimped* consisted of a few tiers of content. Record reviews, live show reviews, and advertisements for fictional clothing and snowboard and skateboard companies I would invent, then drawings, stories and odds and ends from friends of mine. I think there was one poem. There was an ongoing series of drawings I would make with highlighters, white out, and ballpoint pens, and then pages of re-photocopied advertisements following certain characters from the universe of skateboarding and music. I would include reprinted ads that followed a particular character across their appearance in periodicals. This was not unlike Richard Prince in the early stage of his work where publicity aesthetics were used to assemble a cinematic cast producing episodes of narrative within each published magazine—also not unlike a typical teenager in a bedroom. I think I like the previous context. I like to think I was thinking about something larger. How the individual operated an existence relative to these grander, more foreign narratives, depicted in mass publishing.

With the exception of maybe five percent, I'll go as far to say that all zines produced in North

18

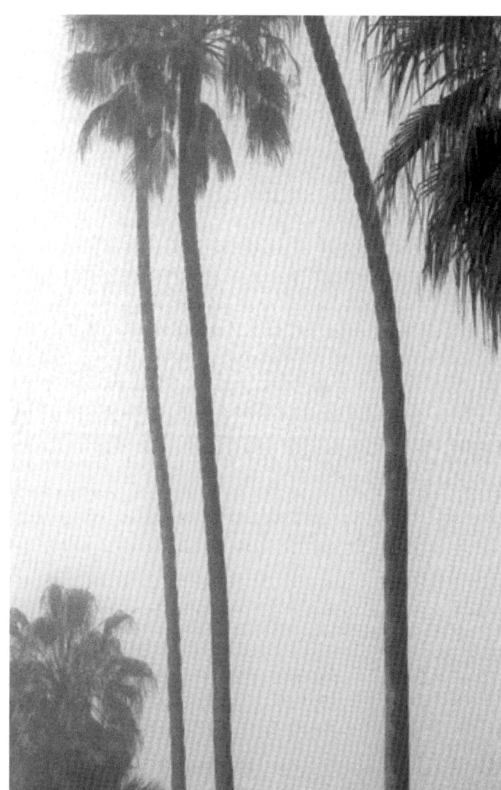

ZT: To use another music analogy, I once described what I do as not unlike Krautrock: establishing a kind of rhythm and then letting it travel and evolve. I love that informal Krautrock rule: no song less than ten minutes. How the music is about elaboration and movement relative to this rhythm that goes on.

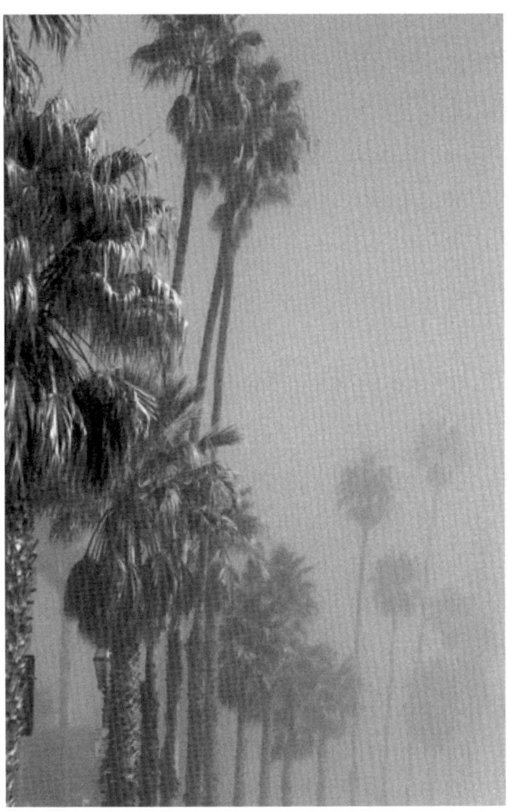

America are made using a standard 8.5 x 11 inch piece of paper, folded on the long side, and stapled together. Thousands of these booklets have manifested through the years. A zine fair could easily be seen as a grubby paper expo.

A zine of the era followed a very basic set of rules. Or at least looking at one communicated a very basic set of rules. This is important to remember: looking at and handling a zine told you how to make a zine. Intended or not, this is what happened. Letter size paper, black and white, both sides, cut and paste text, folded and stapled to emulate a magazine, done. The ingredients of serial production, Xerox machine and paper, were intersected with intent. These machines, existing in every office in the world, were the tools to autonomy. Manipulated to produce a document contrary to dominant economy. That was the idea—an administrative aesthetic hijacked and made applicable to provide a communicative context documenting the underground. Every one of these zines played off of the unit to account its existence. Several sheets of paper, the same kind to print a test, issue a bill, and post a warning were used to tell a story, publish a manifesto, document a scene, and communicate a politic. These things flourished, for every one printed five more would

21

DR: Tonight we're going to see Terry Riley's *In C*. I think it's going to be a blast, because that's it, we're going to see some modulation.

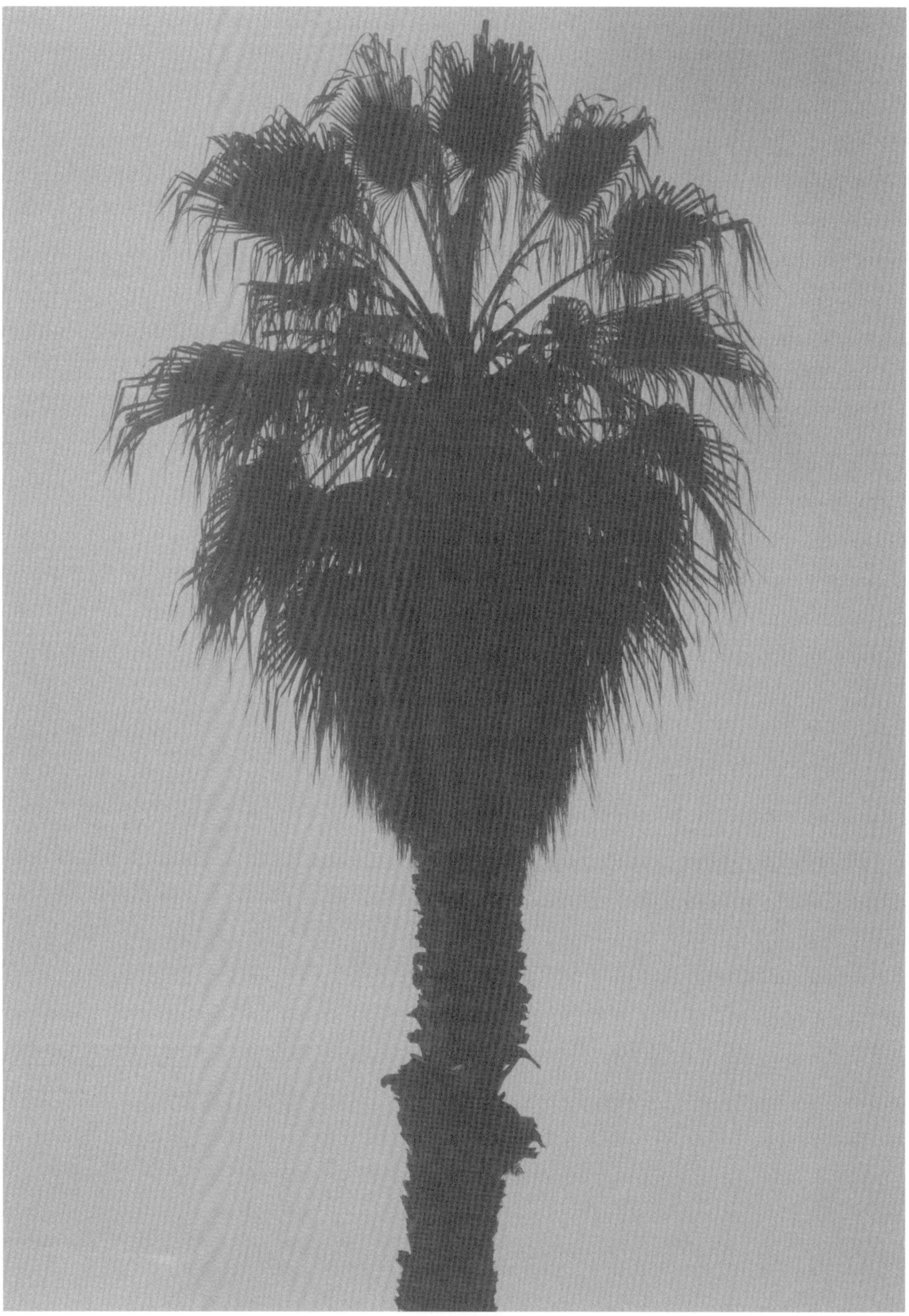

ZT: That's a good word! What is modulation? You take a thing (a subject), and then you move it up, down, to the left, to the right... all the while it's still moving. It never stops. I do one work, or one show—what's it about? If I have to say what my work is about (to give an answer) then that's where the meaning ends, disrupting the discursive rhythm that had been initiated by the asking of a question. If the subject is presented in this manner, it allows someone to say *yes* or *no* to the proposition. I want to tell a big story. I don't want to tell a little story.

DR: Which is sometimes necessary, of course. It's how to continue on. So that answers the question that I didn't really formulate—you want to tell a big story that unfolds over time. One book, with different chapters.

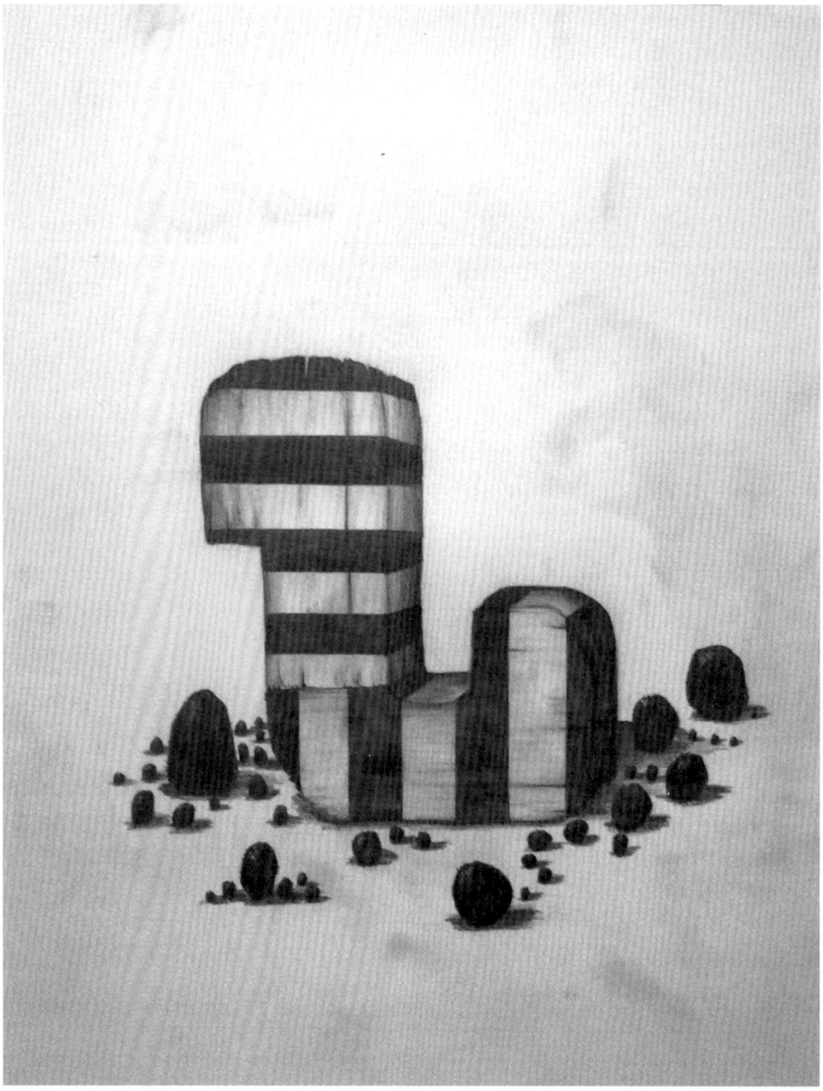

ZT: The plan that came to development several years ago was to make a kind of dictionary. This was after reading Bataille, and his notion of the dictionary of "l'informe," an approach to formlessness as a way to make information flexible. As a response to this, my program has been to talk about everything. I want to talk about everything at least once, and make the dialogue visible. That's why my subjects include underground tunnels, or landscape, or abstraction, stripes and dots: to build a description of a world I want to live in, one that I can invite other people into. I write the stories, or make the stories, for this world in order to build up alternate ideas to think about. All of it comes out of the impulse to create something different, to make a multiplicity out of a singularity. To change that established normative identity a piece of information can be subjected to in order to get it out of the way.

I see those books with 1000 pages—how do you write that? But then Stephen King cranks that out in an afternoon.

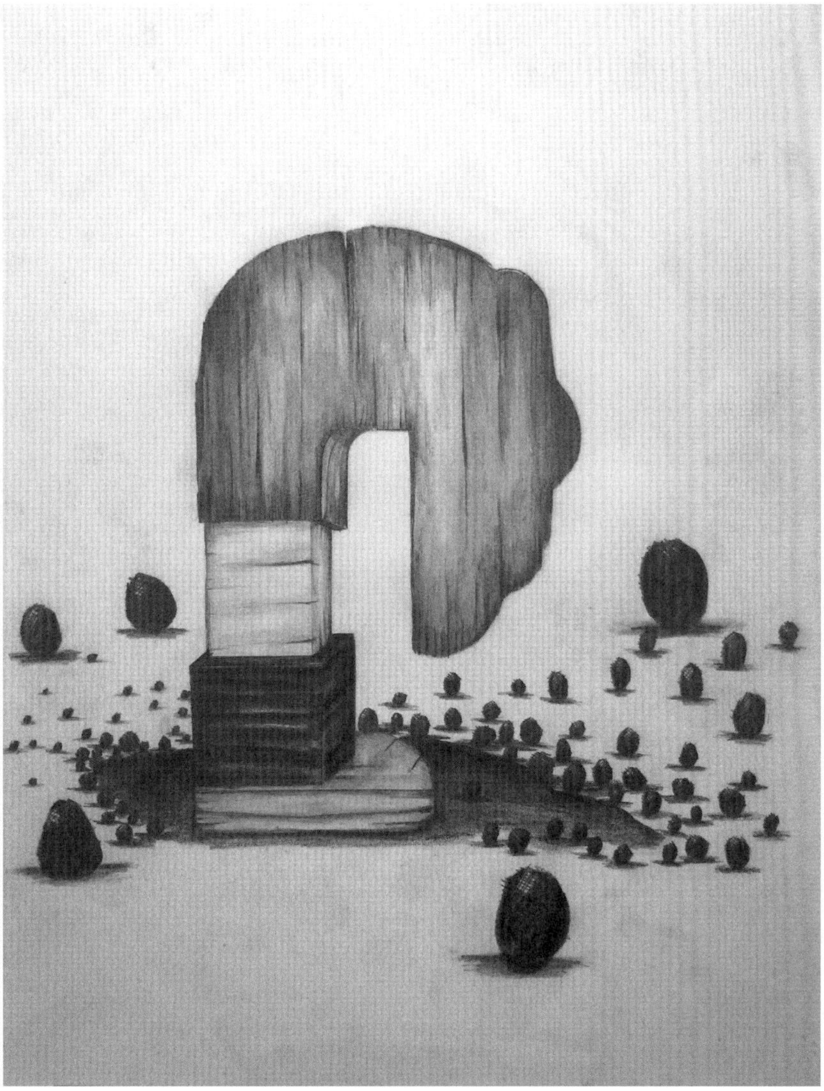

DR: Or it can take twenty years—look at James Joyce. Stephen King's books are about something, whereas the book that goes on and on and is always writing itself is not so much about something, but it *is* something. It's like life in a way, and that's maybe the difference. There is art that is about something, and then there is art that is something. [...]

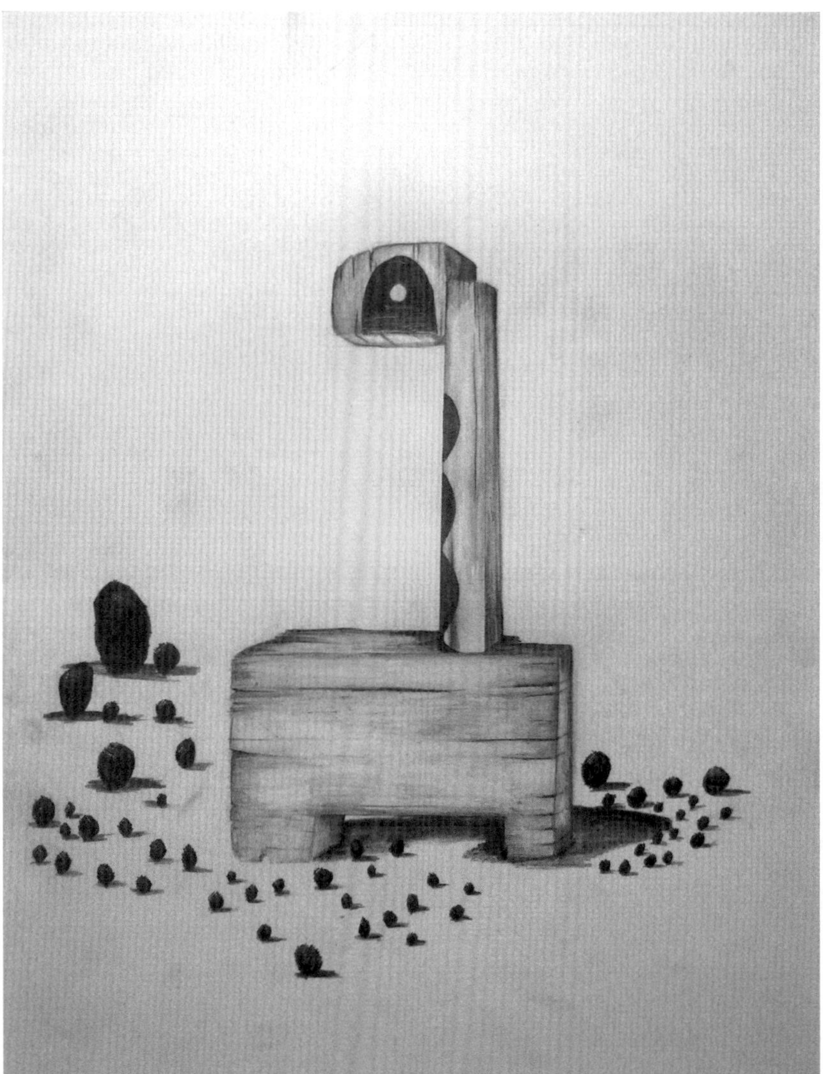

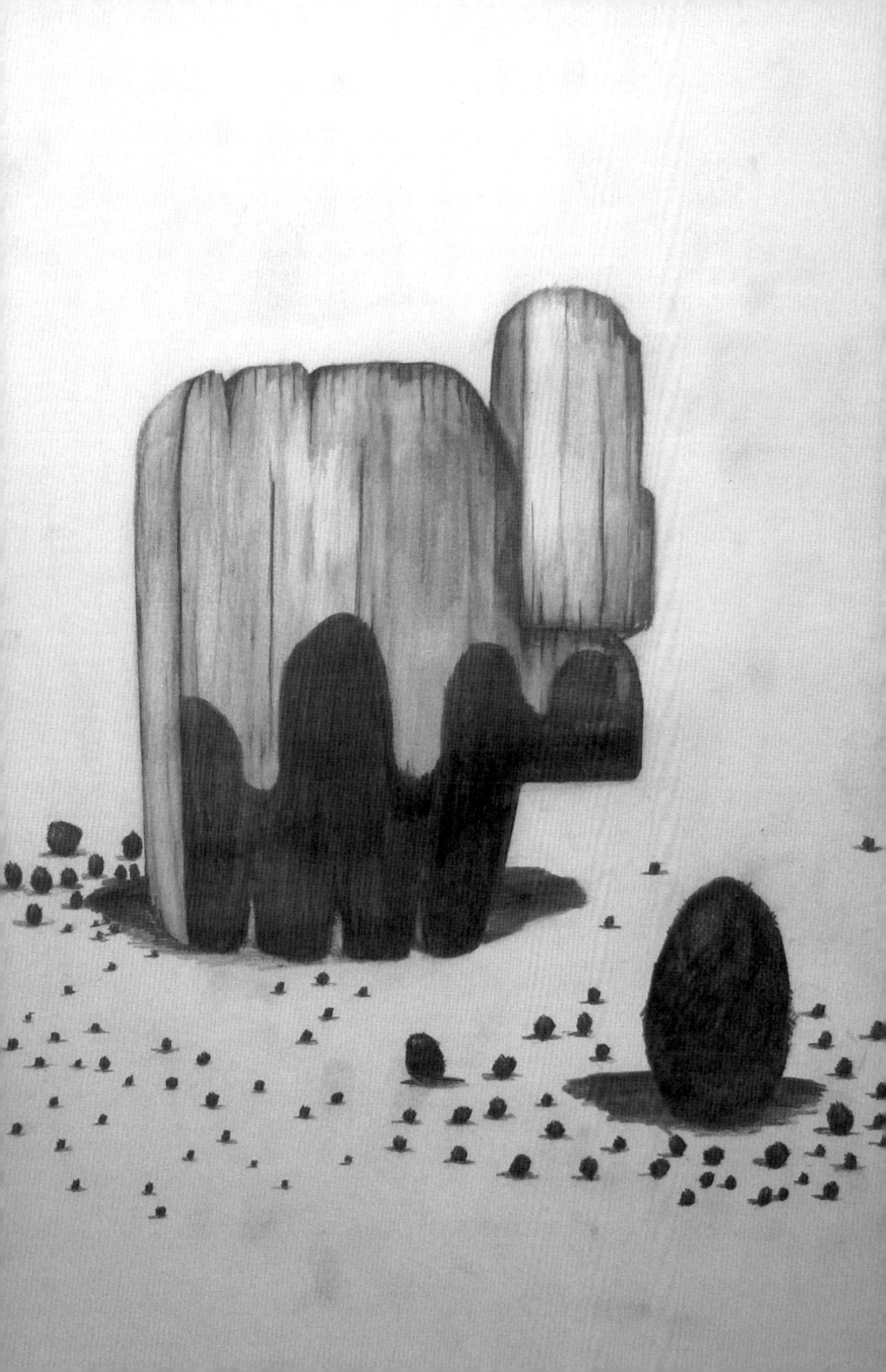

Let's talk about music. I like art, but I love music. You have a particular taste, which you've exposed me to, and I'm completely with you in this interest that you have in the ecology of scenes. I love that shit. The subculture, which is unfortunately a phenomenon that is in weird health right now, I think, is going through a troubled phase that has to do with a variety of massive economic, cultural, and technological factors. I sometimes feel like I was witness to one of the last really great moments in the history of subcultures—youth cultures organized around music. So I do share interest in those kinds of ecologies, and cultures, and the zine. I'm interested in the ways in which people write about music, like in the book that you bought yesterday (*Electric Eden: Unearthing Britain's Visionary Music*), and different types of music, like those records you also bought (*Highwolf*, *White Rainbow*, *Date Palms*). They're all things that I don't know anything about, but you found them at this store called The Dusty Groove. [...]

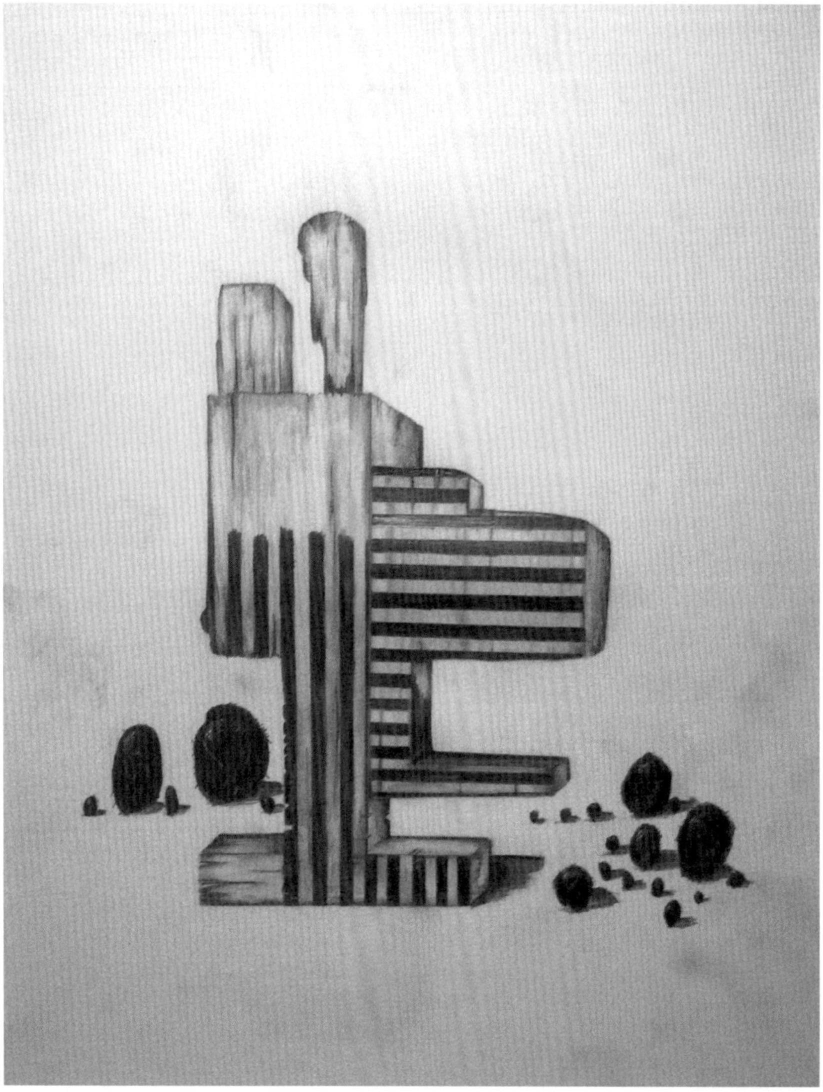

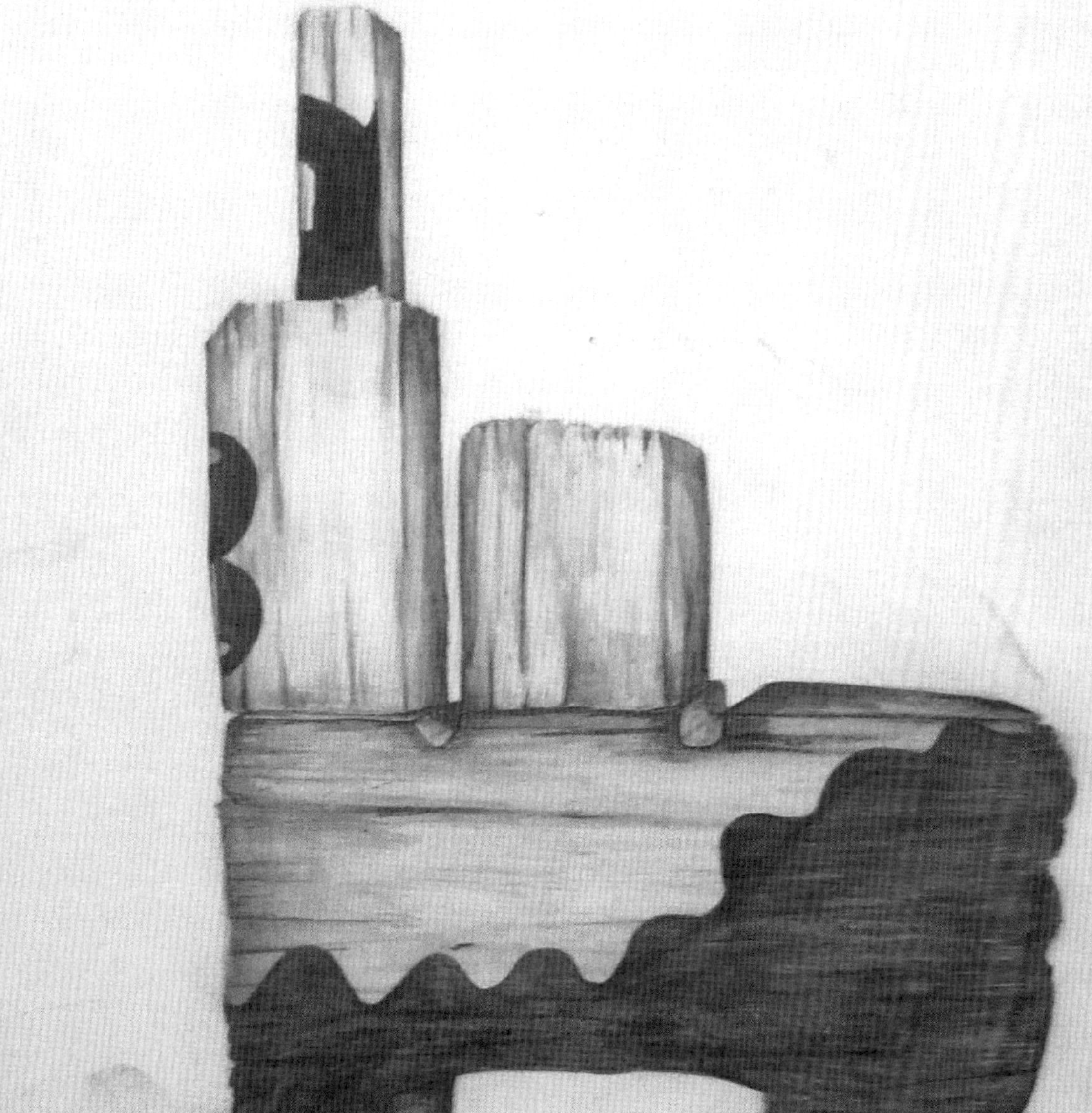

You like a certain kind of sound, one with drones and weird circularities, and a strange sense of plateau—it's eventless, in a way. A lot of the music that you seem to like does not necessarily have climactic buildups and stuff like that, things go on... You were talking about Krautrock, and druid music, and chanting. So I'm curious what that says about what you do as an artist? Are the shapes that you produce and put out there three-dimensional renditions of some of the sounds that you are so passionate about, or is that a little too simplistic? I'm interested in the relationship between what you make and this overriding passion that you have for this particular kind of sound. Because you don't like country music, and I took you to the first jazz concert of your life yesterday.

ZT: I like the immersiveness—you become part of this very long story that is happening. You get to sit down and think along with someone's idea. These are not three-minute pop structures; instead the songs are very long. Sometimes they are entire sides of a record. For instance, the band SLEEP's album *Jerusalem* (also known in an edited version as *Dopesmoker*) is a 66-minute story. I think a lot of what I listen to, what I collect, what I really search out, is being made now by individuals using those histories. The music provides a landscape to walk around with in your brain. [...]

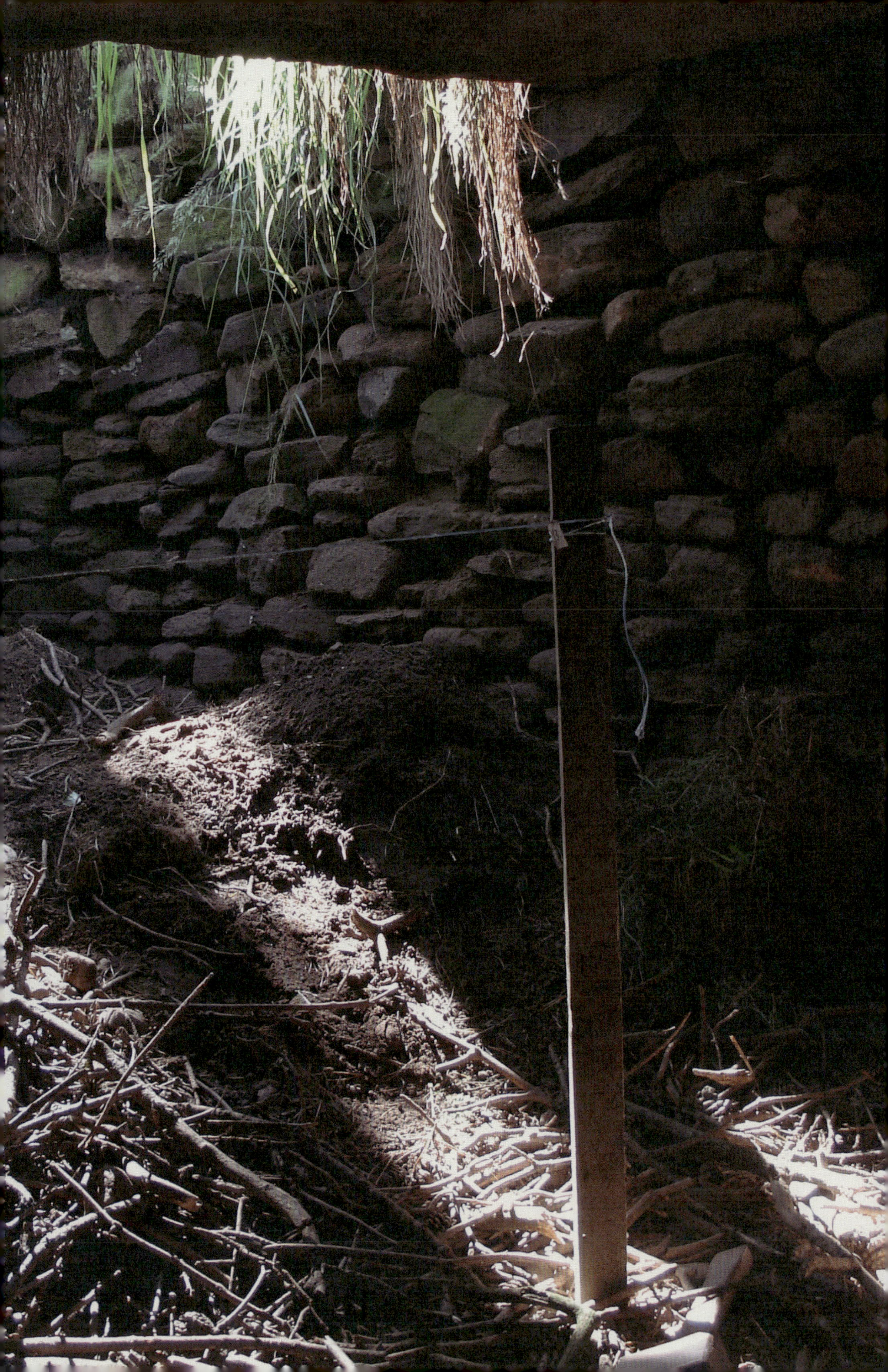

The Flute of Sub came out of my love for this stuff. Particularly the Boards of Canada, a duo of Scottish guys who spent time in Calgary, Alberta when they were kids. Their music makes use of field recordings to create atmospheric narratives, but it also comes from a tradition of psych folk in Northern Scotland where they live. I'm interested in the way they are able to link a sound with pagan culture and the landscape. Paganism, put very simply, is about looking toward the land for answers. To identify that "thing" that you can't really put your finger on that happens when you are in the forest by yourself. It's not the same as sitting alone in downtown Chicago, it's a different feeling. This is about looking to the land, to my environment, as a conversation partner. The works look to the environment to ask questions, while contributing and cultivating that kind of environment at the same time. So I think I'm trying to make ideas similar to how these musicians are trying to make an account of presentness. Where the work, or the album, gives you the tool for doing so. The album is the tool used to experience a version of presentness. It allows you to think along with it, to drop out a bit, by putting it on, and then thinking with it. This is an ambition for the work to develop.

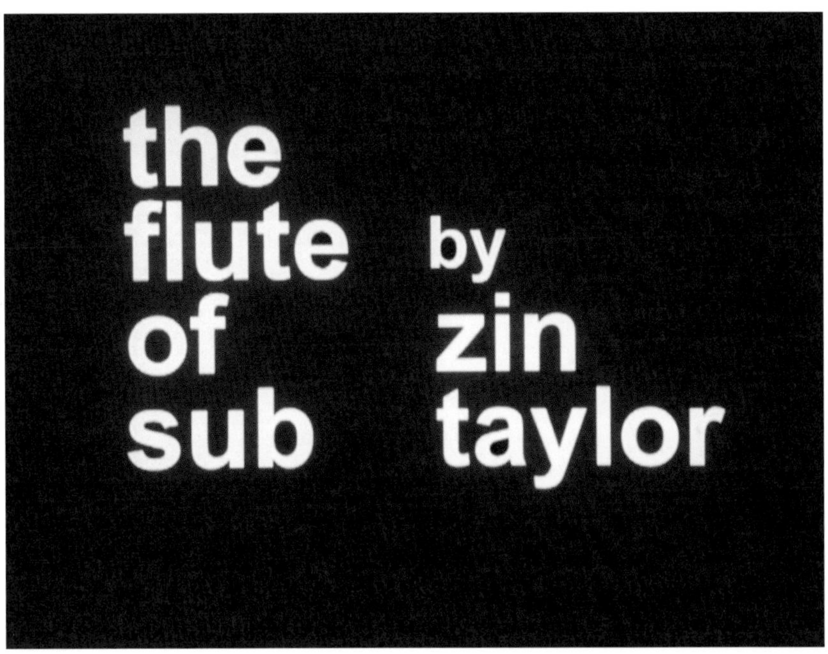

DR: I have two questions. The first one regards immersion, and it's interesting that you bring it up. I have a complicated relationship with immersion; in art I'm a little bit skeptical of it. You don't make immersive installations. You've made the lichen wallpaper, which could be said to be immersive, but you're not Olafur Eliasson obviously. A lot of your work is very frontal. You stand in front of it, it's not around you. I like things to be at a distance, not so as to guarantee a secure space of safety, but it's what I understand to be the basic assumption, or the basic prerequisite, for critical interaction with something, that you have to be able to step away from it. Immersive art works are very difficult for this. Hence my skepticism of immersive art, which has become a huge paradigm in the last twenty years, perhaps because we were entering a world view in which we could no longer imagine something outside of it. We can't really imagine another model than that of the neo-liberal capitalist world order; you can't go outside, there is no alternative. Immersive art installations, to me, replicate this culture, hence my suspicions about immersion as an aesthetic model. But as I said, I like immersive music, and I like taking Gong Baths. Gongs have medical applications. You lie down on the ground and your head is very close to a big gong and a yogi hammers away at it, very softly, like a Tibetan bowl. If you put that on your chest and you go "oooooo," your whole body resonates. I've never thought about your work as immersive, at least not in the physical sense, but you seem to think of it as something that is.

ZT: Well, I think it's immersive in the way a record is immersive, or how an idea is immersive. You can put it on, and then it ends, and then you leave. Or you can hit repeat, start it again by walking around it, or go to another side. You can always leave it, which is one thing that immersive environments will never let you do. [...]

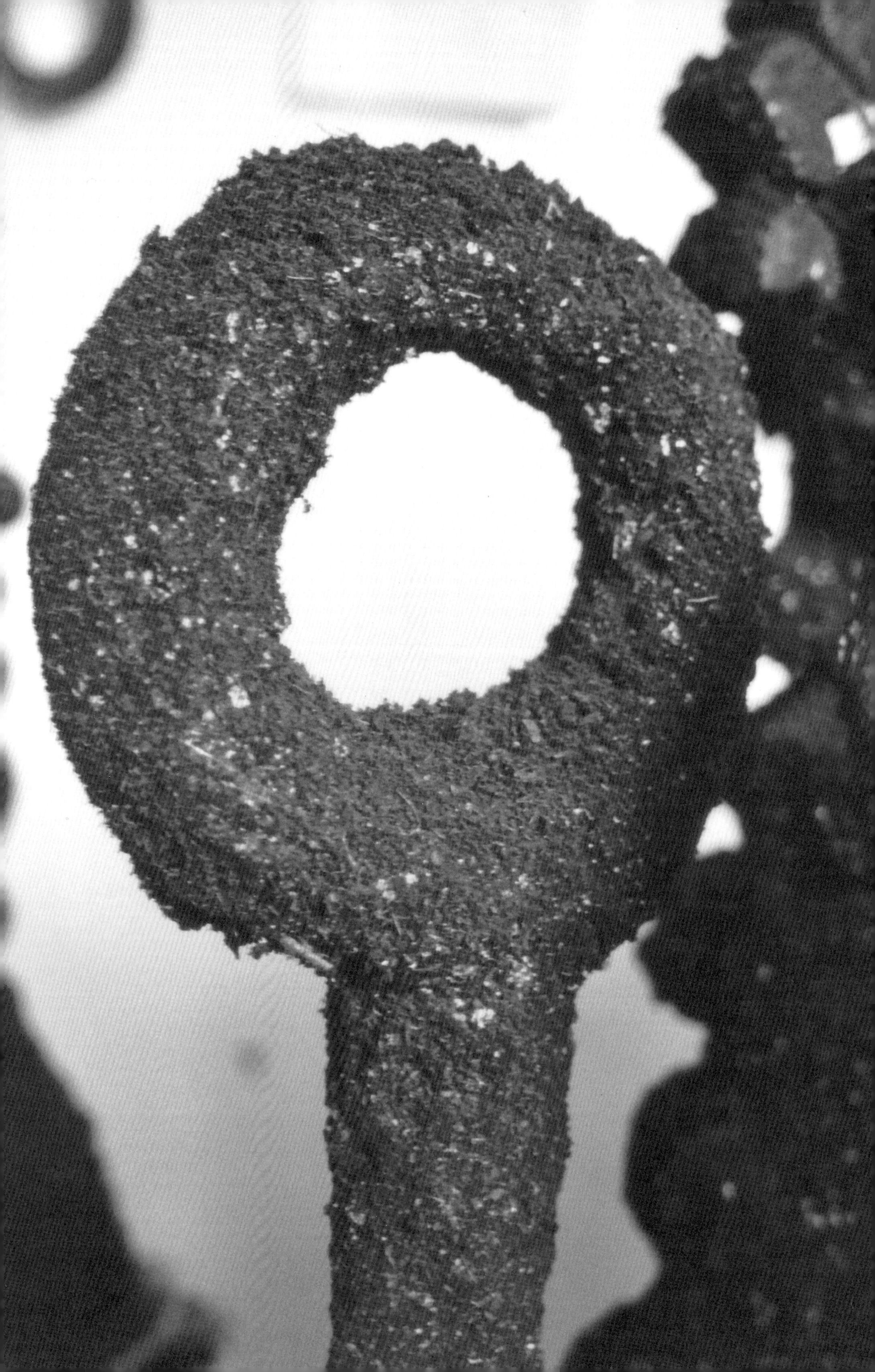

I think it's important to not think about something. To think about something, then to have the option to not think about something. When I made *The Allegorical Function of Dirt*, a video that is 62-minutes long, the full length of Aki Tsuyuko's album *Ongakushitsu*, I couldn't imagine anyone wanting to watch a 62-minute film about dirt, or expecting someone to do so. [...]

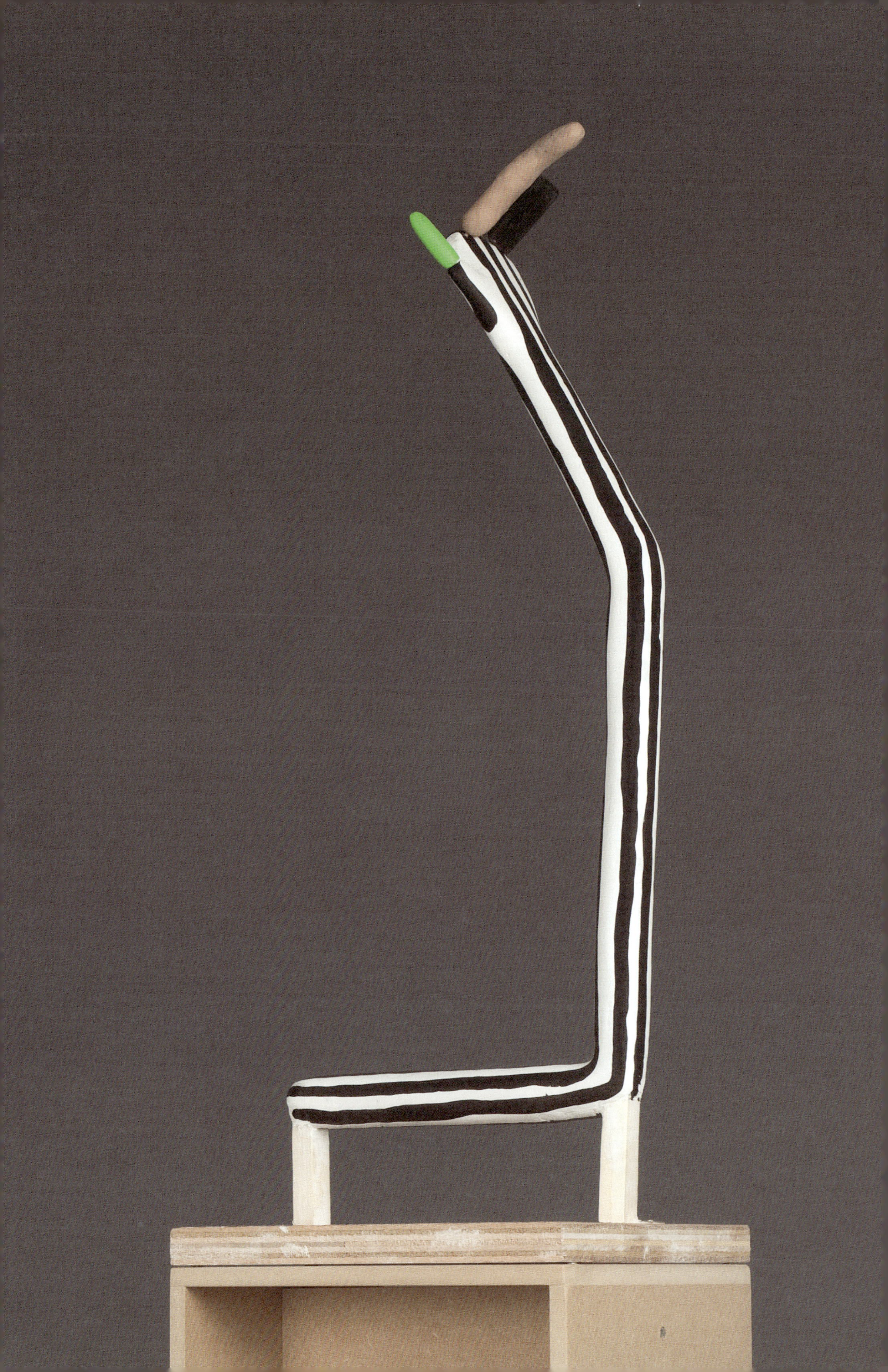

I just found that to be so brutal. So instead, part of that rule for me, that you couldn't make someone do this, also helped to develop the idea. If it's a discussion, it's my discussion, my authorship. You as a visitor, walking in and out, are perfect that way; you get a bit, but you'll never get the whole thing. It may be this part, or that part. The experience is open enough that, as a viewer, you could produce these little subjectivities within your visit. I try to make gestures that you're always able to walk away from. I think that's also why I don't make giant-scaled works.

DR: When you experience something on that anthropomorphic scale, the height of a human being, or its rough shape, there's the sense that you encounter it on an inter-subjective basis, subject to subject. And if you don't like it then you can go. You don't have to stay.

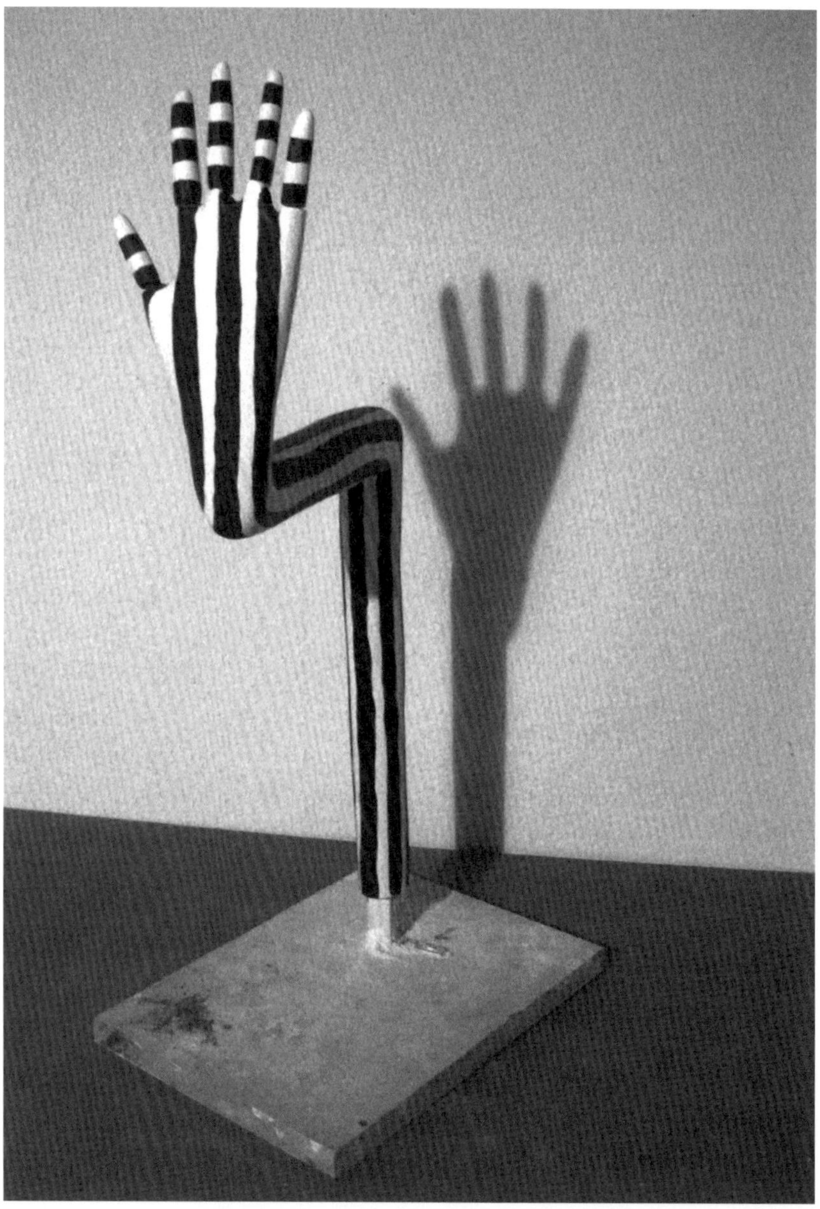

ZT: That approach helps to address the "about" thing as well. If it's about "this" and you don't like it, then it's over. But if it's about being there, with the thing, then it's more about presentness and producing or exhibiting, encouraging thinking—it can be about many things. I'm much more for the allegory, for the expansion, for producing gestures that start talking about abstraction in the thinking sense, not in the visual sense. Returning to music, it's made by people who may live urban, but who are thinking about a different place in a different time, where the music can be an assistant. If anything, it's people trying to think through music.

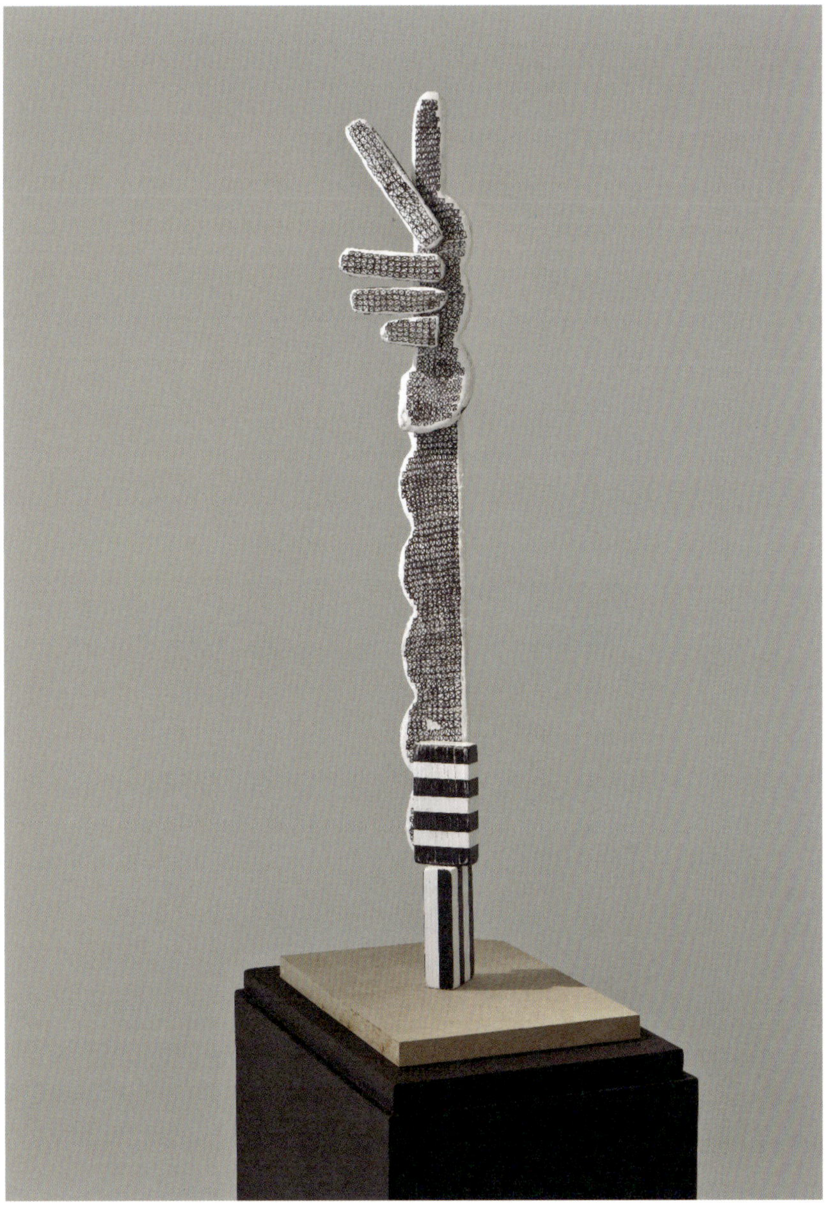

DR: So in regards to the music that you listen to, we've dealt a little bit with the subject of immersion. We've also touched on the idea of landscape, or nature, in music, and how that music is not very urban. The rural aspect is something that I like, a lot actually. That's why earlier today we were listening to the band Cluster. I was telling you about how Cluster used to live on a little farm in the German countryside in the '70s, and that I wish I could put on my sandals and join them. But I like this notion of a landscape that slips in here: the pastoral, the rural. Obviously it's not something that is very visible in your work at all, but it seems to be there perhaps in spirit.

ZT: I come from a relatively culturally remote place: Calgary, Alberta. There is something incredibly pastoral about Alberta and the prairies. You can see the mountains from the city, but what you are surrounded by are the foothills, a kind of desert flatness. It's very flat, and it's very empty—a void in that perfect Japanese Buddhist-void kind of way where what you think comes into being. It's you within this very big theme of nature that continuously cycles every day, a lot closer to something very elemental. Being at such a distance, you learn things from all over the world by reading and looking. You learn about history, philosophy, or critical theory through reading books, and then walk outside and become immersed in this contrary environment that is your everyday. It has a different effect on how you conjugate information.

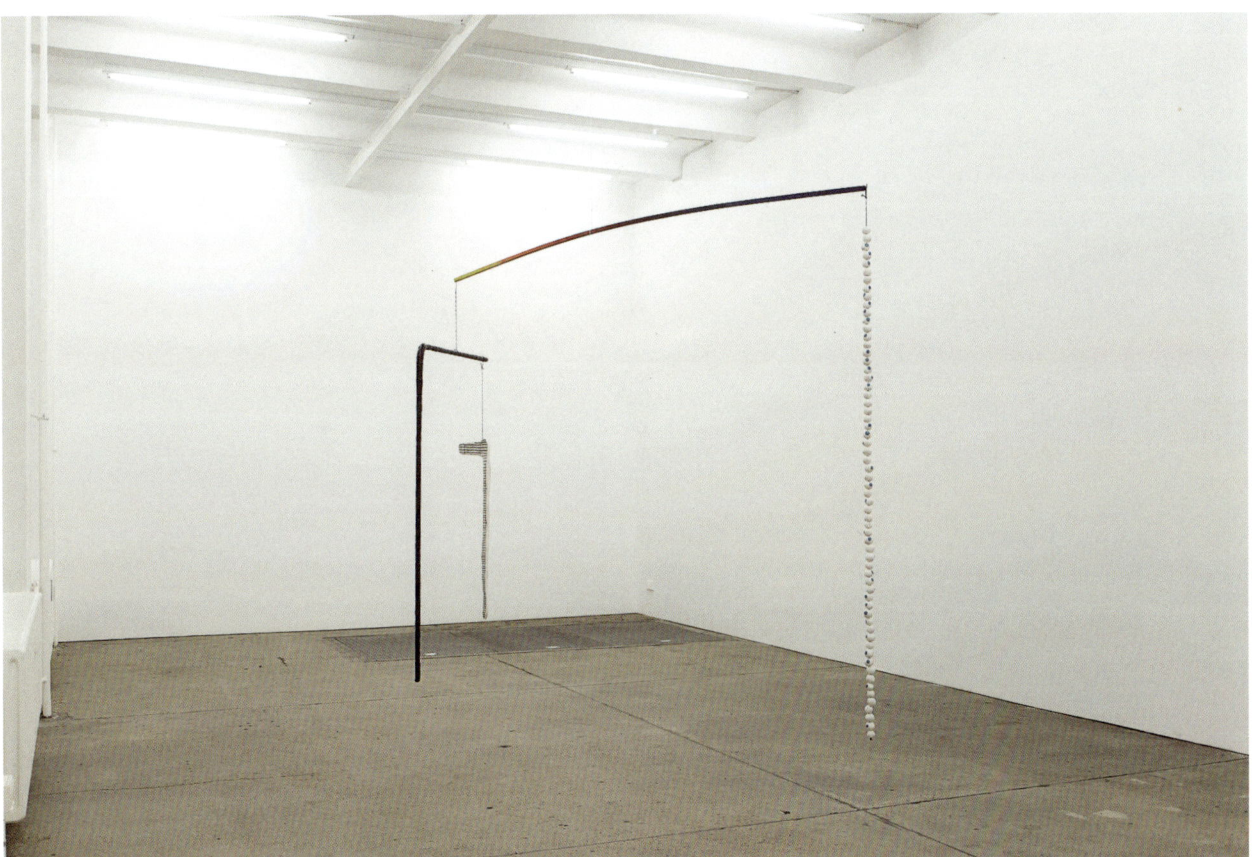

DR: Conjugate information. That's a great term. You thought about that.

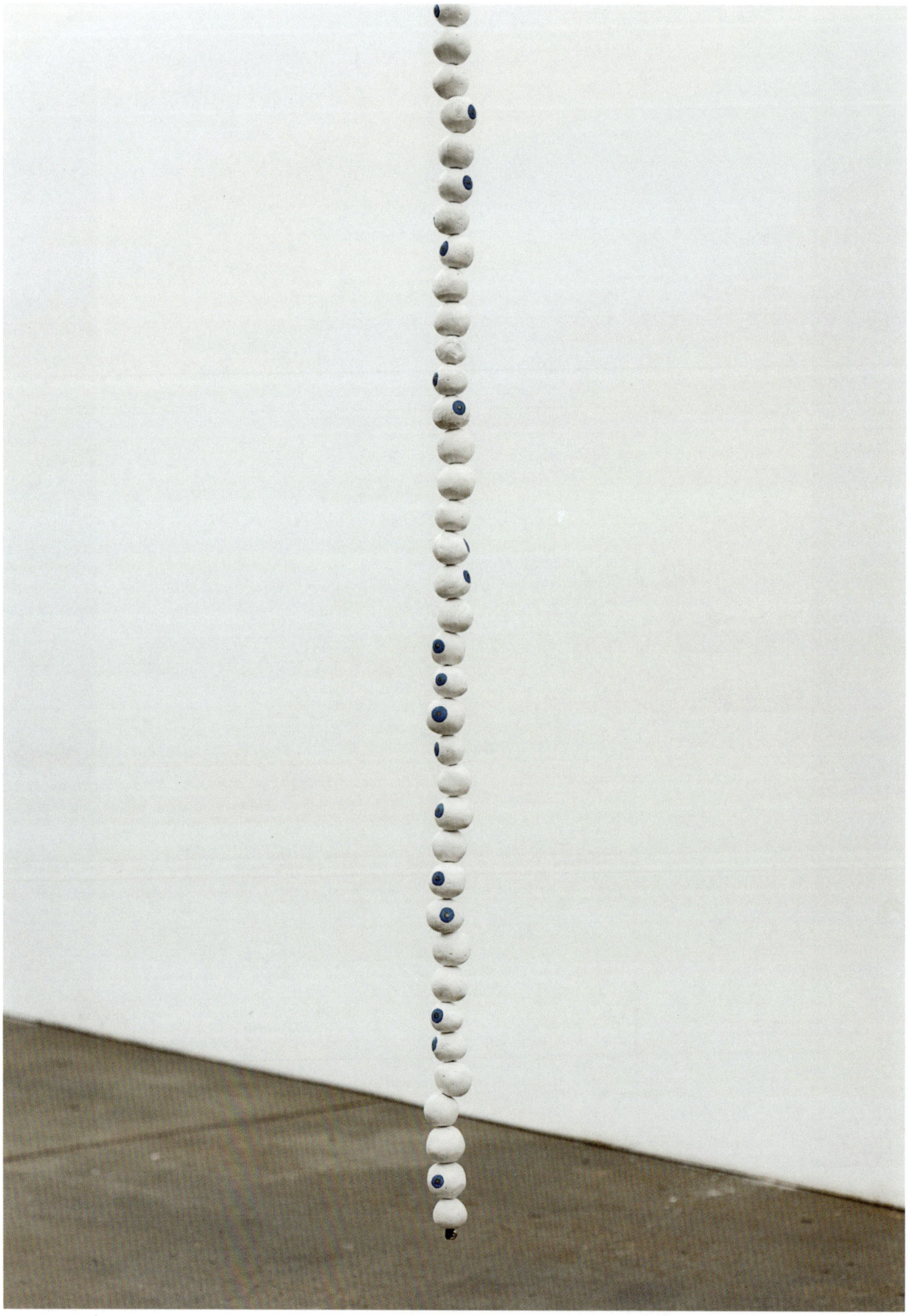

ZT: I tend to use these words related to grammar and speech to describe how I make forms. A discursive form, for example, is a form talking about its place at that moment with what it's directly engaged with. A conversational form is one that elaborates and takes on this movement away from the source. To conjugate, how did this one subject navigate all this other influence and information into being right there by its self? In my mind, it makes perfect sense.

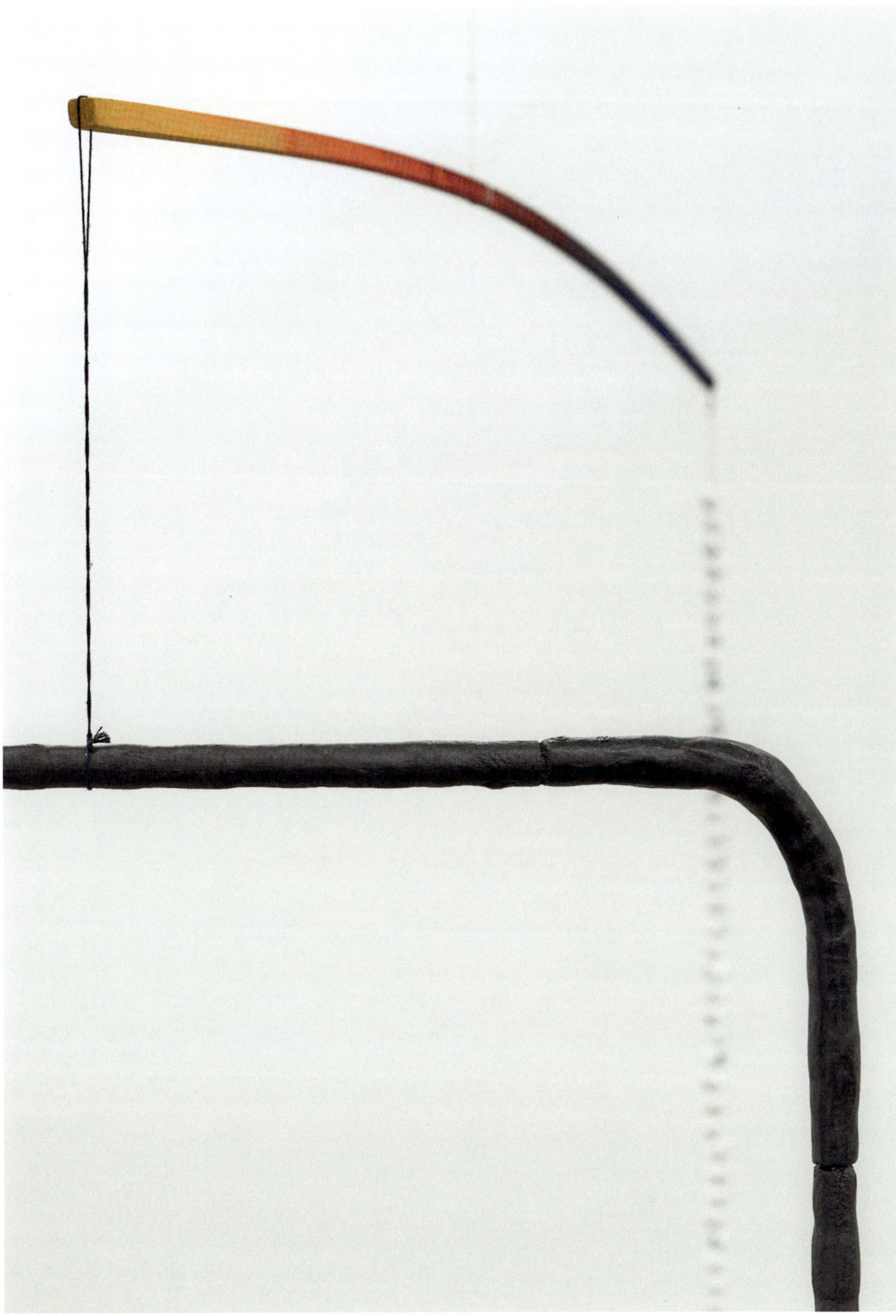

DR: Inter-function / interpunction. Grammar.

ZT: It's a kind of structure to adjust and account for the ordering and understanding of information. Words like *form* and *narrative* can almost mean anything. Thought, but what kind of thought? What's that thought trying to do?

DR: Your work was perhaps more language-dependent in the past than it is now. If you think of *The Allegorical Function of Dirt*, or the Kippenberger video (*Put Your Eye in Your Mouth: a conversational documentary recording Martin Kippenberger's Metro-Net sculpture in Dawson City, Yukon*), or *The Flute of Sub*, and the *White Pearl Sunshine Summoning Charm*, narration is much more integral to those projects than what came after. [...]

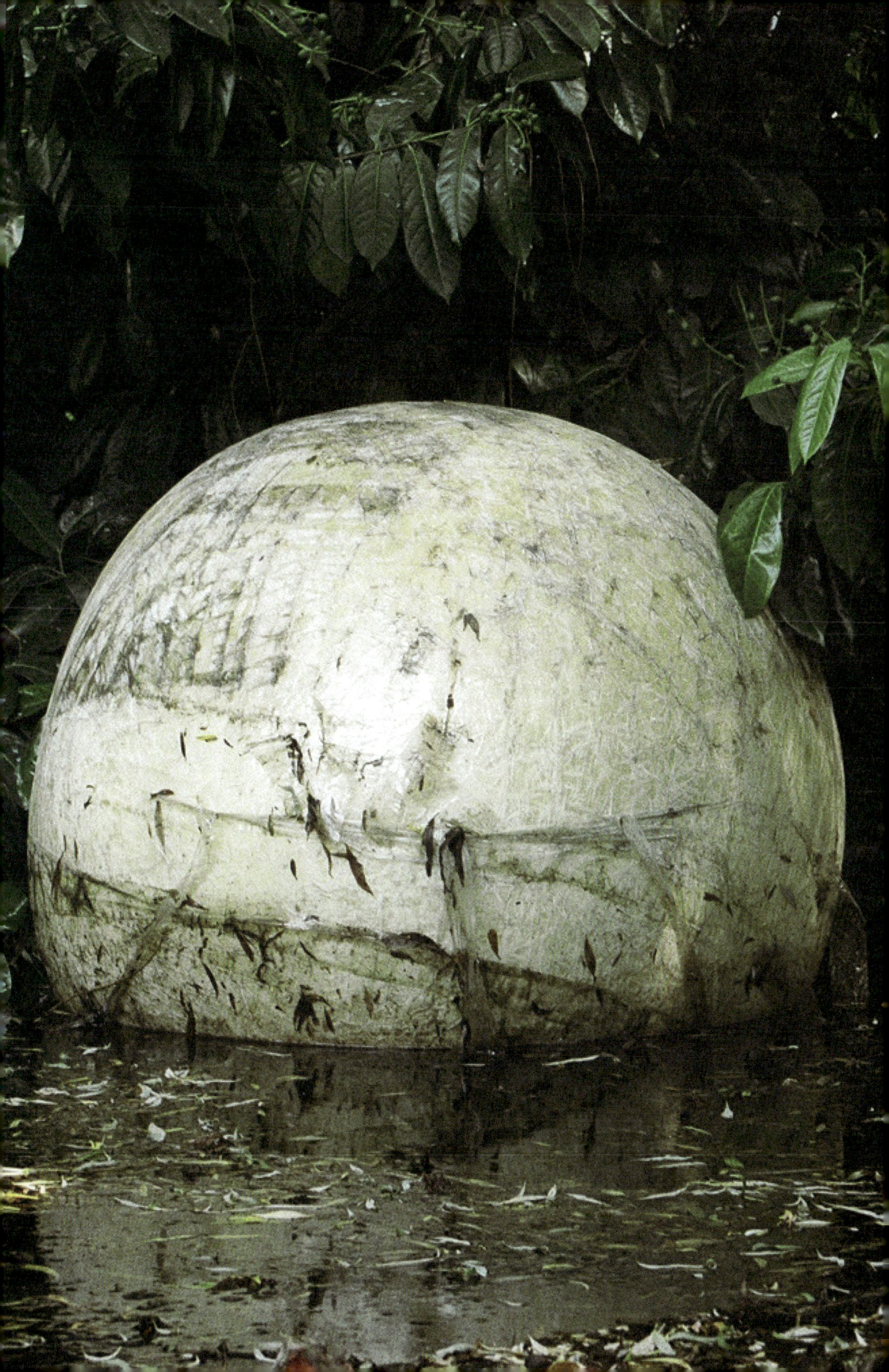

It would be nice to know which works signalled the break, but of course the break is probably related to the fact that you moved countries, and you moved linguistic contexts, and you moved traditions. [...]

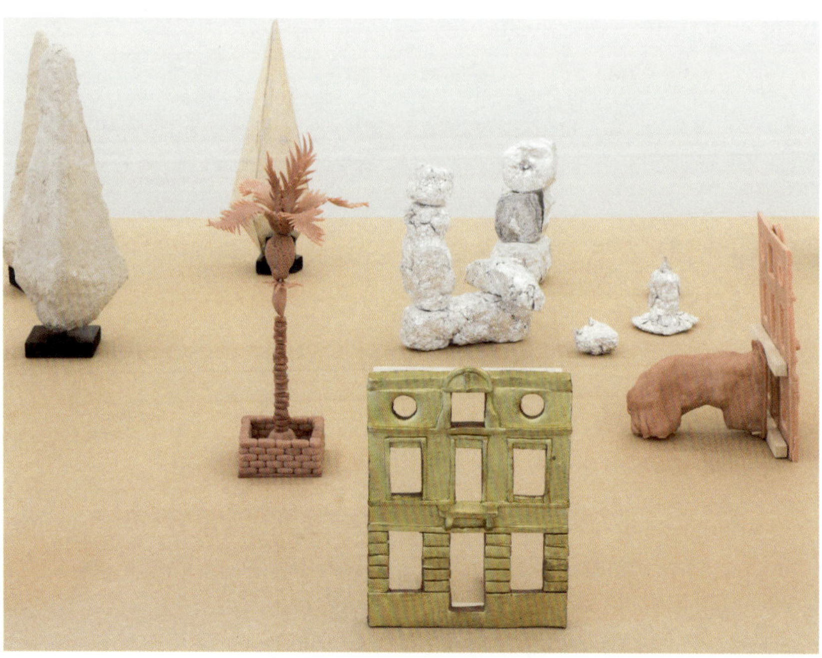

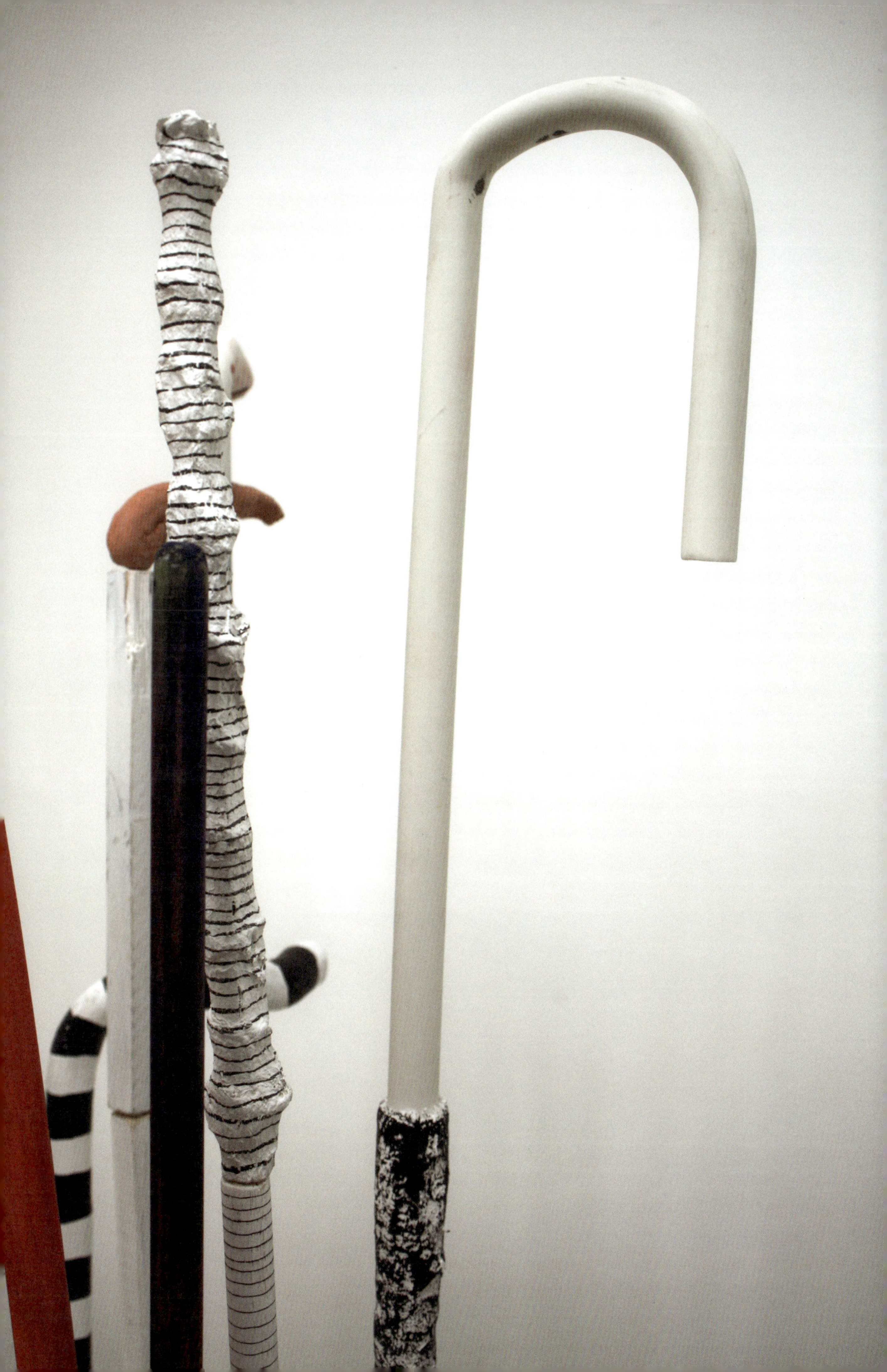

You left a certain kind of tradition behind in Canada, which I think is much more discursively academic, and then you came to Belgium. [...]

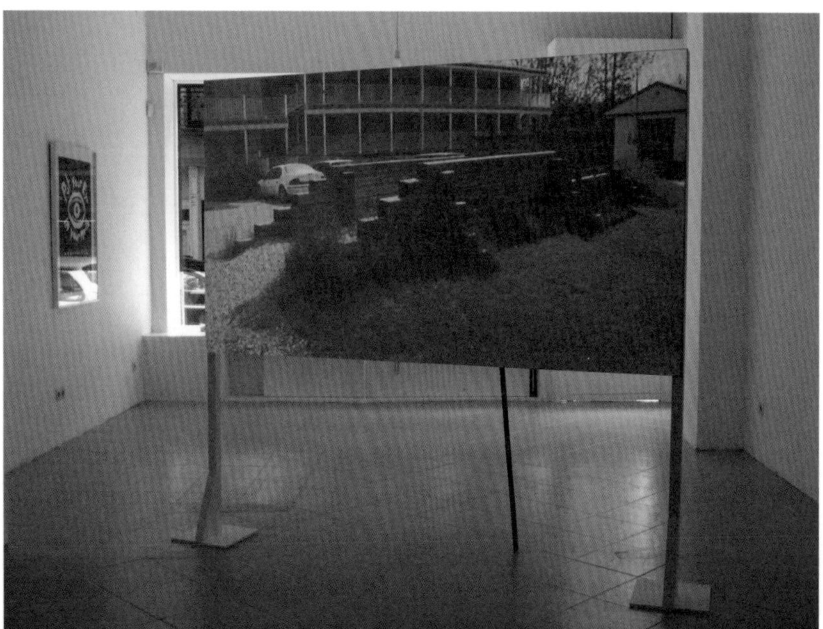

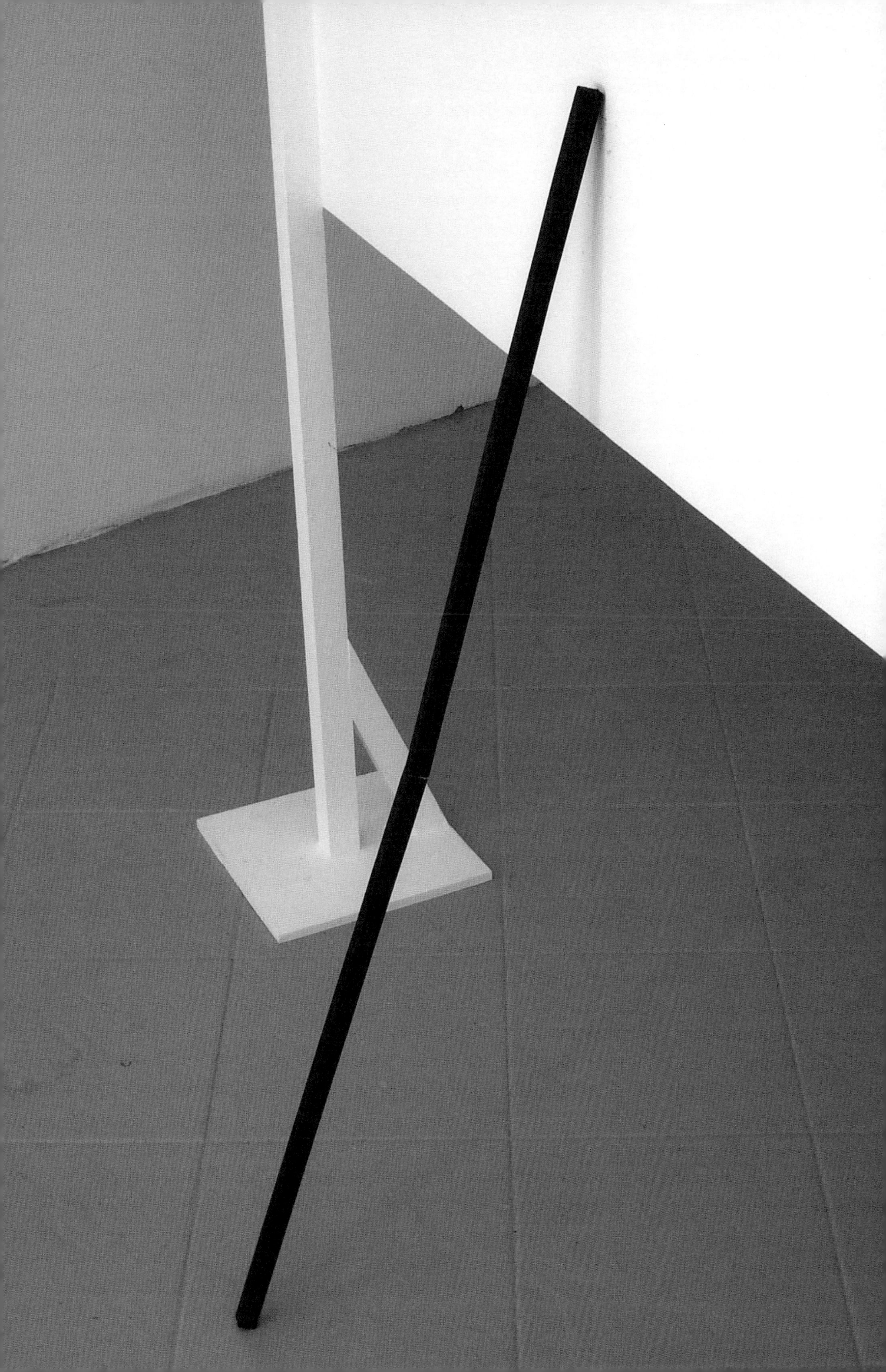

First, can you talk about what moving did to your work and what the change from one language context to another did for your work, how translation figures into this whole problem? And second, are these contexts not just abstract notions?

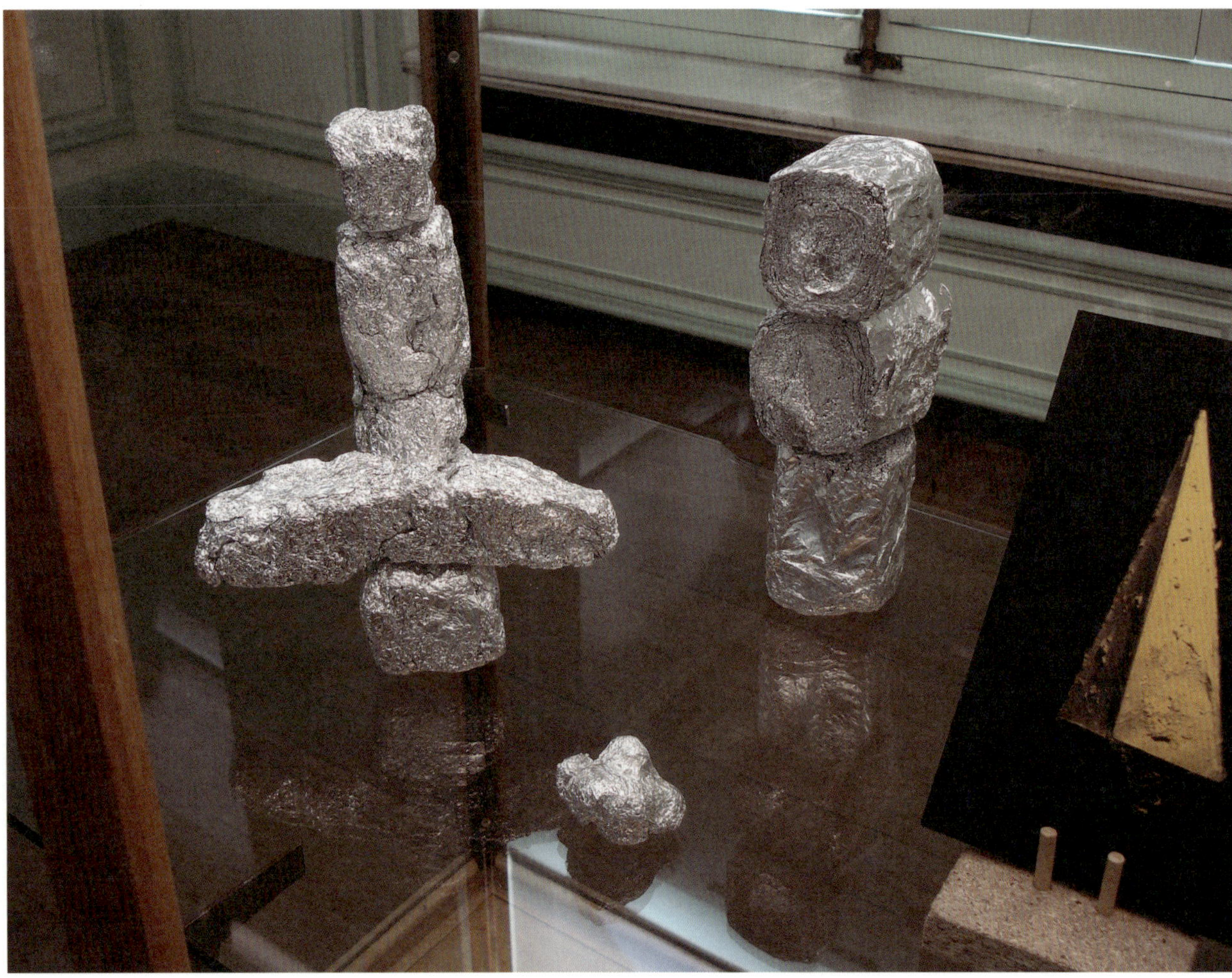

ZT: The work that was my “bridge” between Canada and Belgium was *The Crystal Ship*, a narrative addressing what was happening in late ‘60s Antwerp with A379089, an artist space. It incorporates the idea of the avant-garde and how spaces produce art forms within them, similar to how a cave would produce stalactites inside of itself using runoff water from the surface. [...]

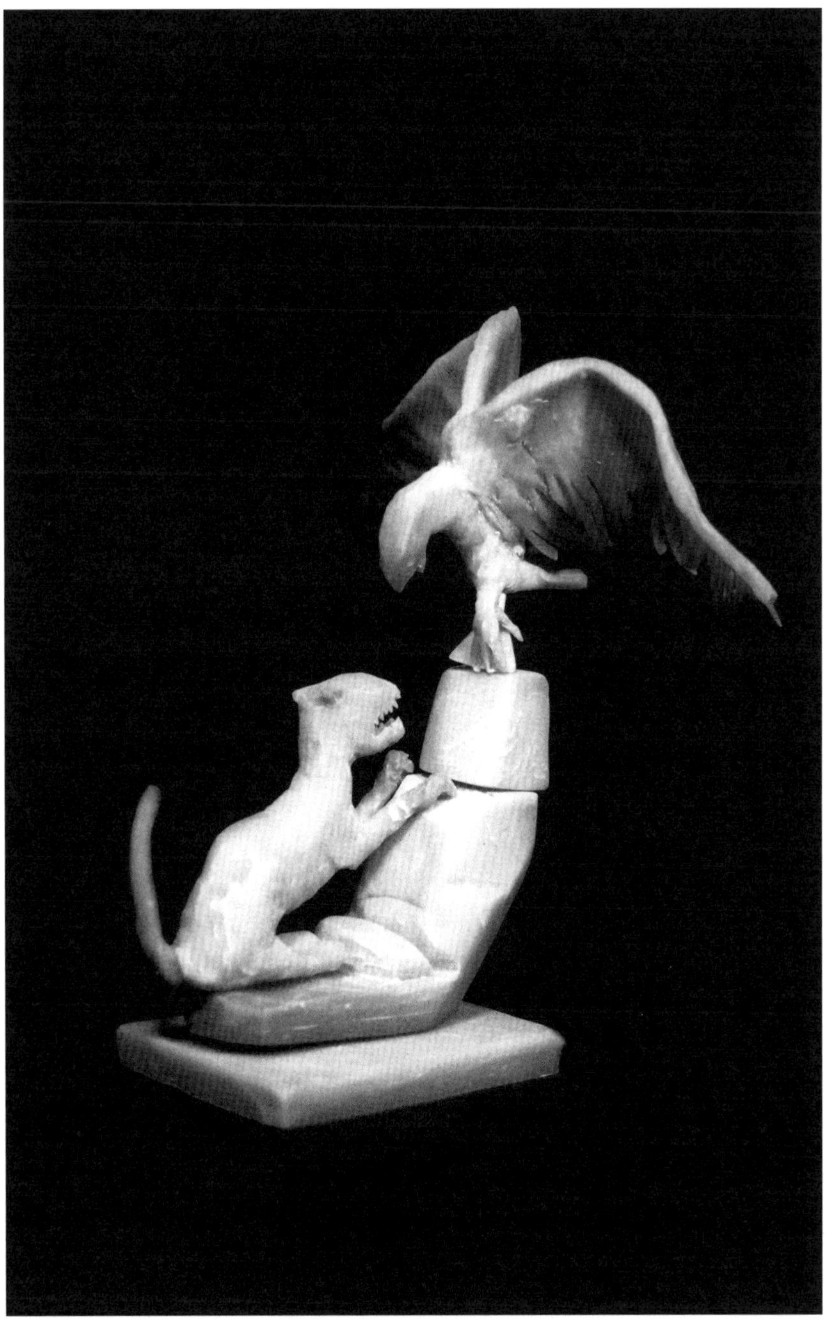

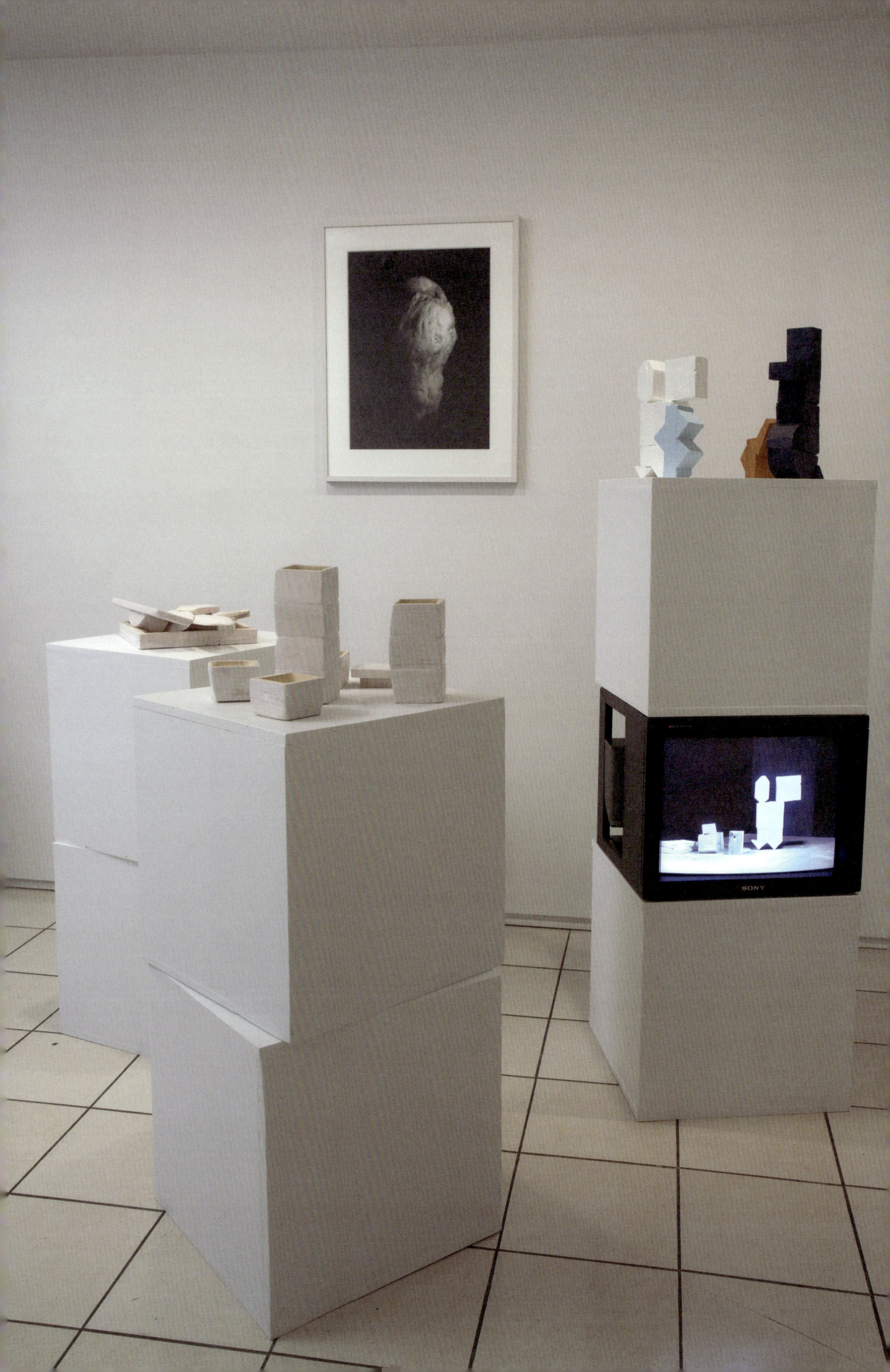
SONY

The first work I made while in Belgium, and this is kind of interestingly important, was *The Bakery of Blok*, which completely dispenses with any kind of comprehensible language, instead substituting it for abstract sounds.

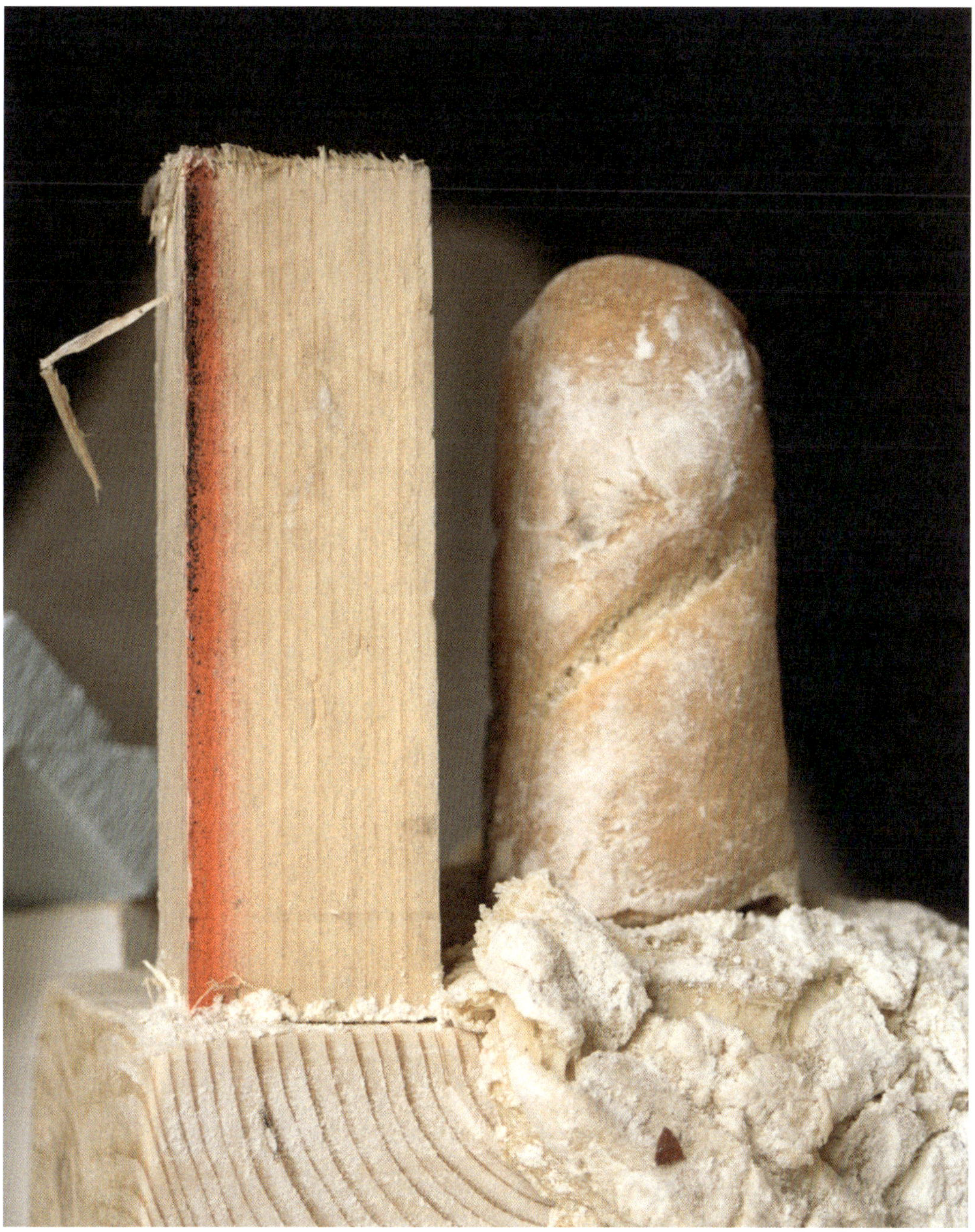

DR: With *The Bakery of Blok*, you made a pilot suggesting that this could be a television show with characters that say "Ooo ouuoo ooOoOooooo."

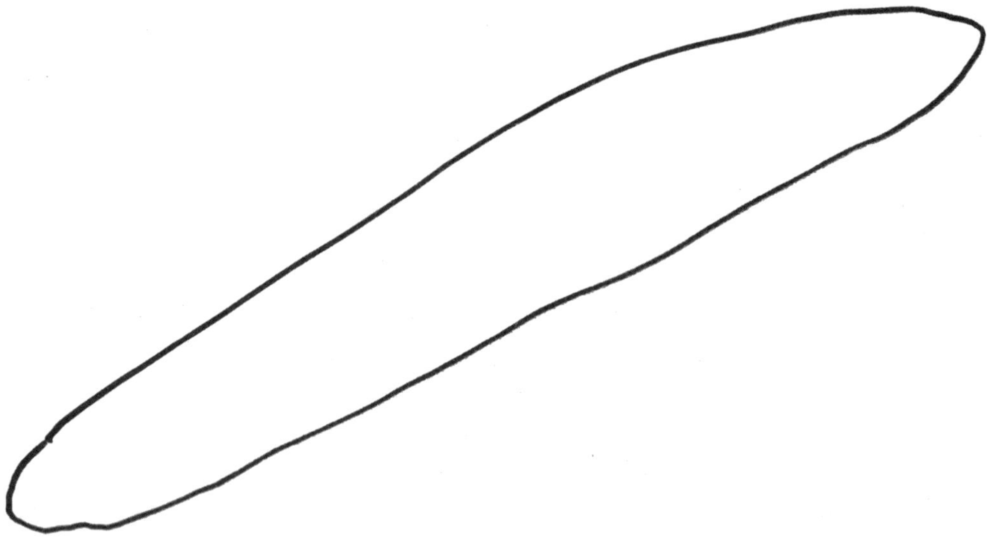

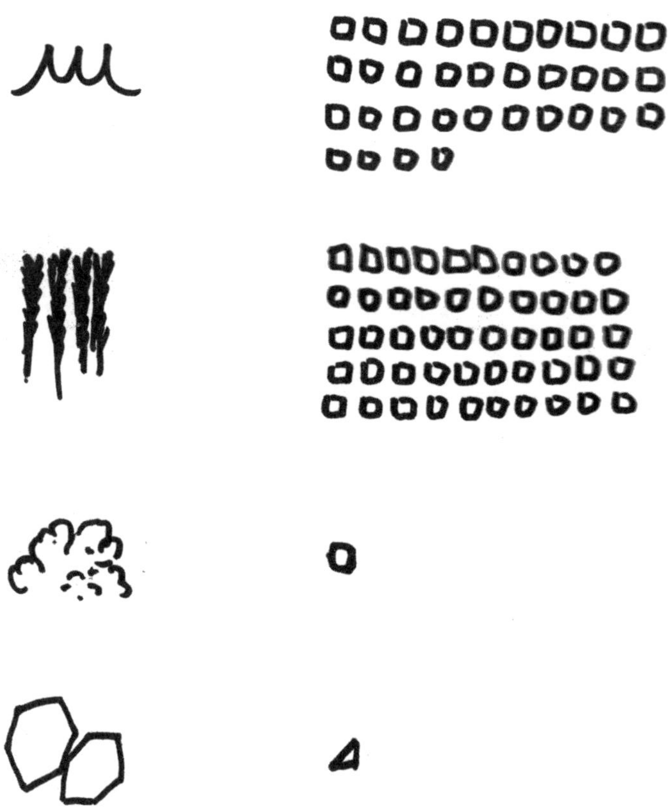

ZT: It's the sounds of wood and the sounds of bread. Wood speaks wood, bread speaks bread. This decision came from remembering something I had read years earlier, maybe in *The Economist*, or some sort of news source like this, where the article talked about *Pingu*, this claymation series, and how it was the most franchised, widely purchased, television series in the international market because it doesn't need to be overdubbed since the characters speak gibberish; there is nothing to over-dub. This introduced a proposal where abstraction became the most economically viable way to communicate. Something you can't understand is actually more accessible because it puts this relationship upon the audience of projecting content and meaning into what is going on in front of them.

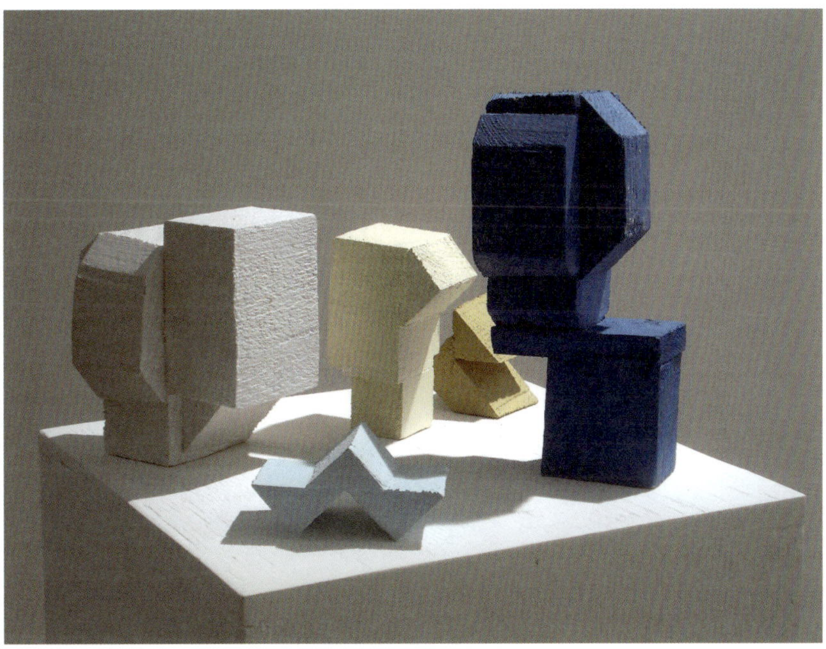

DR: And you don't have to involve any translating, or translators, you don't have to translate yourself. There is no internal meaning, all the meaning is external.

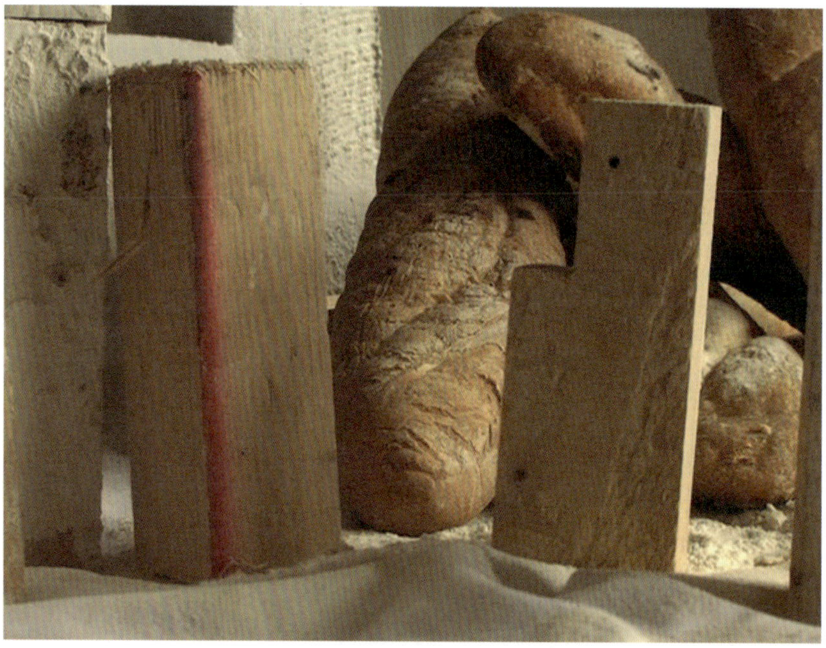

ZT: There isn't something to "get" in the literal linguistic sense. Comprehension occurs at that moment of looking and thinking, which I thought was an okay thing to work with. This work definitely came about from moving to Brussels and not understanding the languages that were going on around me (Flemish, French, Arabic), yet still having to conduct my daily business within it. I found that an impulse took over to assume a stereotype about a situation, not to make a decision as to what something is, but in order to get started. You need to assume it's going to be one way, in order to be proven wrong, to learn another way. Afterward this is augmented and adjusted to what your idea is, or what your conception of something is. But in order to get somewhere, you need to begin. Part one, the *Eight Pilot Episodes for The Bakery of Blok*, was shown at Jessica Bradley Gallery in Toronto in 2009. Part two, *The Bakery of Blok and the Three Forms of Unit*, was shown a couple of months later at Miguel Abreu Gallery in New York. [...]

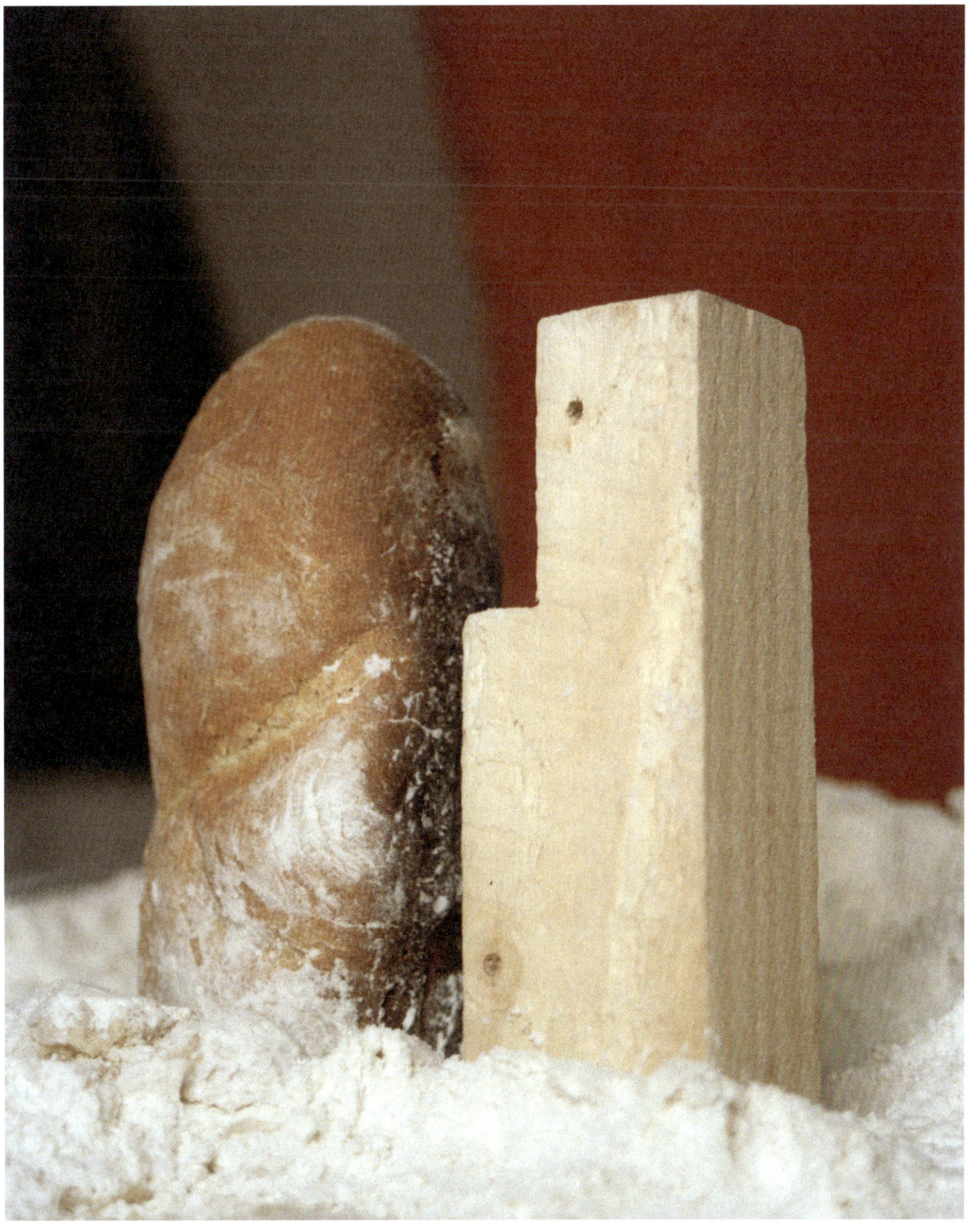

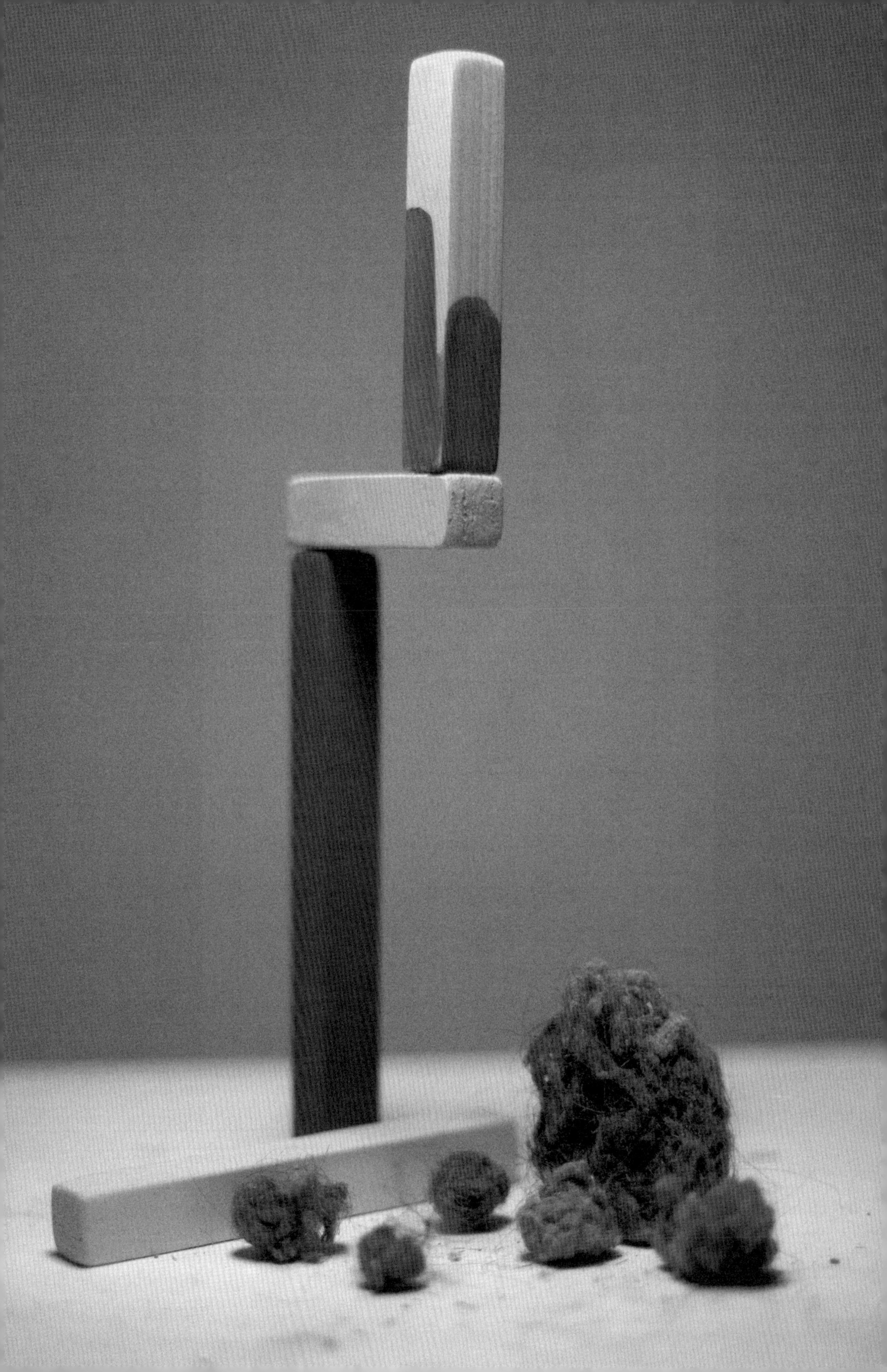

Coming back to Belgium in the fall I wanted to make a work that I couldn't say anything about. I dove into studying what a form does, how does it talk, and how can it talk differently? Communication was central. Around that time I did the *Wood and Dust* series, arrangements of wooden units into sculptural characters.

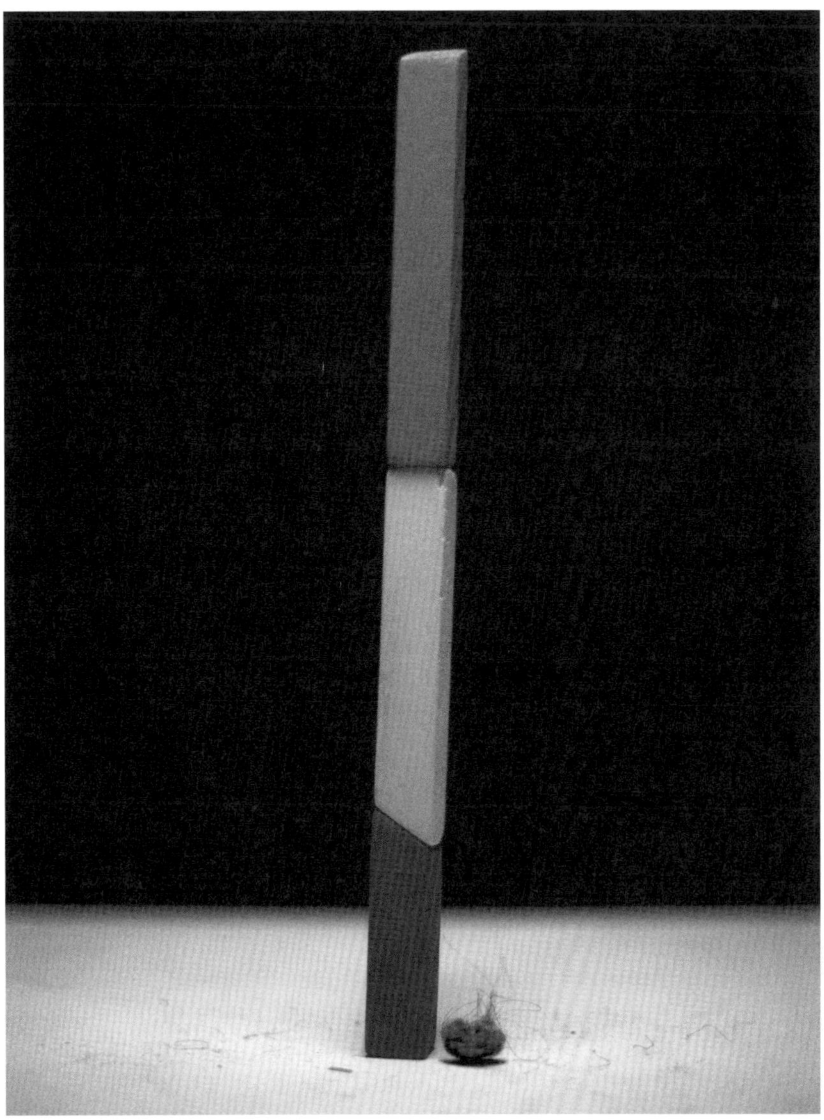

DR: And *Snake with a Wig*.

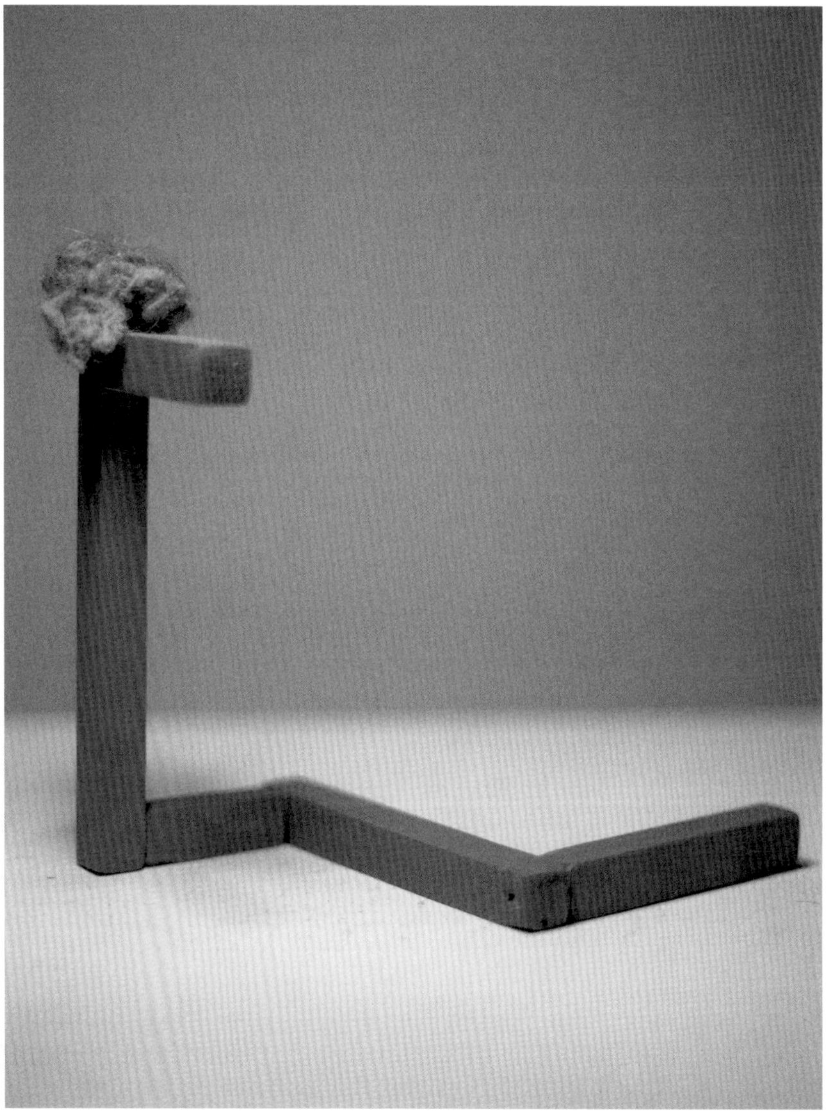

ZT: Right, where the wig is formed by a collection of dust, of debris. The second works I made were the painted arms, *A Structure for Language on to an Organic Form*.

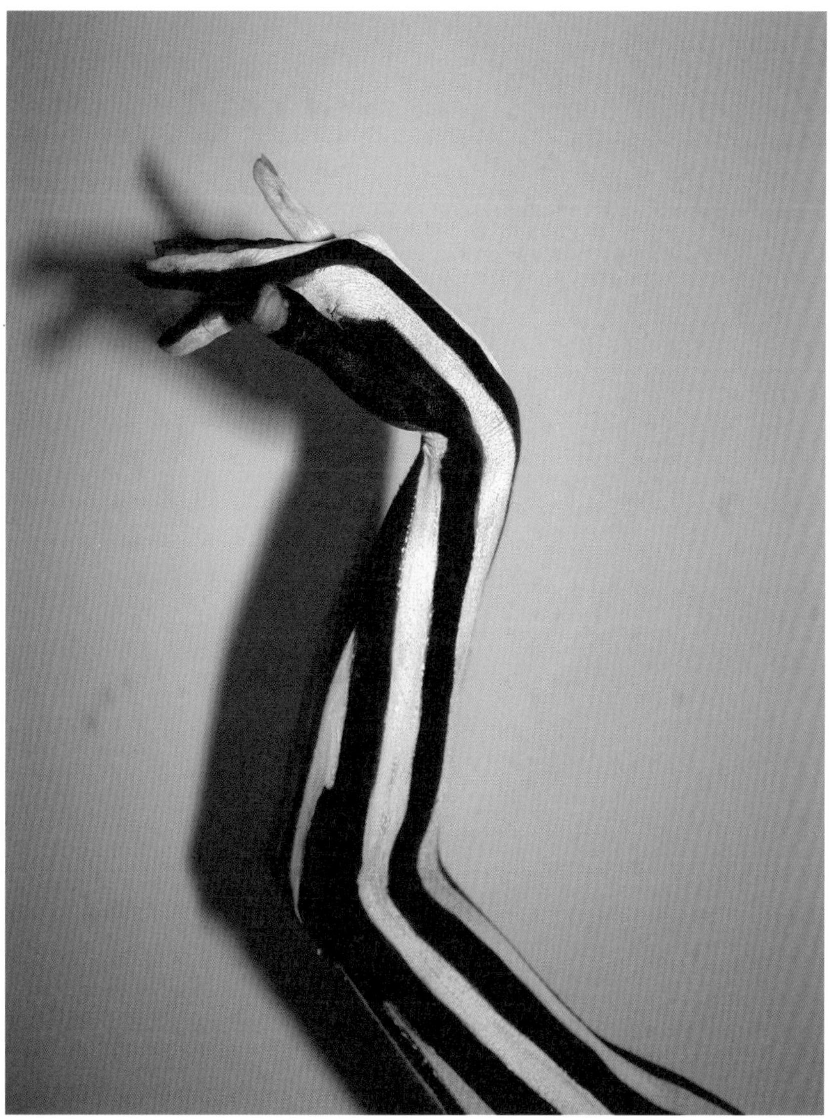

DR: So you wanted to make works that were not going to solicit people's questions as to what they were about, they just *were*?

ZT: It was something about the forms, with the surfaces on them. Those arms were about the proposal of a surface. The idea came from looking at a magazine called *Poupi Whoopy*, a photo zine produced in Antwerp that I saw at Copyright, a book shop I visited. It was one of those thinking days, where I spend the whole day walking around a city, and then after I come back to Brussels with an idea. Before returning I sat down in the Witzli-Poetzli, a tiny bar in the centre of Antwerp. I remembered this zine I had seen earlier. In it was a photo series of a lady heavily painted with body makeup to create a giant eyeball on her head. The form of the body was renegotiated with makeup, with a kind of fiction applied to her surface, temporarily weirding her body form.

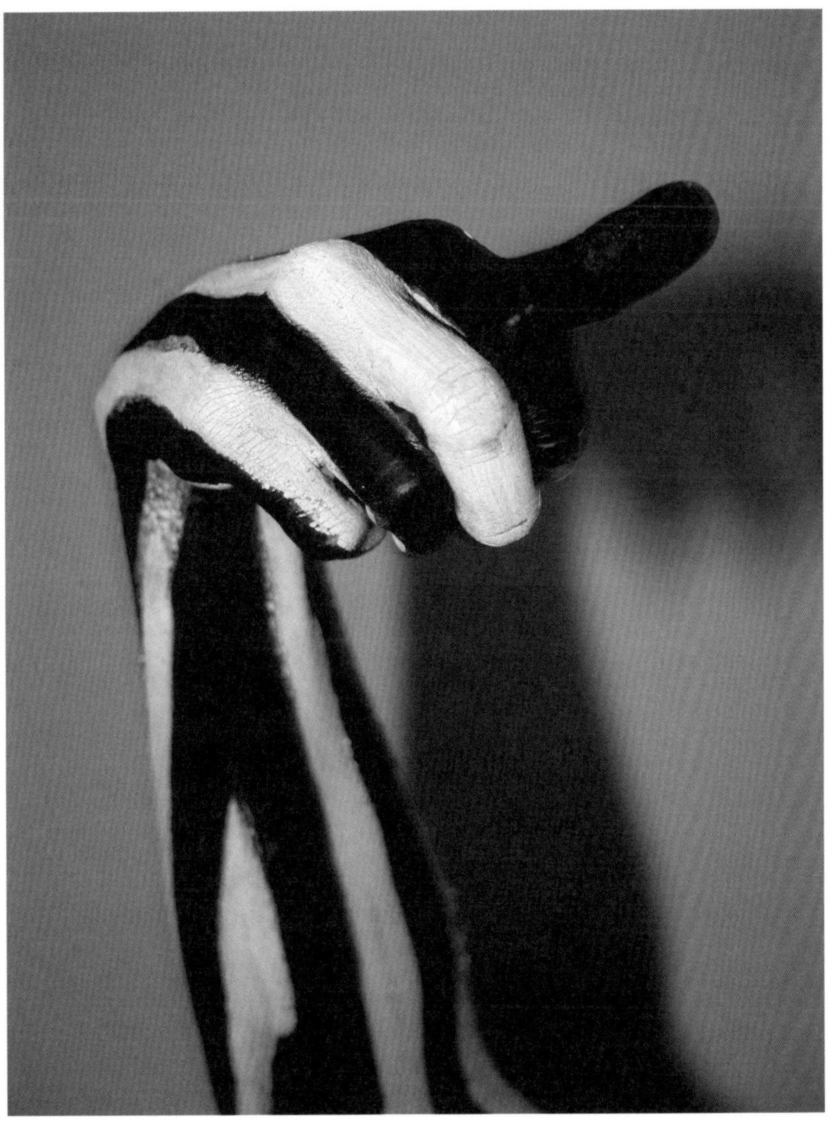

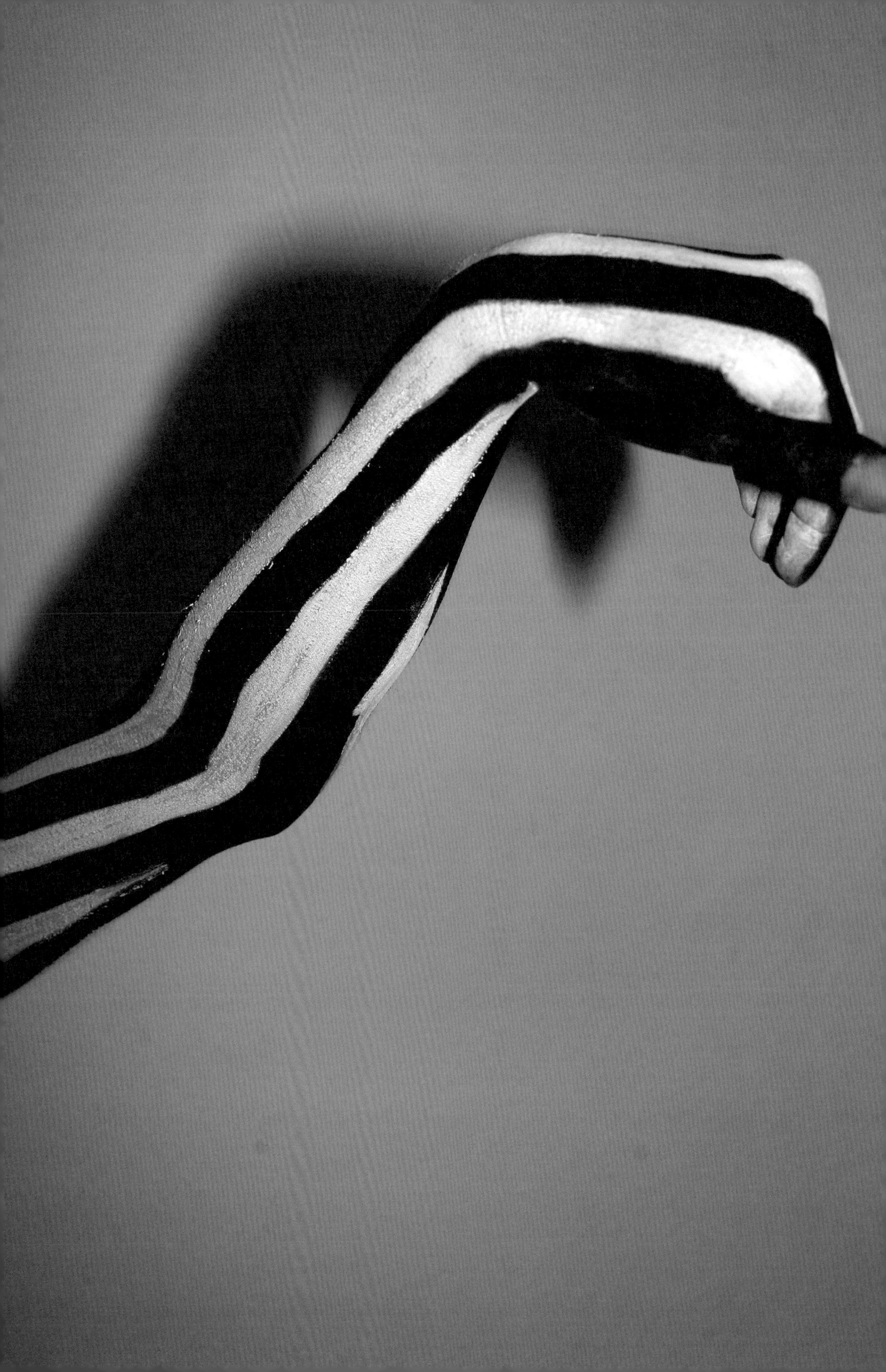

You asked earlier what goes into making a new work—sometimes I sit down with a list of things that I would like to have in every work, and from then on, it's about trying to find an alternate way to tell a story again, to present another proposition of a story, of an idea. In the case of the zine, I asked the question: what can I do to a surface that would temporarily make it different, but still readable? I had already decided that I wanted to do a photograph. I decided to paint a body part, an arm, a thing that you can never really understand because it's living and thinking. Although temporarily, through the use of surface, you can assign this form a new job, a kind of role. A friend's arm was patterned with black-and-white stripes using body paint. As the arm jerked around throwing poses, the gestures were captured by the flash of the camera. The photograph froze compositions of white and black, verticals, horizontals and diagonals, using the recognizable form of an arm. The body is a fact and the surface is a fiction. It's a body doing something, a form talking. The forms featured in the photographs have a similarity to the strokes of letters in an alphabet; a font of gesture, if you will.

DR: Can you talk with a little more detail about this move and your sudden immersion into this world where you didn't understand things anymore? You talked about how *The Bakery of Blok* was something that came out of that experience. But it was an idea that you maybe had before that immersion was triggered. [...]

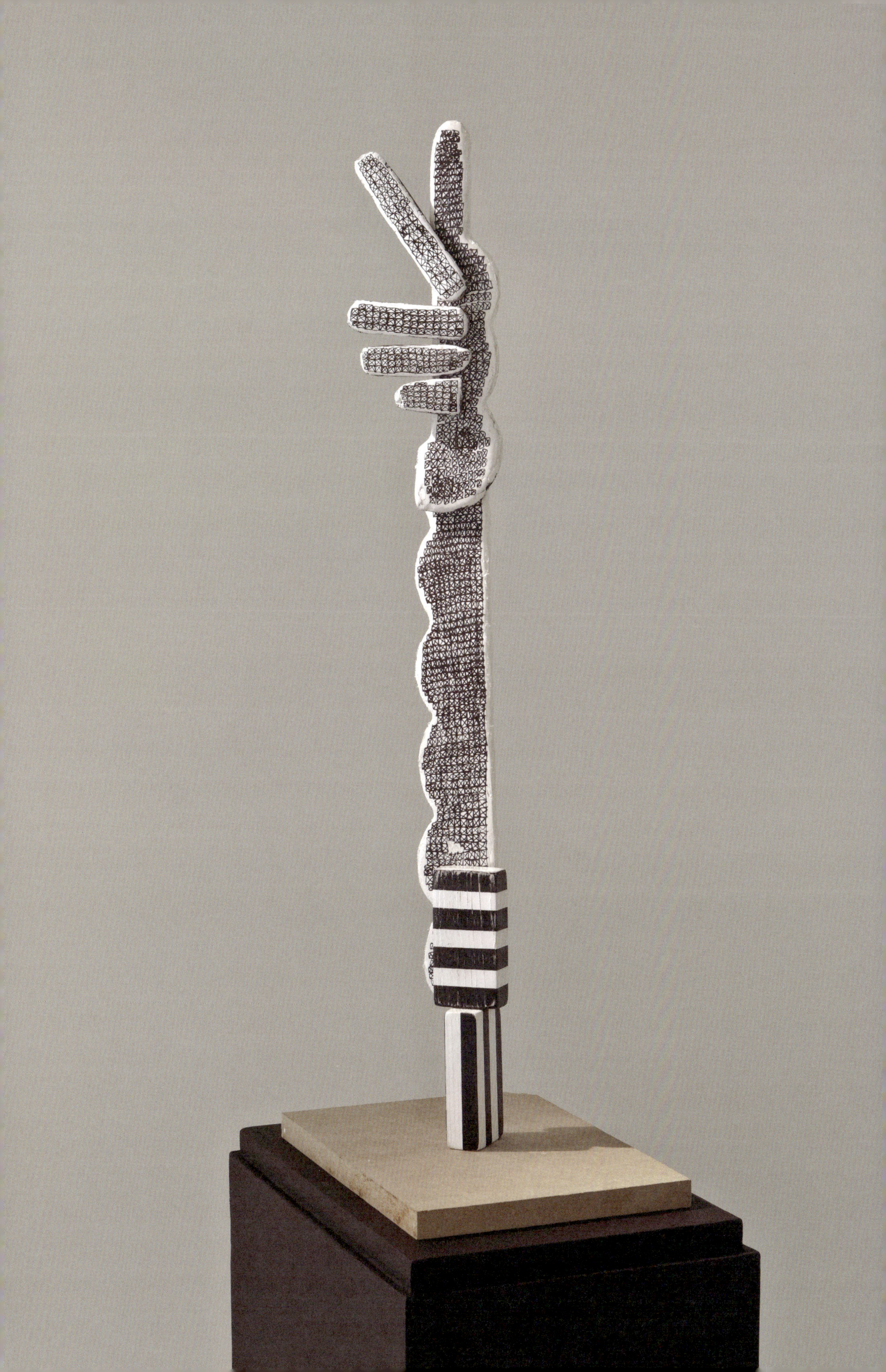

You have lived in Brussels for eight years now, which is a long time—it's obviously your home and it seems to be that your work is now a little bit Brussels, a Brusseleir. It's a good fit. But, to some extent, it has to do with the dominant ideology of art making in Belgium, which historically, has been something quite visceral. Magritte is probably the most important artist of the twentieth century. He's not a really visceral artist, but in *The Treachery of Images* (*Ceci n'est pas une pipe)*, there is a very strange discord between word and image, between the eye and the mind, and it's a foundational picture of the Belgian imagination at work. If you think of recent contemporary art history in Belgium, for the longest time the dominant figure in terms of a museum context was Jan Hoet who is a super intelligent guy, but for him language didn't do it. If he had to express why he liked something he would say "euurrrhhhhmmppphhh." He would always gesture towards his gut, euurrrrhhhhummpphhh. I grew up with that as the basic philosophy of Belgian art making and art appreciation, the gut. [...]

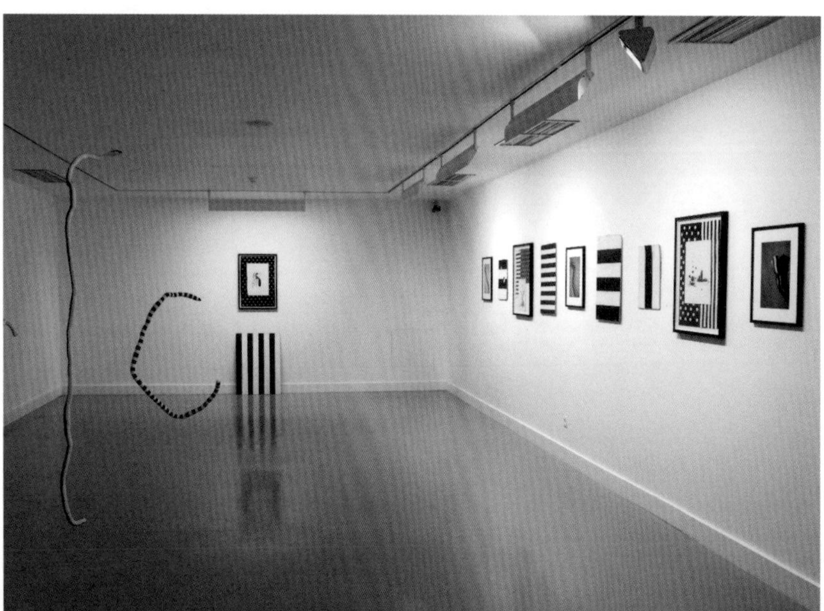

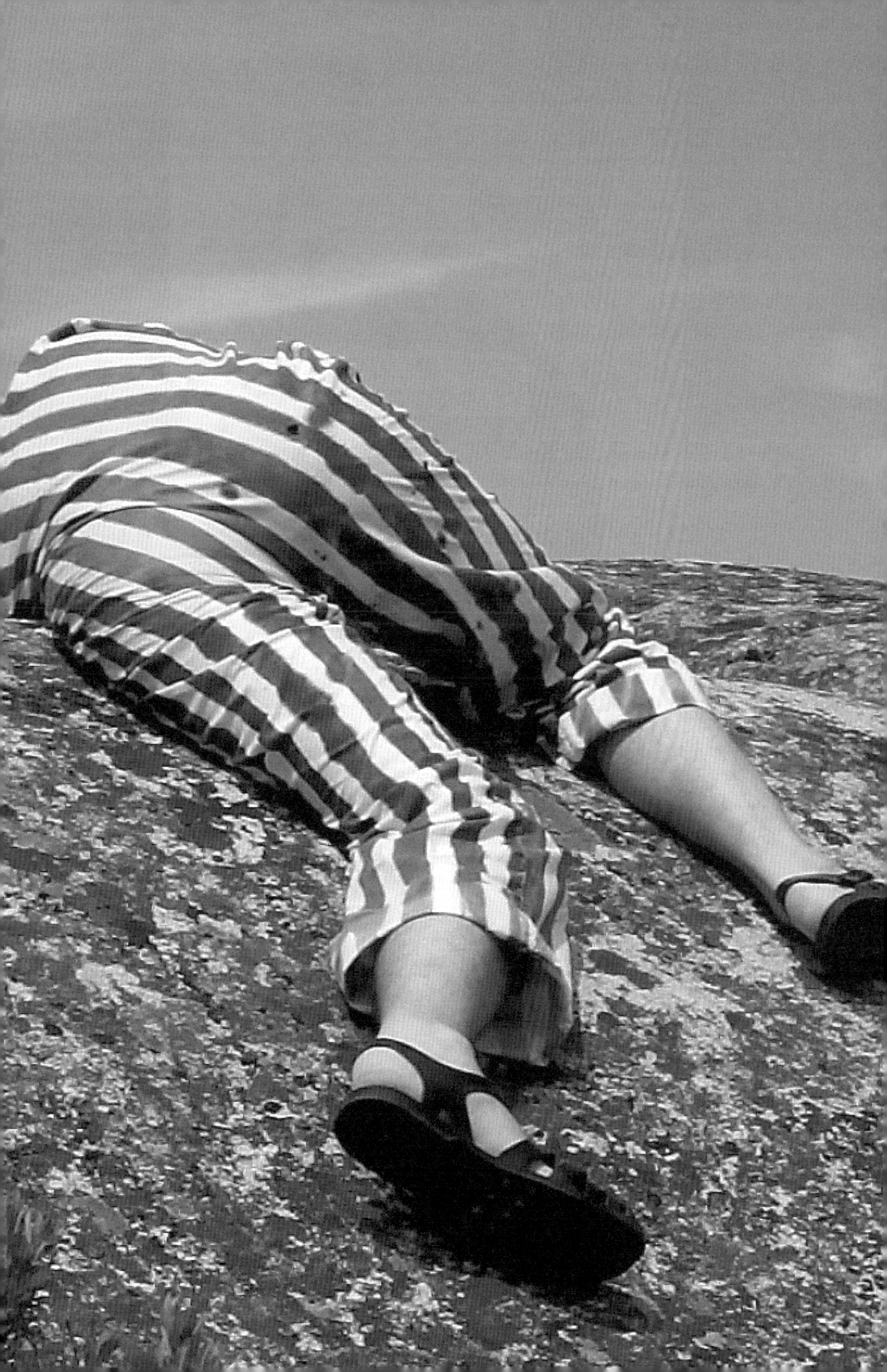

So it was something kind of wordless, beyond words, before words, behind words, but it was definitely a-linguistic and at times even quite hostile toward words. The attitude was anti-intellectual to an extent, but it's an anti-intellectualism of intellectuals, actually. Guillaume Bijl, Panamarenko, Jan Fabre, Luc Tuymans, those are all really great artists. Tuymans is very loquacious, eloquent, and articulate. But with these guys, it's all very intuitive and instinctual, not gestural but guttural—not just as in a sound that comes out of their throats but also guttural as in of the gut in a way, no? And all of a sudden you're there and it's a good fit in that sense. But your work is very different in many ways. I'm curious if you can talk about coming home, about feeling at home in Belgium?

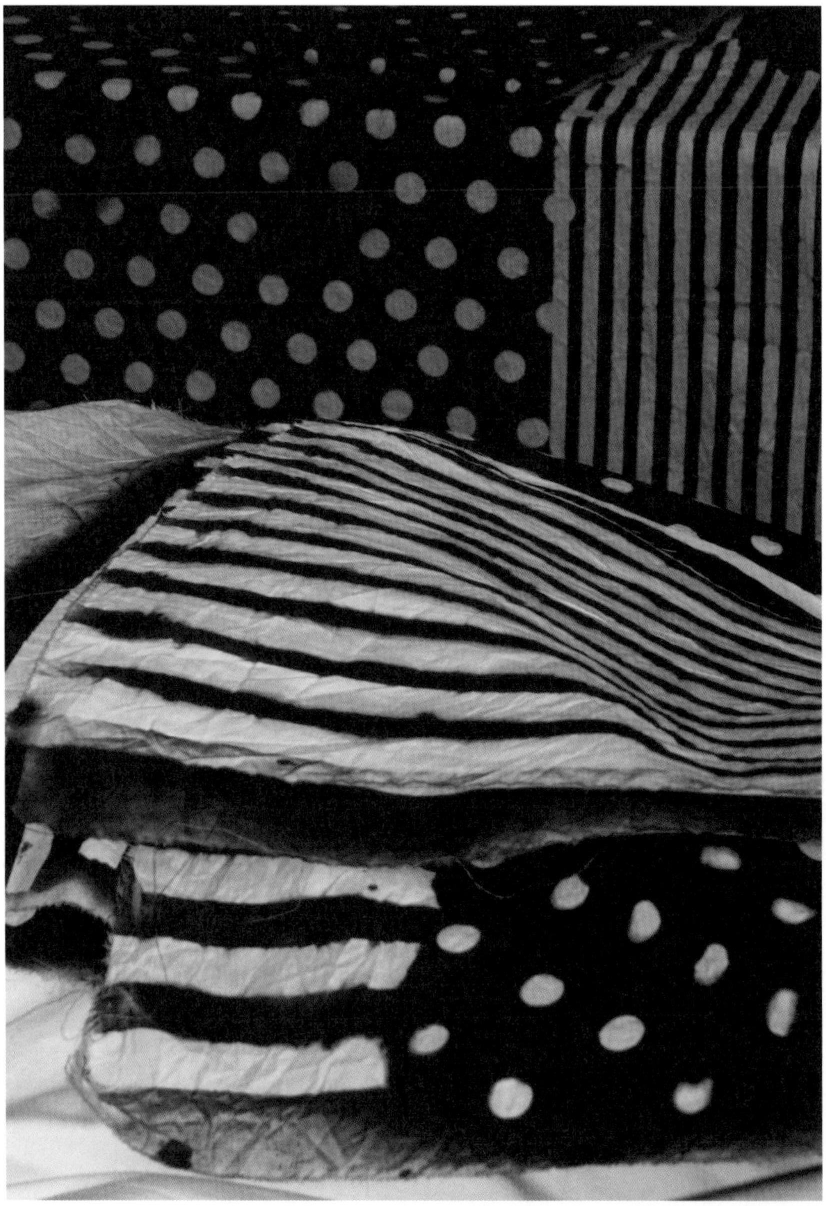

ZT: There is a weird influence that persists when you're living in Brussels and involved in this environment. What is that *thing* going on that's not there, but it is there in an imaginative way? I've described the place as having a bent of magical realism. There is a wonderful tradition of the sublimely surreal. If you were to look at James Ensor as someone doing realist portraits, that wildness coming out of his depictions is the *not* in Magritte's pipe. That's the guttural. There is a psychology to making, and there's a humour to making, and it's a dark one.

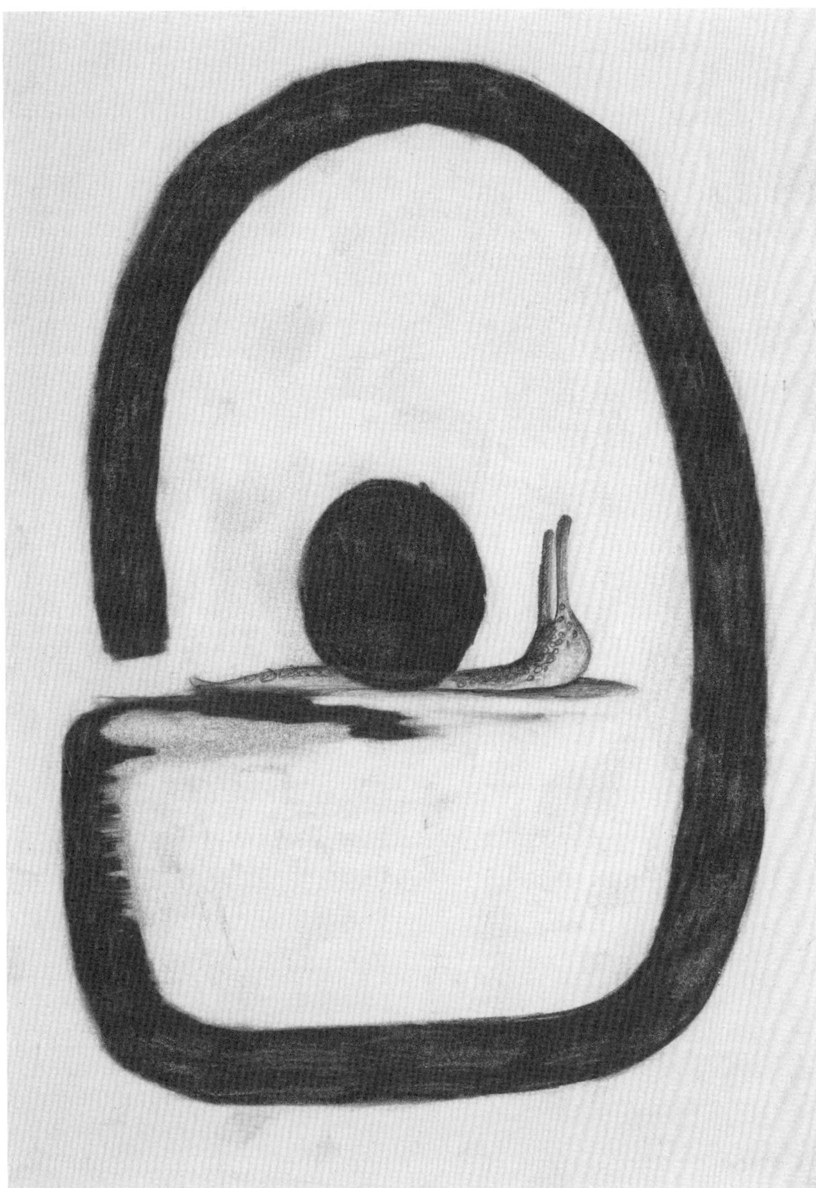

DR: The shadow of Marcel Broodthaers hangs over *The Crystal Ship*, and Broodthaers is the most direct heir of Magritte. In a way, Magritte turned conceptual art into a visual pun. But there are slightly darker layers underneath that. Just a couple of days ago I was having a conversation with someone who is obsessed with how Marcel Broodthaers has become such a canonical figure in America. It comes namely from his institutional critique—Broodthaers as the critic. But there's also Broodthaers as the poet, typifying Belgian identity in a way... there's something very analytical about him. [...]

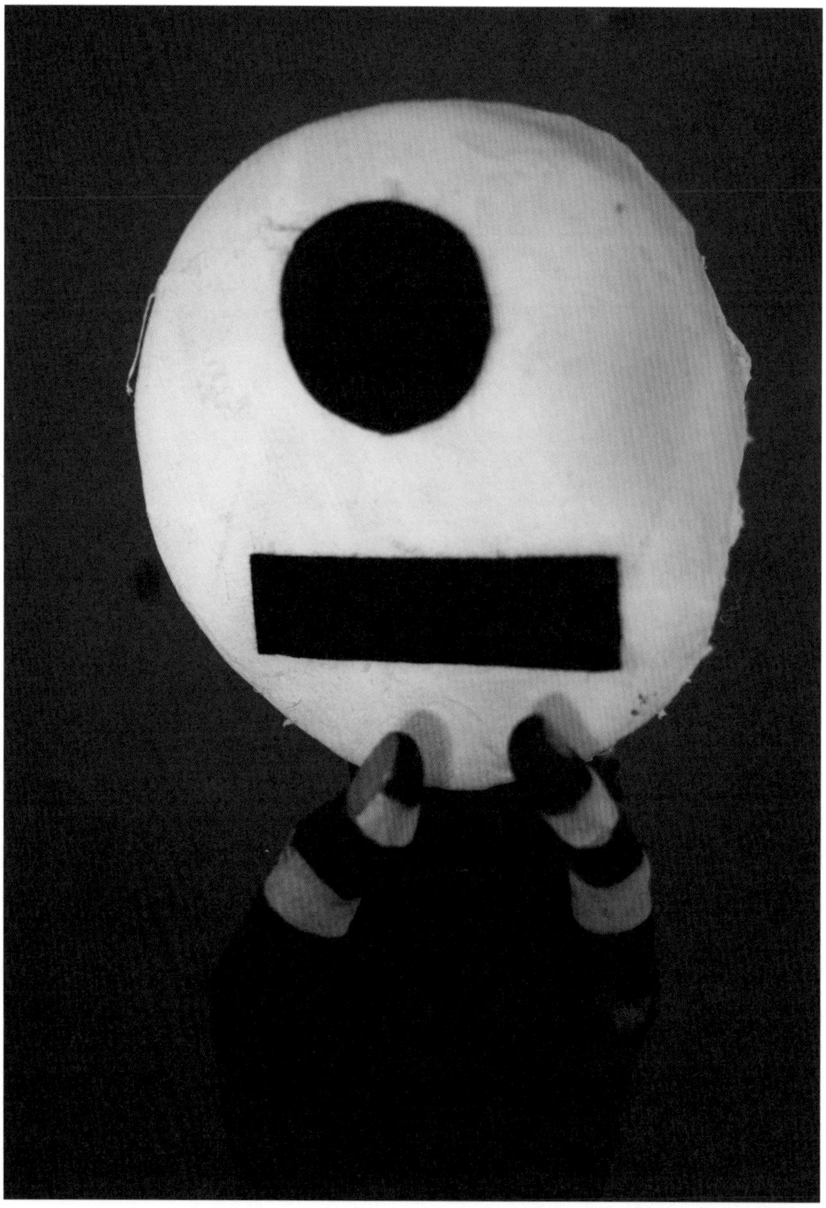

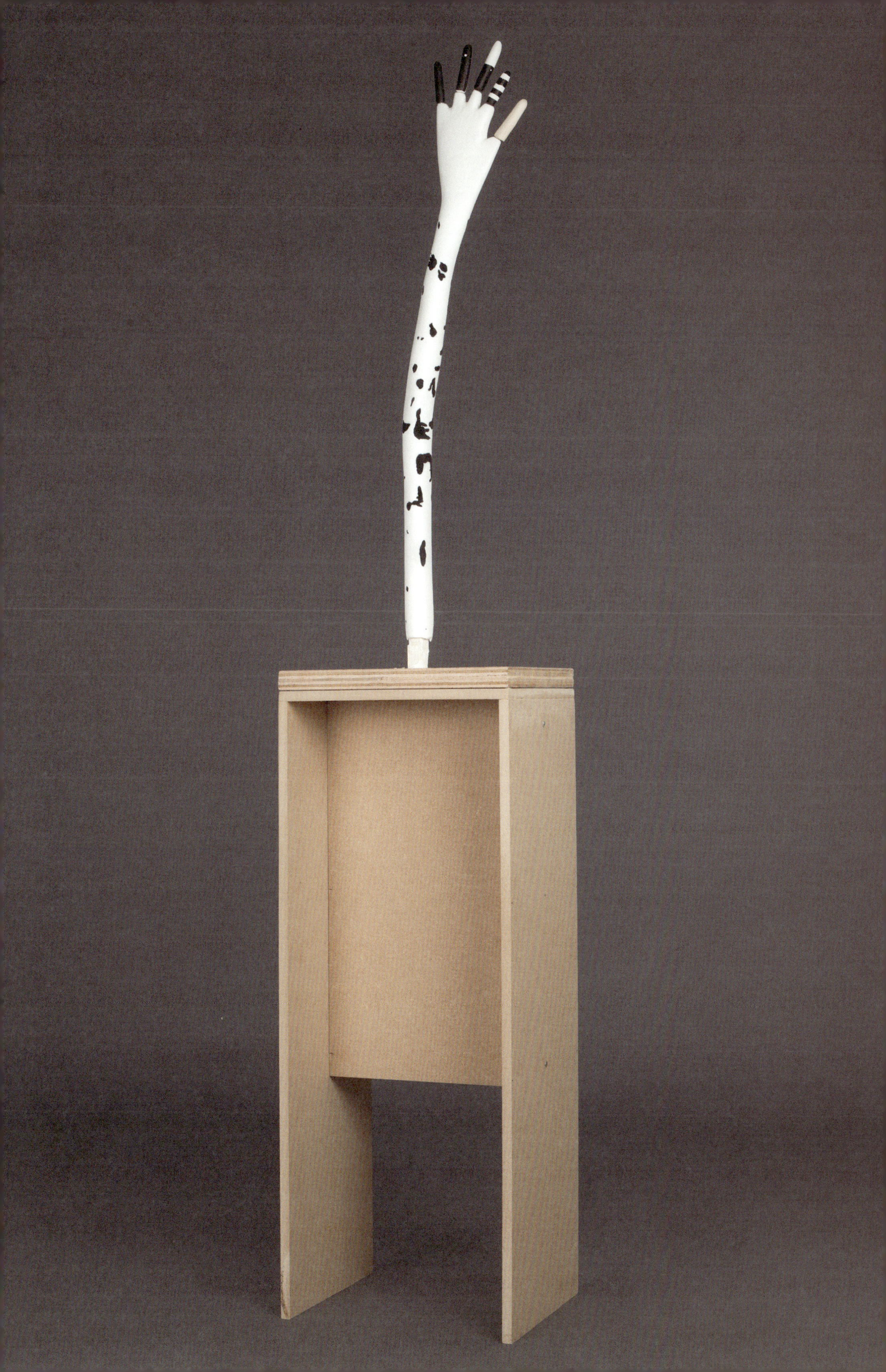

What I like about Broodthaers is the decision: he was a poet, was interested in art, he wrote about art, but he was essentially a poet. He published his poetry and nobody gave a shit. I don't think it's bad, probably not. People just didn't pay attention, and then at age forty he decided to give up poetry entirely and he made the unsold copies of his last book, *Pense Bete*, into his first artwork. It's an incredible sculpture, and an incredible title, *Pense Bete*— "reminder"— first it was the title of the volume of poetry, but then it became the title of the sculpture. So it reflects the double decision of "I quit": I'm no longer writing any poetry, from now on I will become an artist.

You said something earlier about *The Crystal Ship* as a break, a pivotal moment—a point of transit, or a portal. You said something nice, that you were looking at this historical source material about this avant-garde gallery in Antwerp and a place that produced certain things and certain art, much like a cave producing stalactites. That sounds like a really fresh way of thinking about how you relate to art history, that you look at it as a natural or geological process. A city produces art like a cave produces stalactites. That image is also a nice metaphor for your work in general, no?

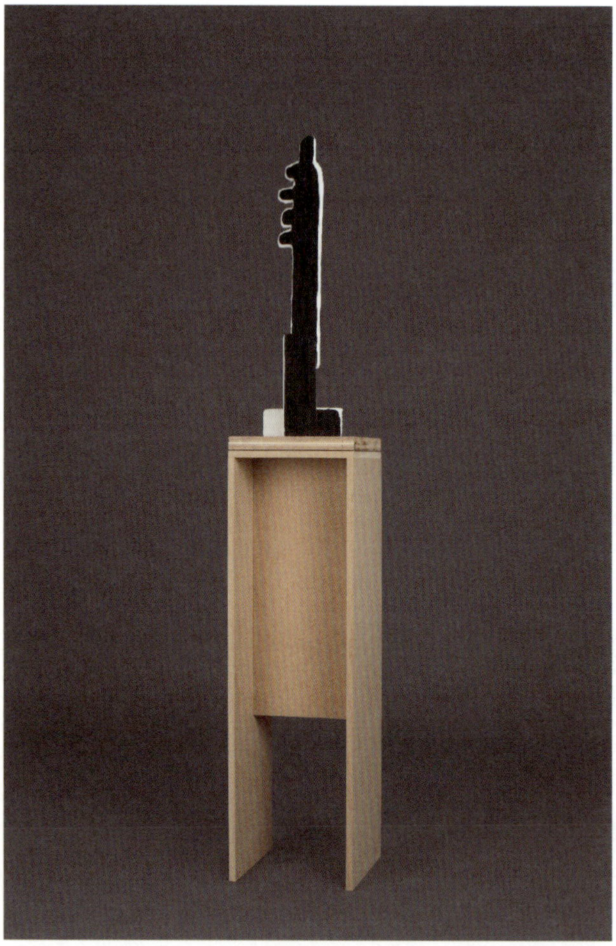

ZT: I would carry that one step further and say thoughts produce forms. Those three words, in one sense, are so boring, they could mean anything. But when I say them, my mind is using everything I've ever done to inform and back up that statement. This relates to my feelings about intentionality, that it's the thing that happens to information after you consume it. It's forever changed because you've developed a relationship to that piece of information that has now adjusted that information; it's been changed to fit into everything else you know, it's been turned into a unit. [...]

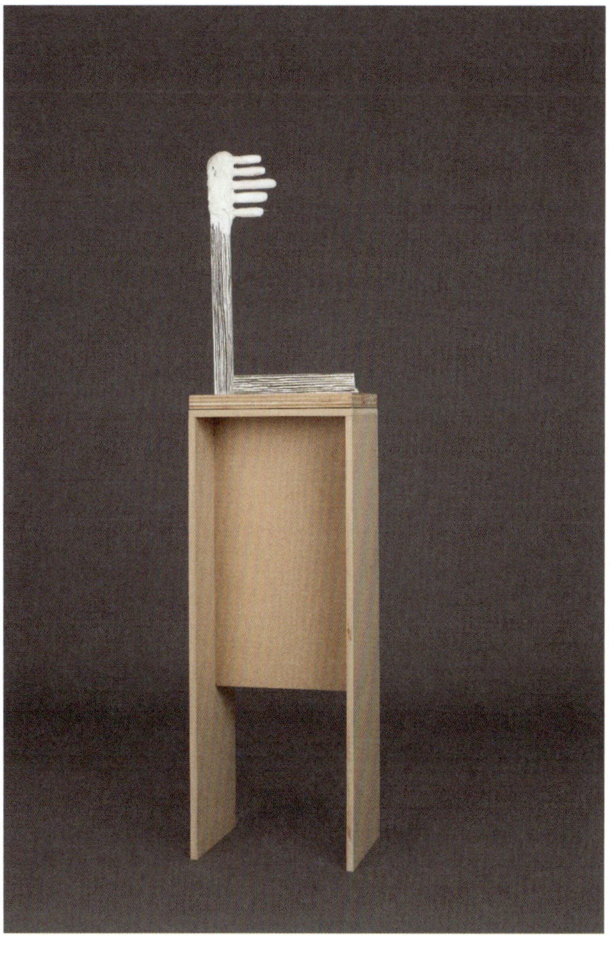

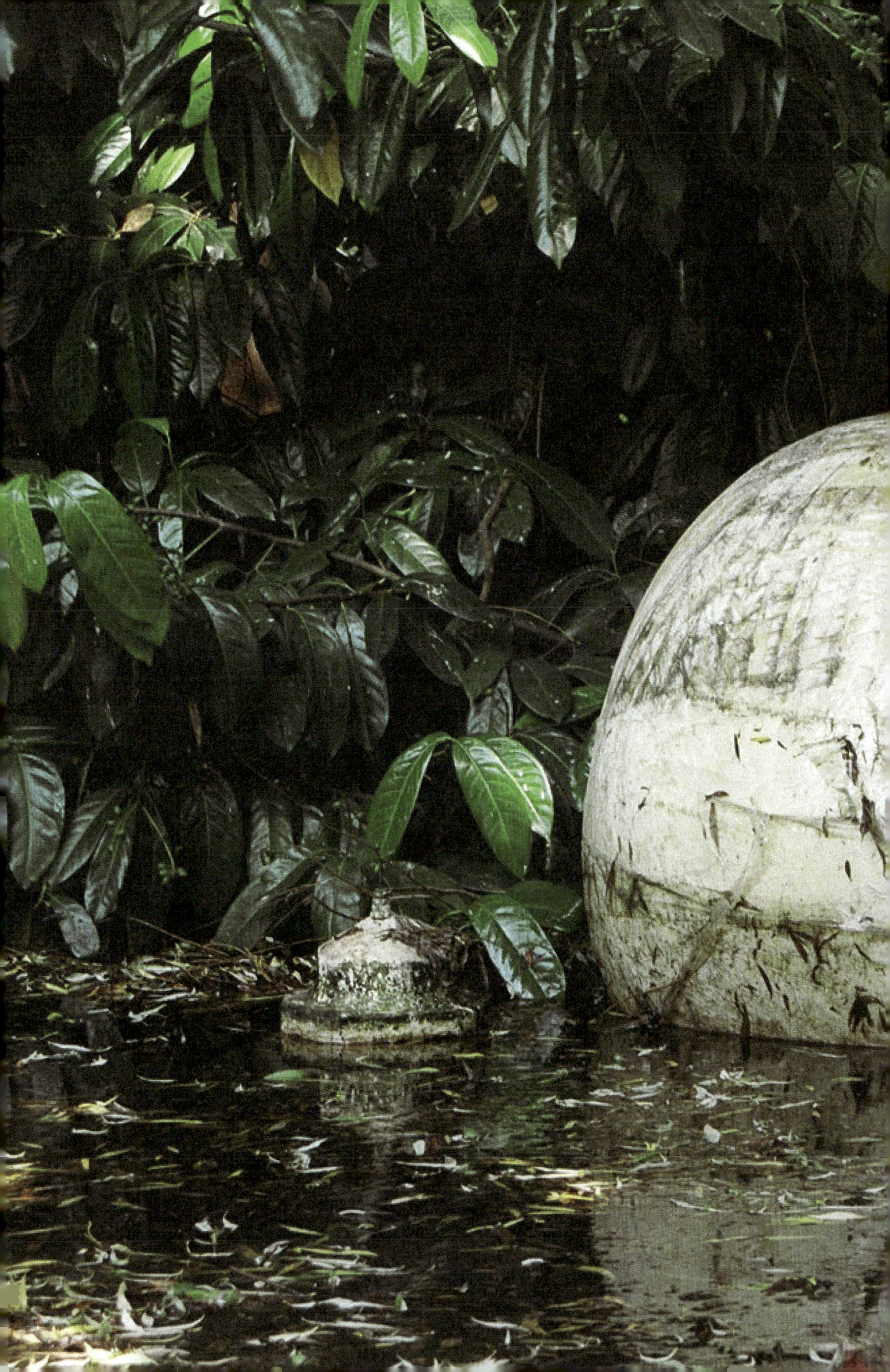

When you were curating my exhibition for the Ursula Blickle Stiftung in 2011, you wanted to do something that I had avoided relative to a description of my work, and that was to find one word that would describe it as a whole. I hated that idea of reduction. *Growth* was the word that came out of the discussion. Specifically, that growth was the thing that is exhibited. This goes back to the work not necessarily being about something. Instead, it's about a projection forward. Thoughts about a subject, turned into forms about a subject, and that what is exhibited is the growth occurring from this process.

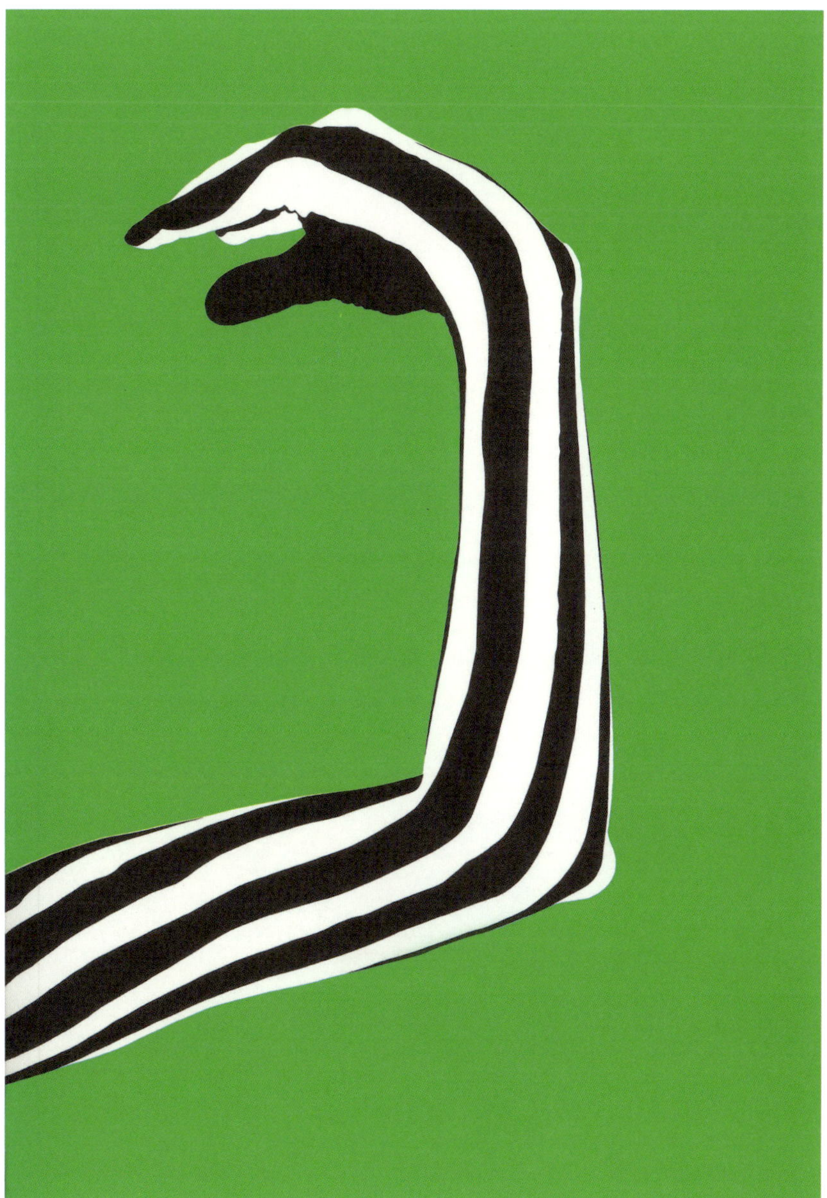

DR: It's a picture of organicism. You talk about landscape and the rural—of forests, trees, sounds—and it kind of vindicates my picture of your work as the story of organicism in a way. You mentioned your distrust of fabrication, or certainly of over-production, which perhaps has to do with the idea of inner forces, that your work has to manifest itself naturally. There is something completely natural about your work, and you've used imagery culled from nature to explore that dimension: caves, lichen, moss, dough, all of those things. There are straight lines and angles in your work and there are some shiny and hard surfaces, but a lot of the work emerges into the world as if it was an organic growth.

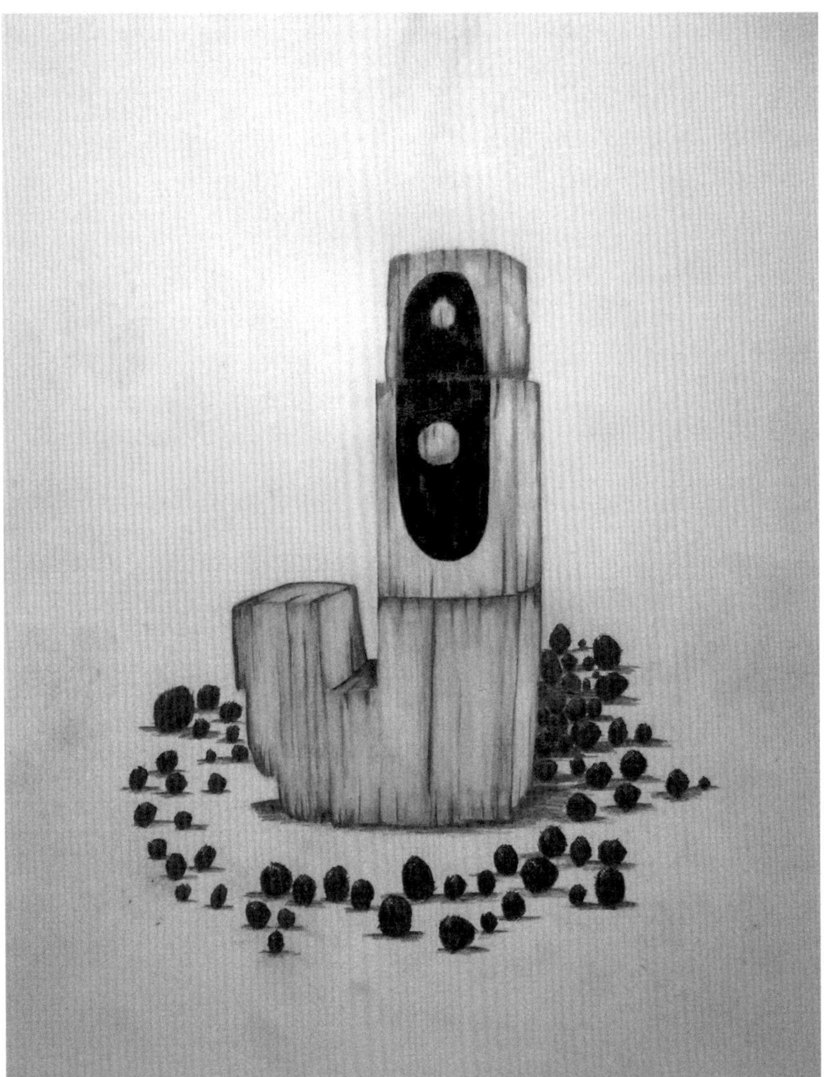

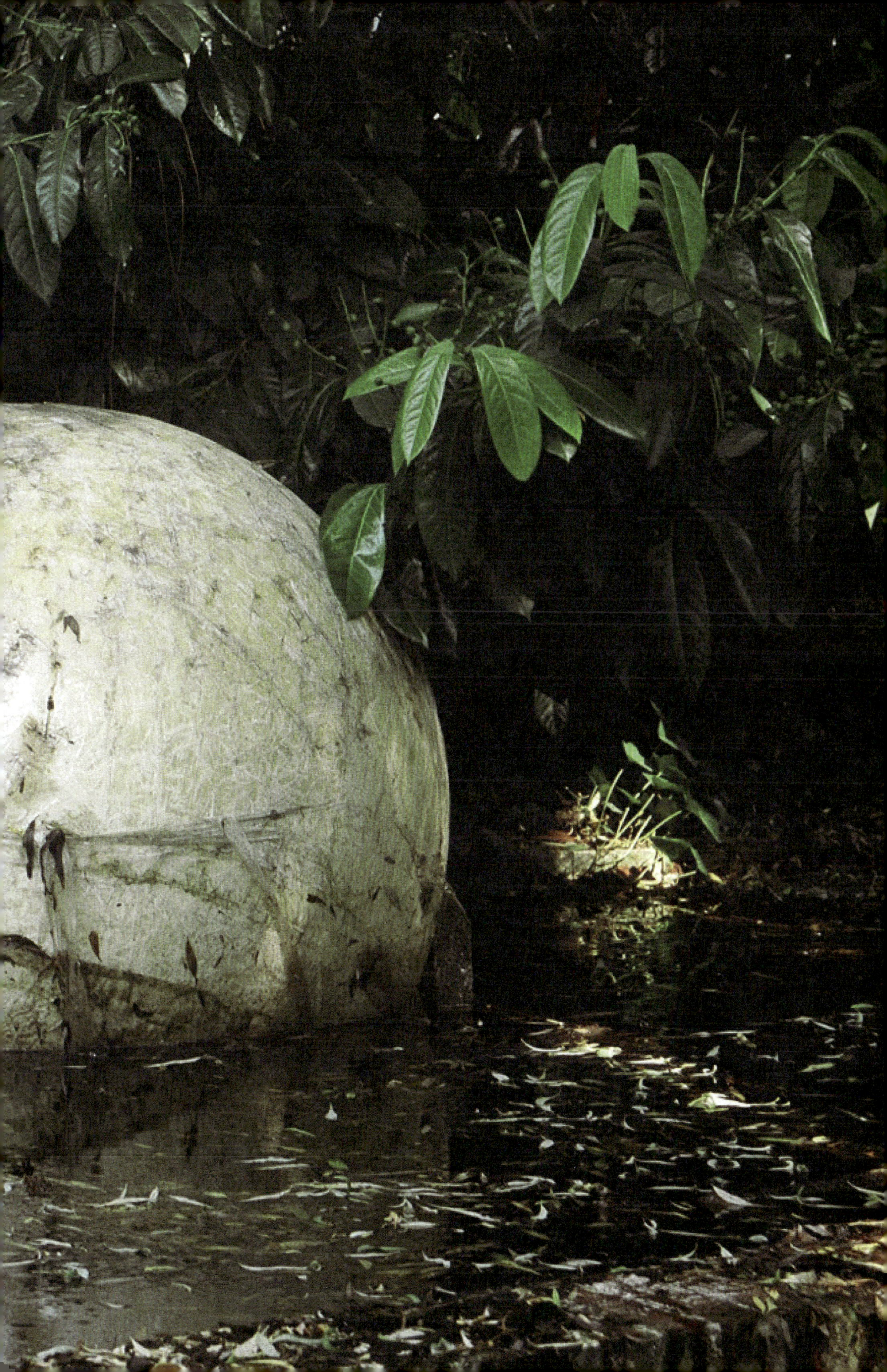

I like this idea that the artist is a means to an end; the artist is not necessarily the source, but the tool for the expression of some things. These things exist in the world and they are looking for some way out and they find an artist named Zin Taylor to express themselves. You're almost like a hand puppet, or like a mouthpiece, a ventriloquist... Can you talk about *Plants do things*?

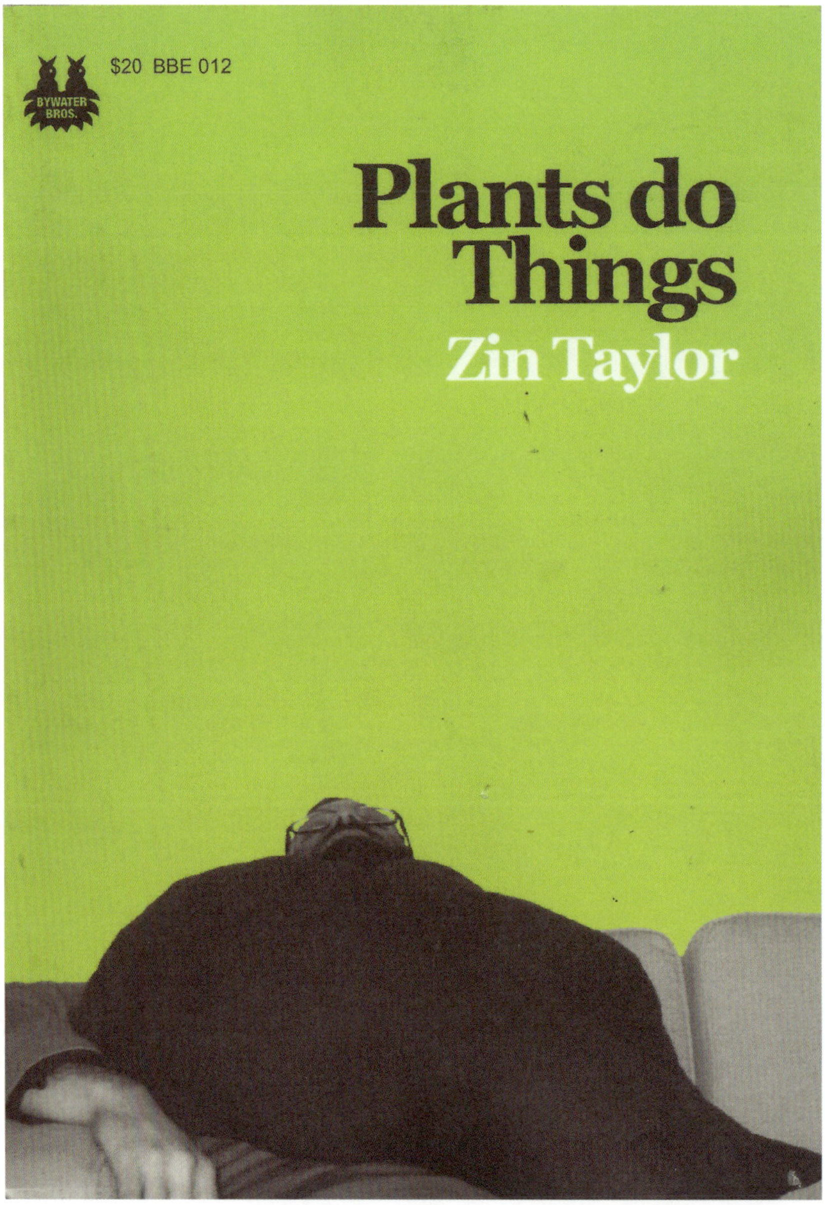

ZT: *Plants do things*, a book which is a compilation of photographs I took of plants doing things, reflects exactly what you said about how these instances seem to find me. I was looking through all my photographs and I knew I wanted to do a photo book. Someone once said, why is it that whenever you come back from a trip you always have the same photographs? No matter where I go I manage to find these lumpy, organic, nightmare-like forms. These photos are part of my growing archive of stuff that I love to think about and work with later on. I started organizing these photos into folders, and the plants folder was the biggest one. [...]

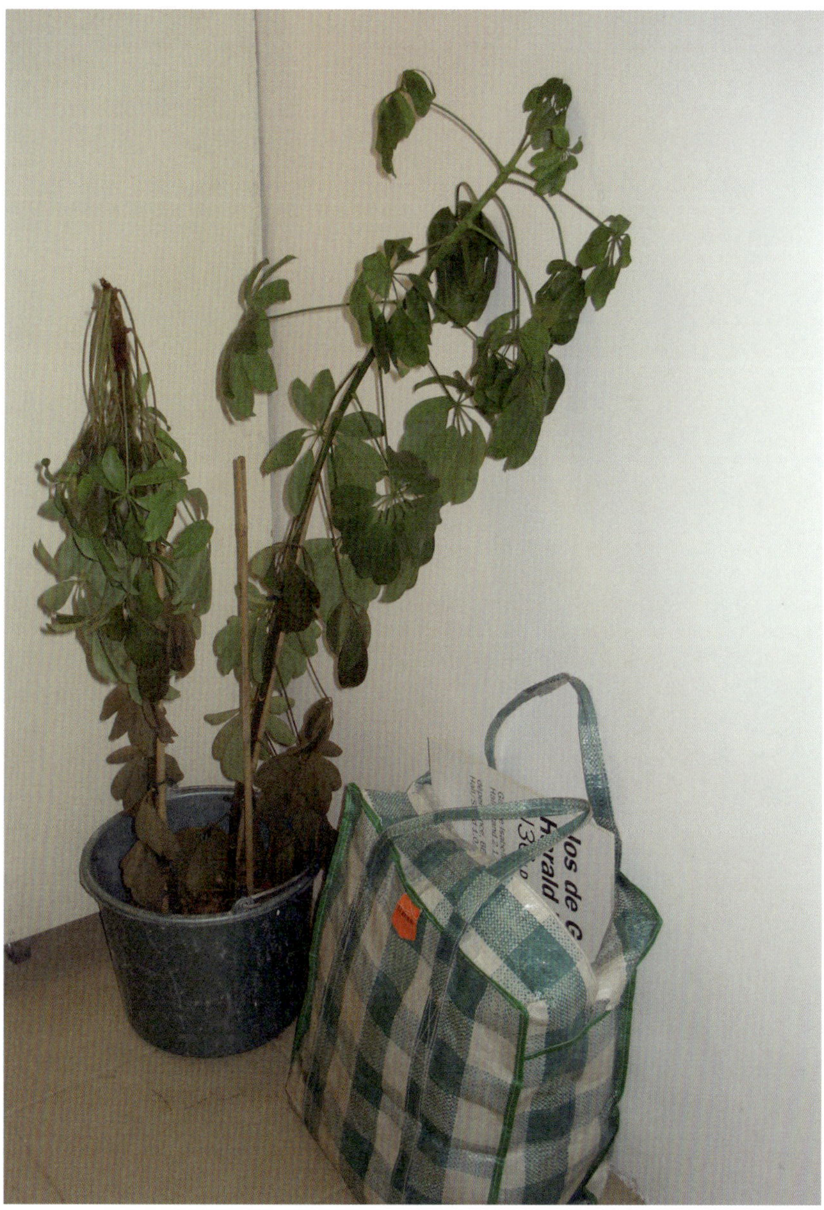

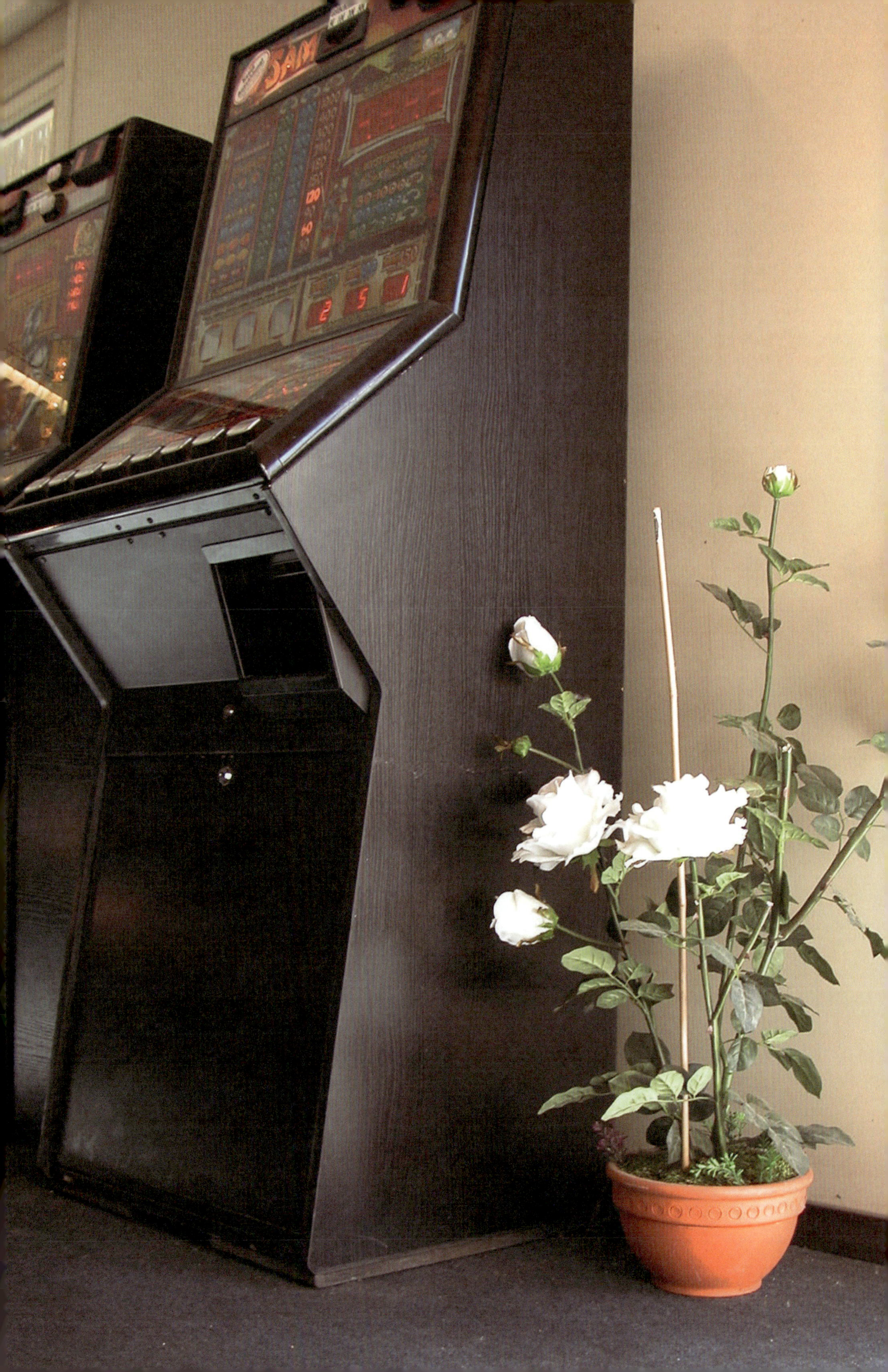
SAM

A photo of a plant gambling that was taken in Berlin; a plant reaching to touch and make contact with an image of Einstein; a plant jumping into the picture frame in the background. The theme presented a way of using the plant as the stand-in for the imaginative in space, the spirit in the space, the thing that's not physically there. It's the smoke that's not in the pipe, or the haze in the air. This was a way of talking about a kind of landscape, a material relationship to documentation, to your environment, and putting that idea in there. If the thought can be a plant, which grows and records its environment, or sits there augmenting its environment when you visually look at it, maybe that can work as a kind of metaphor for growth.

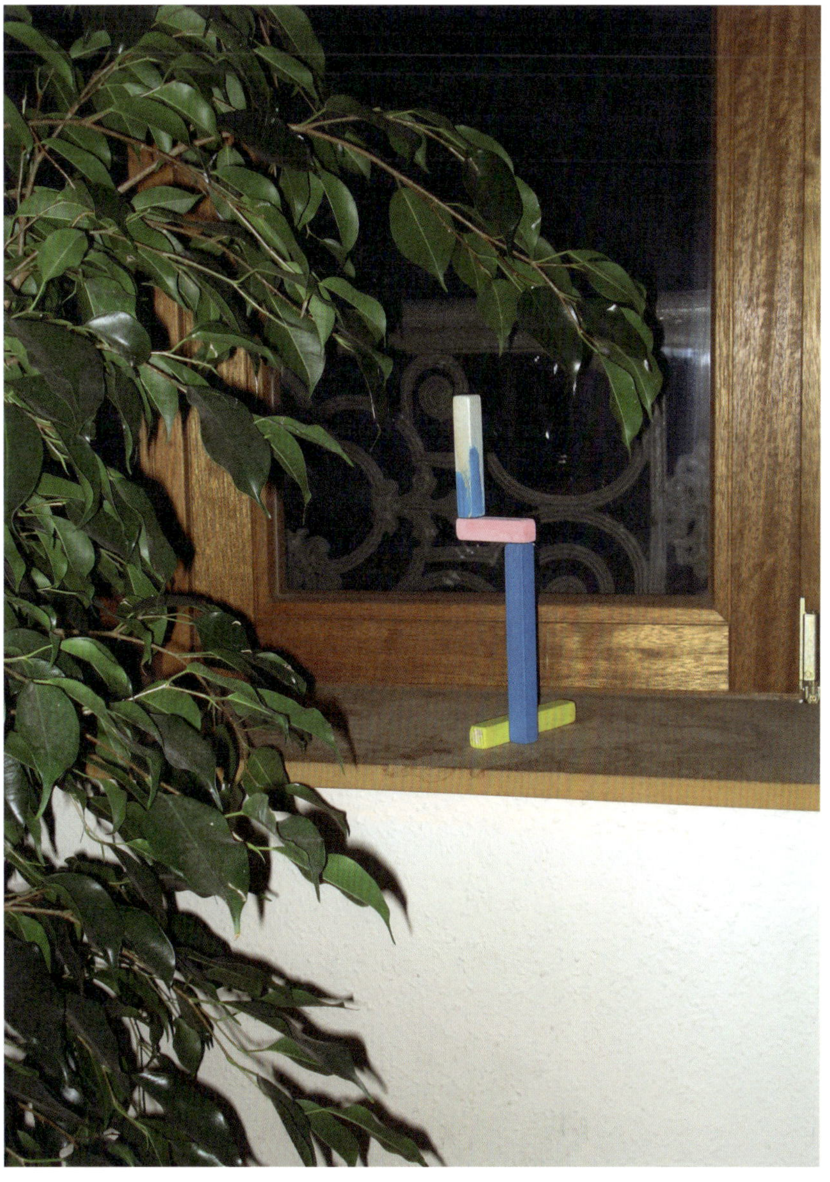

DR: The vegetative is a powerful and interesting thing. I love that book *Plants do things*, it has a picture of you stoned on the cover, which references the ingestion of plants, of vegetable material. You smoked a plant. It’s amazing how plants can have that effect. [...]

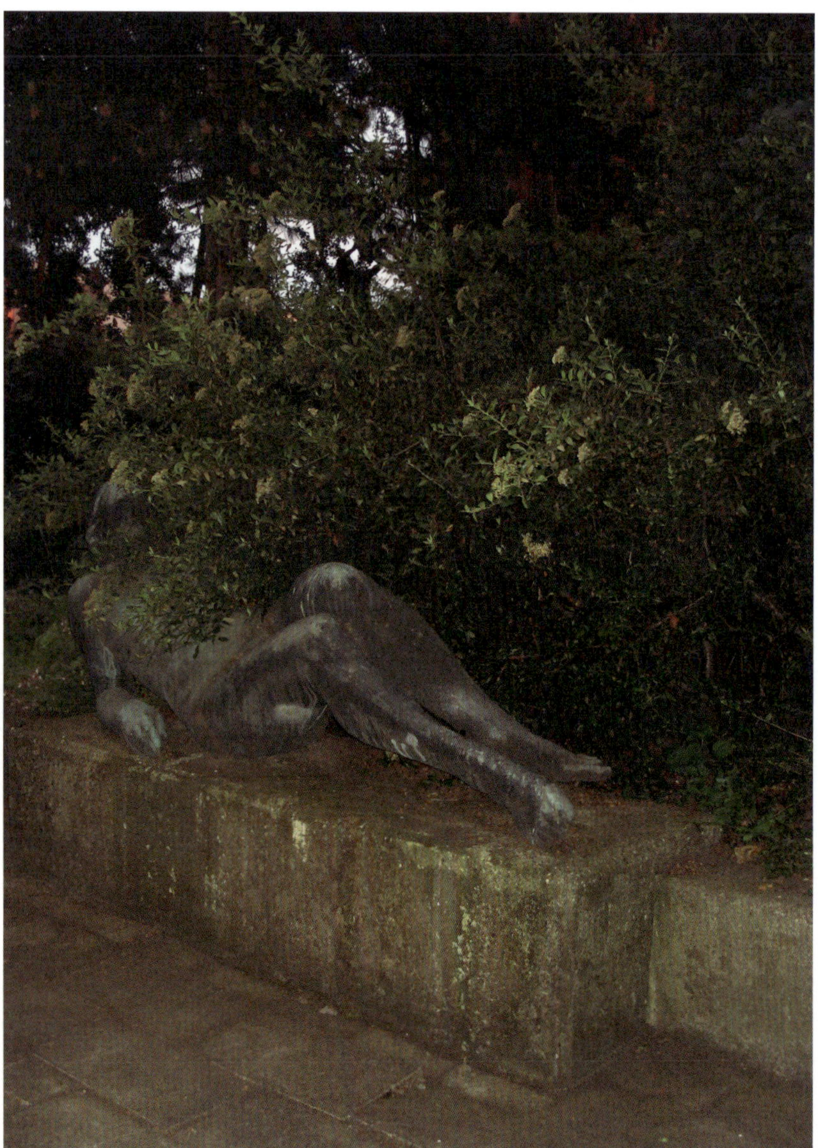

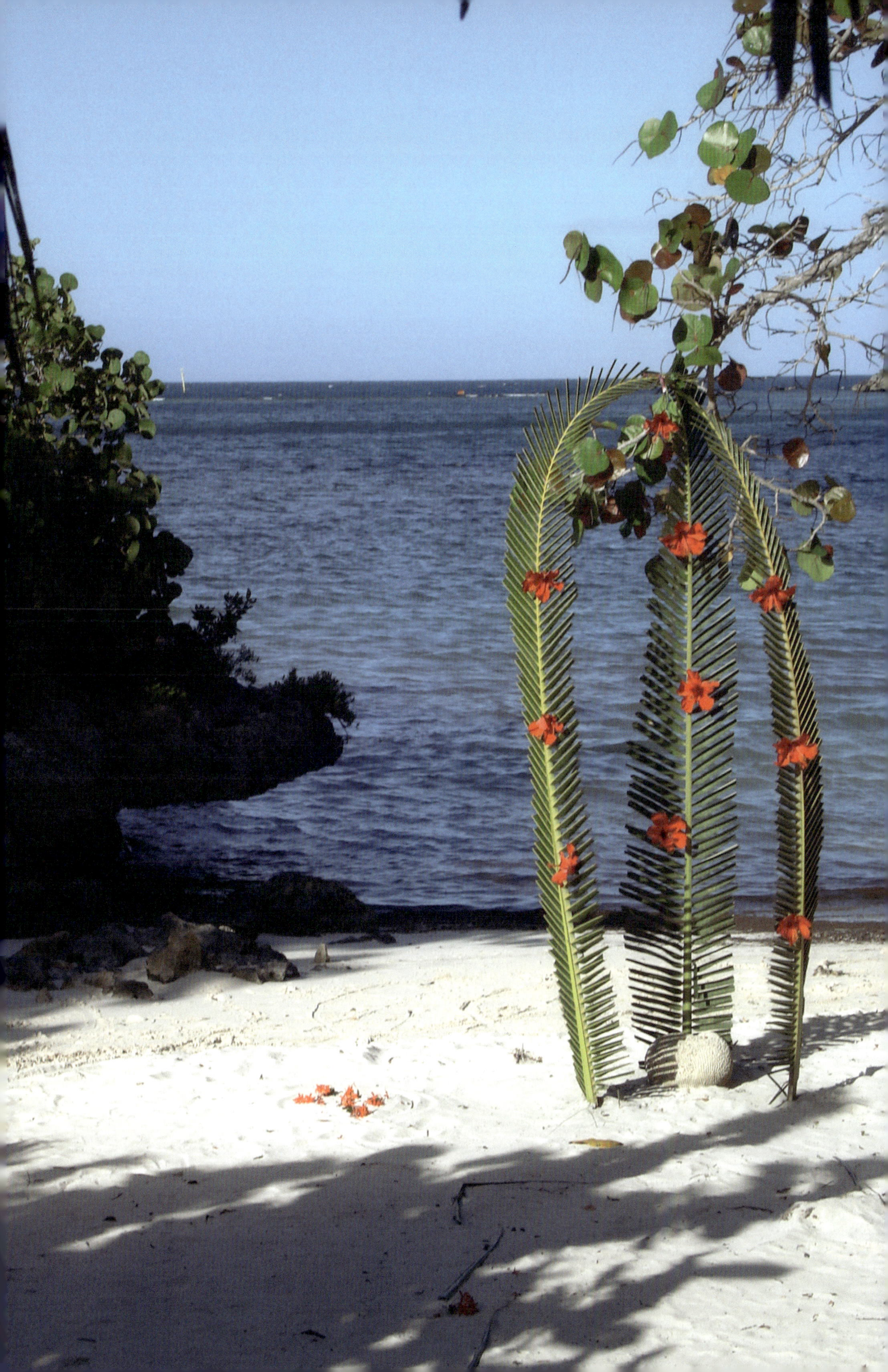

We're sitting here amid the trees in the quadrangle of the University of Chicago and there is nothing that I love more than a tree. I would love to be one. I think that I fell in love with Rodney Graham's work because of the singularity with which he was able to grasp the significance of *tree*—his inverted oaks, which if you stand on your head are just pictures of trees. We're sitting here underneath a tree and there is a little circle of eight trees, they're young, with a couple plants in the middle, so it's not like a circle of elders, not like a grove of ancients, it's more like a campfire with teenagers. Or maybe they're in their late teens or early 20s and they are moving, just really slowly. So fucking slowly, and maybe they are talking to each other, but in a frequency that is inaudible. They grow so slowly to our eyes that there's no way of knowing whether they speak or not, communicate or not, and if they do speak it has to be, because of the slowness of their growth, on a frequency so low that we just can't hear it. So that is what I thought about when this notion of growth appeared in the discussion of your work. That trees seem so static, and they are so *there*, absolutely present, sunk in the ground, quite monumental, and not very mobile. They are beings. They are not really becomings, but they are in fact becomings because they grow. They develop, but so slowly, that they strike us as these unalterable entities and I'm interested in that dynamic in art, on an incredibly crude and basic level. [...]

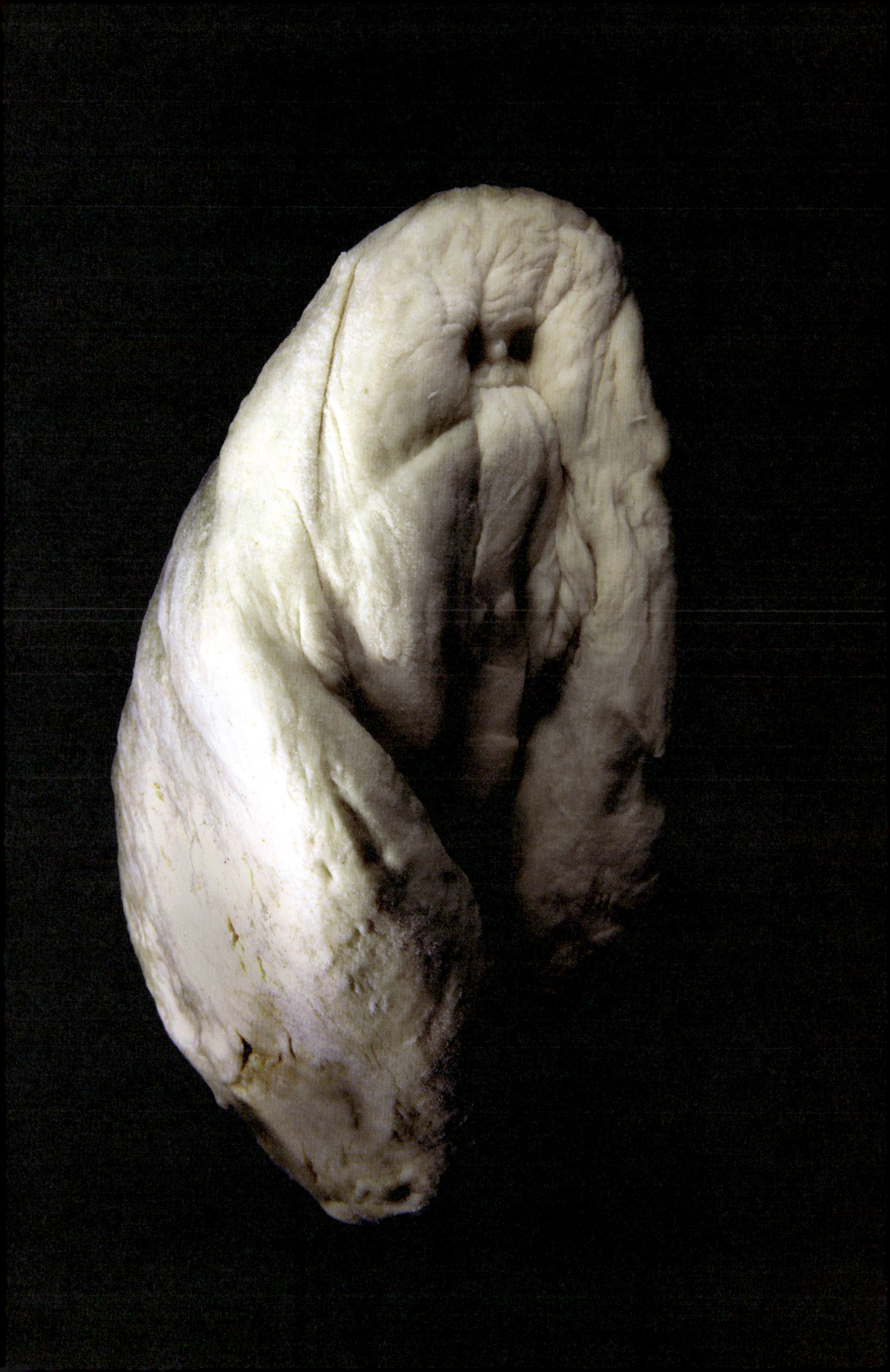

I think I've written about this in the book *Growth*, that I'm a bit weary of motion in art, and art that moves. One of the qualities I like about art is stillness. I love stones—you were stoned on the cover of the book and that's such a weird verb. Why would it be *stoned*? To be like a stone, to be more like a stone. There's this amazing poem by a Brazilian poet Carlos Drummond de Andrade that begins: "In the middle of the road there was a stone." It's a very simple, weird, poem. It's so amazing. It's a poem that appeals to my love of stones. What I love about stones is not unlike what I love about trees: their absolute there-ness, their non-negotiable presences. If we pick up a stone over here somewhere today, it is so much older than anything else. It's been around for fucking ever, and it's going to be around until the world ends. And when the world ends, in a way, it's going to go on, because how is the world going to destroy all these stones? It's cosmic debris. Yesterday you showed me a picture of the rock sculpture that Fischli/Weiss made for the Serpentine in London, and we talked about how we both like "the Bean" (Anish Kapoor's *Cloud Gate*, the infamous public sculpture in downtown Chicago), and I'm not sure if you've ever worked with stones...

ZT: One of the first works I ever did was called *The Dub Roc*; it was a giant rock that played dub music, that I had composed, on a pair of headphones. I covered the surface with a simulated fauna that was made out of paper —little paper flowers that I spent a summer making. Each flower was a hybrid species of four different flowers that I discovered in researching plant properties. The idea being that I wanted the viewer to slow down. This idea of slowing down was a way to exist longer. You could live with this thing, and slow down with this thing, in order to have more, to do more, to take the time to see the nuances in something. To be put into someone else's rhythm. Thinking along with a tree, thinking along with a plant, thinking along with a stone...

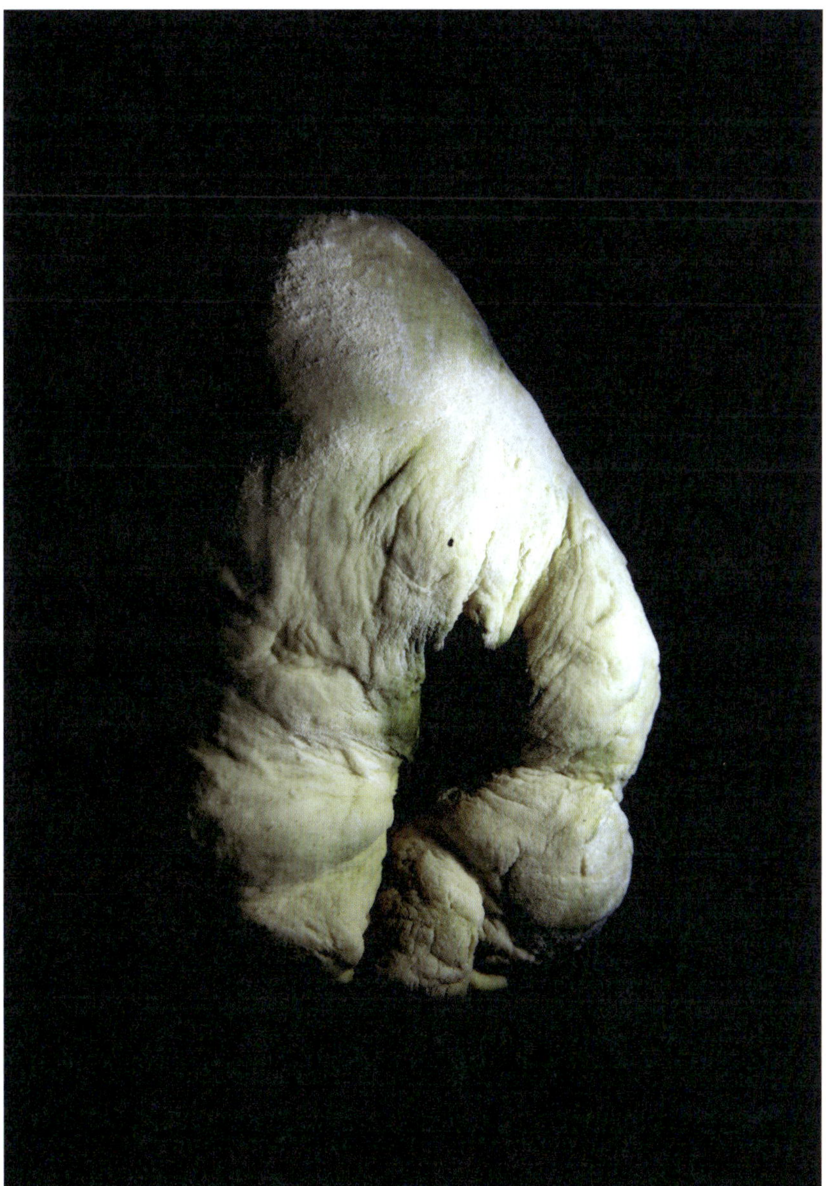

DR: Extrusion. That is a very different kind of thinking, but it is thinking. I was trained in a certain way, intellectually and academically, so of course I'm always aware of the dangers of these romantic projections onto natural phenomena, they are essentialisms. But I do think that trying to think like a tree, a rock, like moss, or a 'shroom, or whatever, naively perhaps, still has a very elemental core of ecological awareness in it. Art for me is the product of a semantic triangle: the artwork, the artist, and the viewer. It comes down to those three relationships: an artwork and artist against the viewer, viewer and artist against the artwork, artwork and viewer against the artist. All those combinations are possible, but you have to have that basic triangle in art. That is the schematic basis for a contract that you could say exists in the experience of art. The most basic question that I have to answer for myself, is why am I looking at this? Why are you asking me to look at this? Because an artist makes things for themselves, but also, to share them with other people, to show them. Not necessarily to tell something or to communicate, but they do want to share, they do want to add something. There has to be a reason, there has to be a why.

ZT: You've described some art as being like observations, fuelling thoughts that wind up in forms—that's more my triangle. I've talked about the work as a version of a Trojan Horse, in that I put one thing into another in order to get it someplace else. In *Put Your Eye in Your Mouth*, I used the subject of Martin Kippenberger's 1995 installation of a METRO-Net station in Dawson City in order to talk about a relationship to landscape and how forms come out of an economy of thinking and acting, an economy of response. [...]

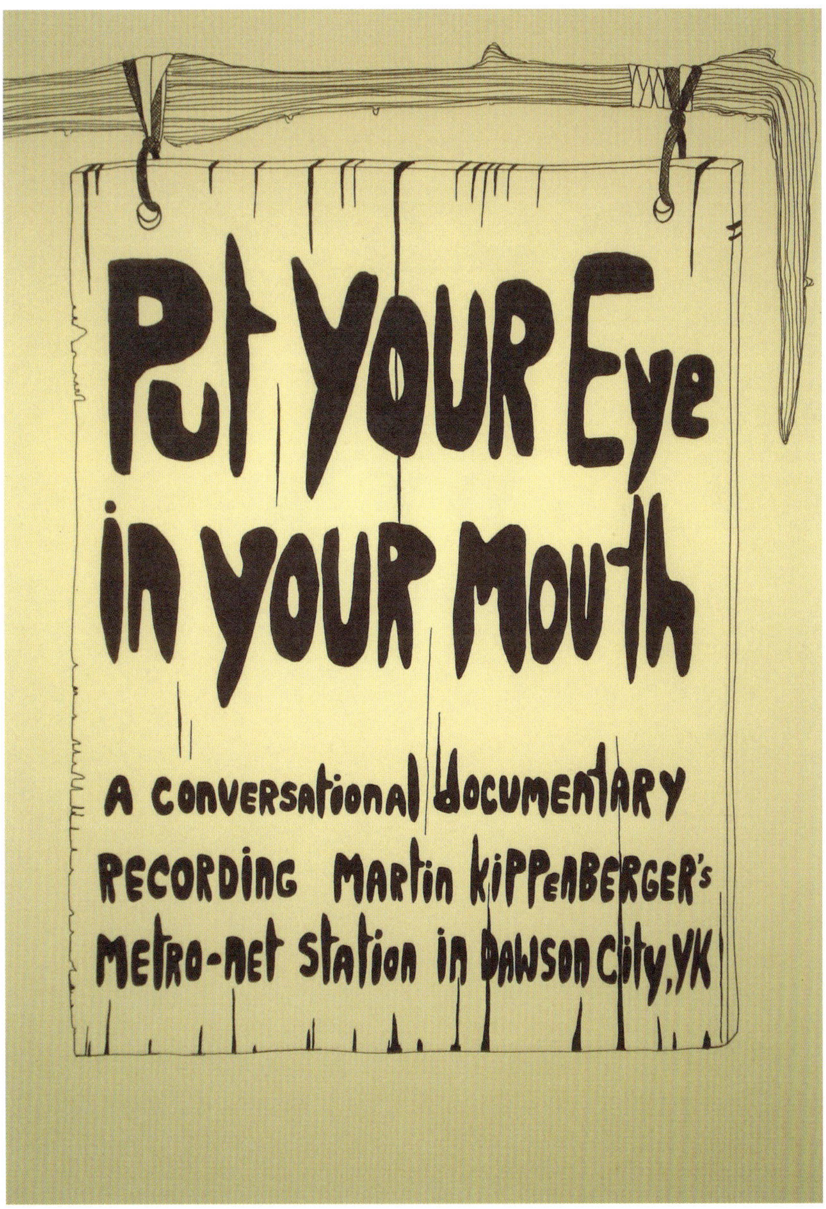

Put your Eye in your Mouth

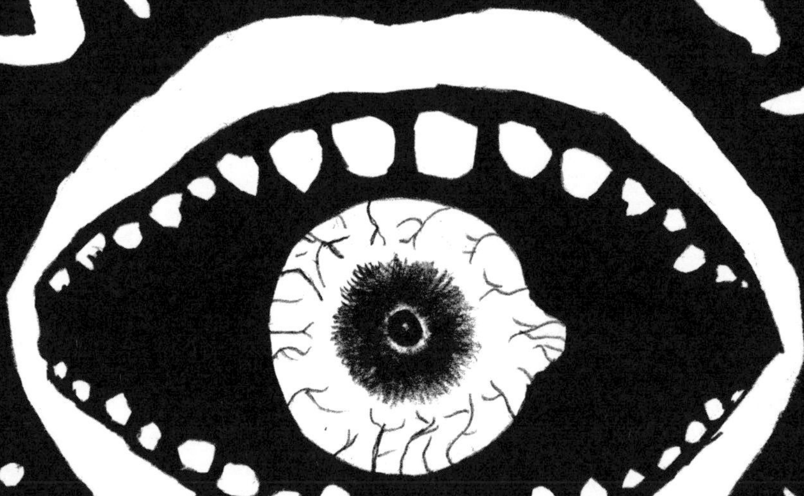

A conversational documentary recording Martin Kippenberger's Metro-Net Station in Dawson City, Yukon

When the gold rush happened in the Yukon, people moved to the west through the United States (Manifest Destiny) to San Francisco. From there they started exploring north because people needed to make money. Eventually, they discovered gold in what became known as the Klondike, in the Canadian north of the Yukon Territory. As a result, more people came up, and they needed things to survive: tents, food, supplies, etc... So a city was built to accommodate the growing population. Dawson City was the first fully-electrified town in the world because they had so much money and there was such a need for it. As the population grew, people weren't just there searching for gold; someone needed to run the hotel, or the brothel, the bar, the trading outpost. These structures were built bit-by-bit from the surrounding materials. The architecture was constructed from the landscape, and that was something I related to in the construction of Kippenberger's METRO-Net: it was built from the same material that every other building, dog house, boat, whatever, was built from. There was an economy of response; the back and forth of dialogue that created the physical forms.

DR: I think you do something quite smart with references. It's a problem in a lot of contemporary art, but you're moving away from that, no?

ZT: Certainly.

The Crystal Ship used Marcel Broodthaers as the Trojan Horse to talk about underground caves and actions of resistance in the late-'60s in art and how these actions led to the production of new art forms. These two figures became my stand-ins in order to get more attention for these whimsical, propositional ideas I was suggesting. This reminds me of the Oprah Winfrey Book Club. The thing with the Book Club is that Oprah would put her stamp on a book and that book would then sell millions of copies. She engineered a segment of her show to encourage Americans to start reading again. She brought African American Feminist writers to light as well. She really activated the audience that she constructed. My Oprah analogy is that you can use names like Kippenberger or Broodthaers, which are historically significant within contemporary art, in order to pass along this information. I'm going to slip you *this*, by making you pay attention because of *this*. Through the years these figures have been substituted with my own language, replacing source characters with much more familiar subjects that can then be used to produce an allegorical reach.

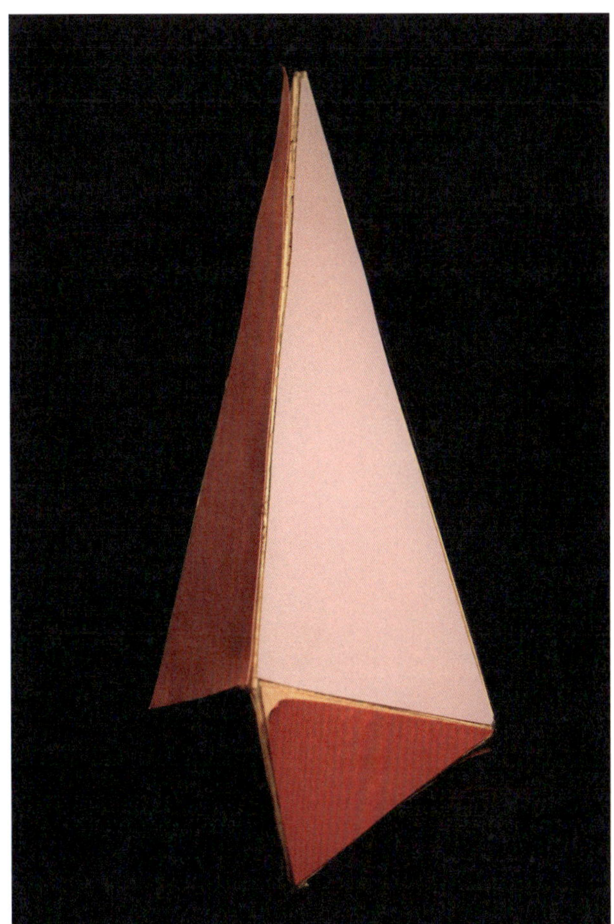

DR: You like that word, allegorical. The etymology of that word is based on the contraction of two Greek words: *Allos*, or *allon*, which means "other," and *agoreuein*, meaning "to speak." The word is based on the idea of saying one thing, while meaning the other, or to talk through other things to talk about one thing.

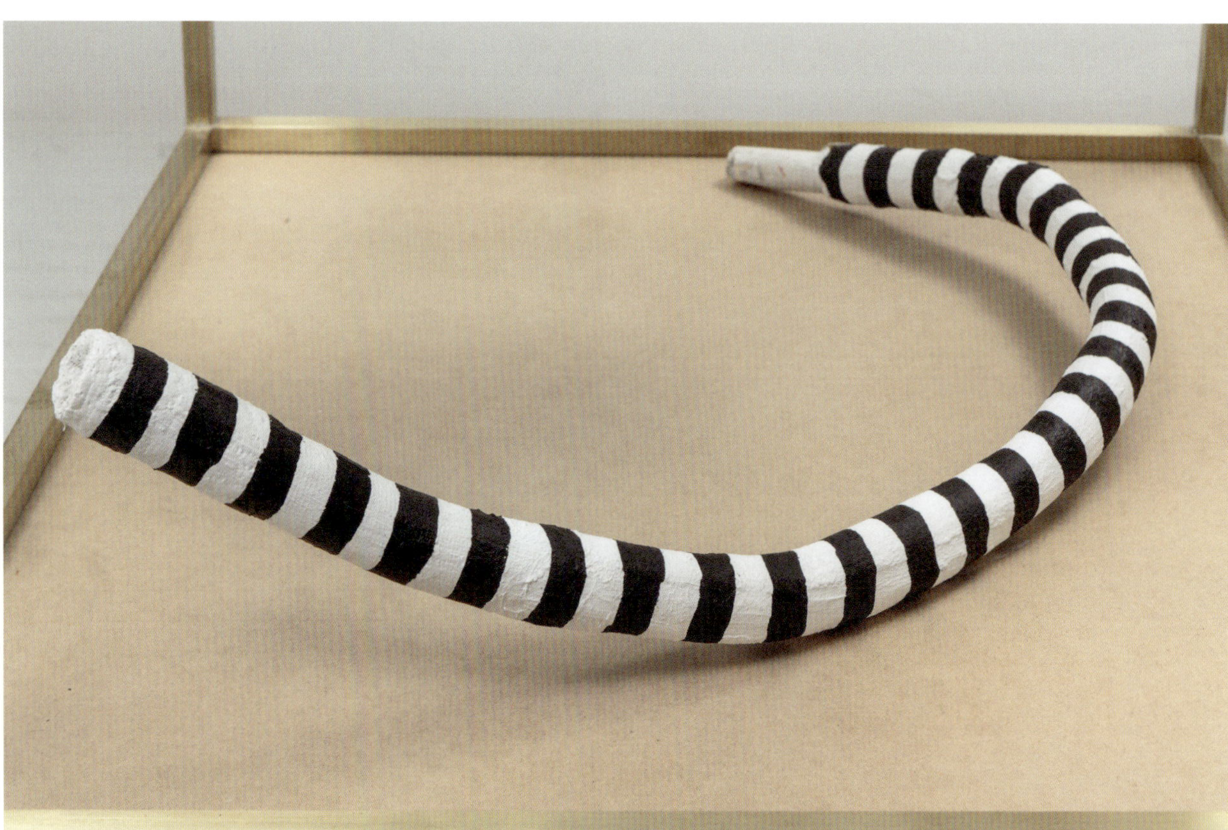

ZT: It's like having an artwork operate as a transitional device, as a translator for thoughts, where at the end of the day it becomes a tool with which to talk about other things. It *is* the allegory, and it *is* located somewhere. I like the approach of locating an idea within a form: you can pack away that thing, bring it out again, leave it alone, walk around it, or turn your back to it. [...]

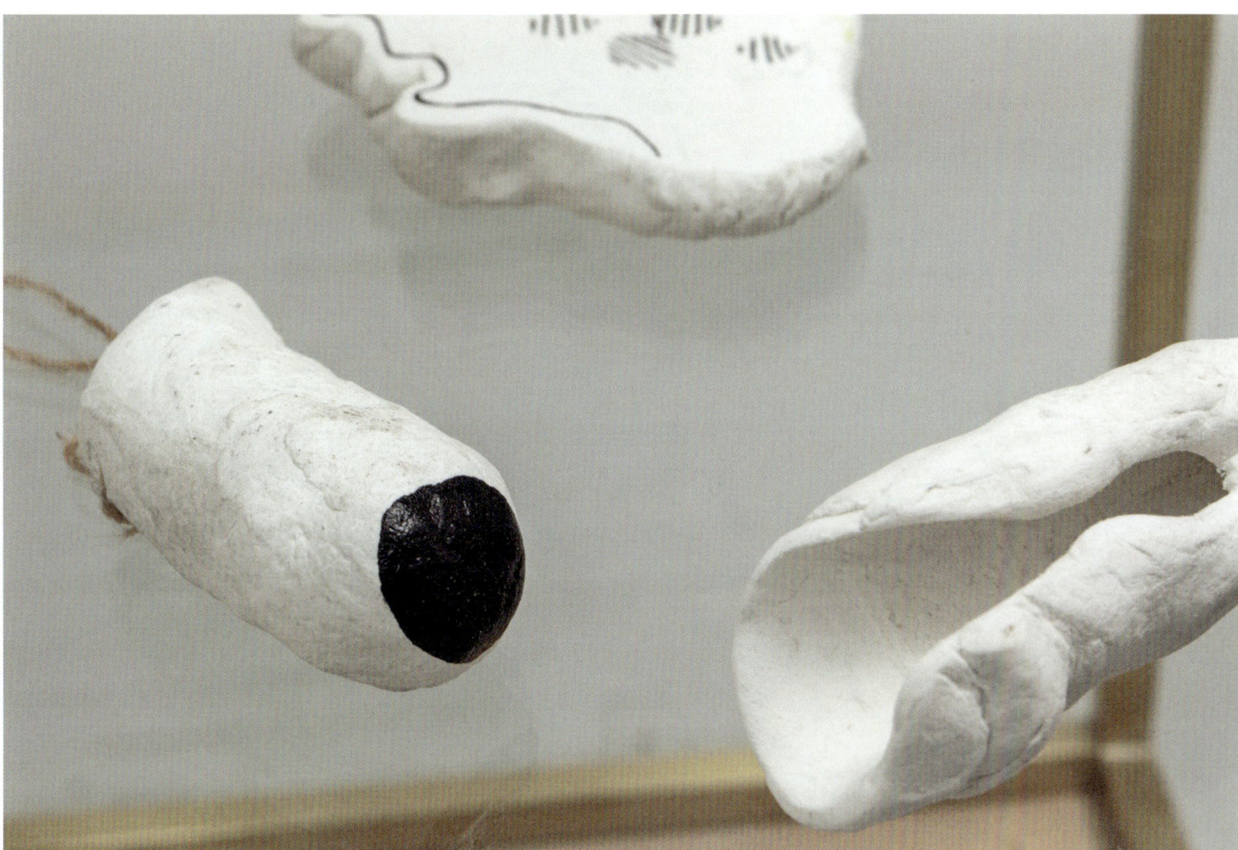

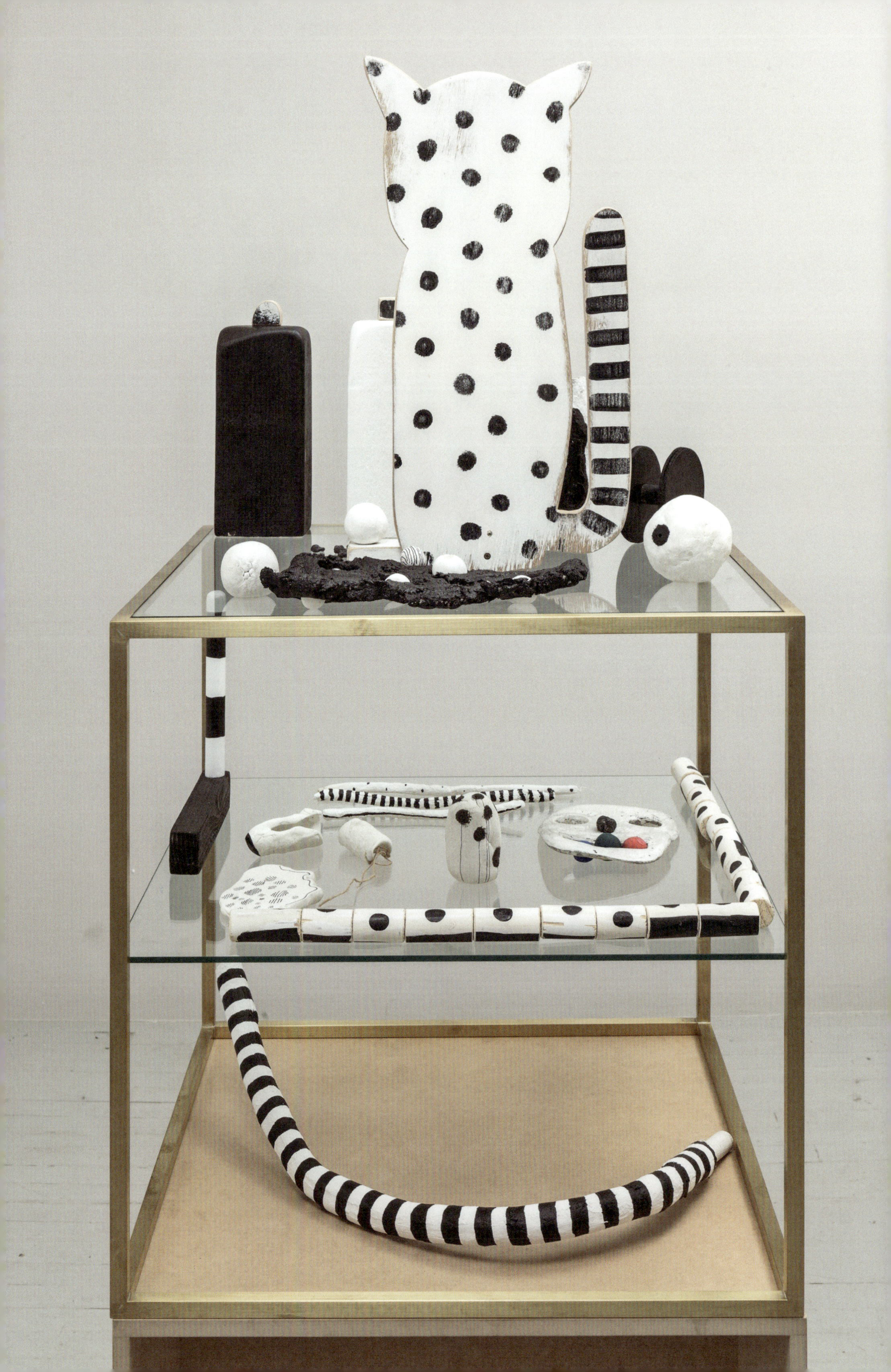

With *The Story of Stripes and Dots* I was able to talk about the allegorical unit as something to insert into a conversation. The artwork was an opinion, and a suggestion, using familiarity as a tool to express difference for a subject. As a result, I was able to quite confidently make a black-and-white stripped panel, like a Daniel Buren, but with my own language and narrative world operating to develop the object's story.

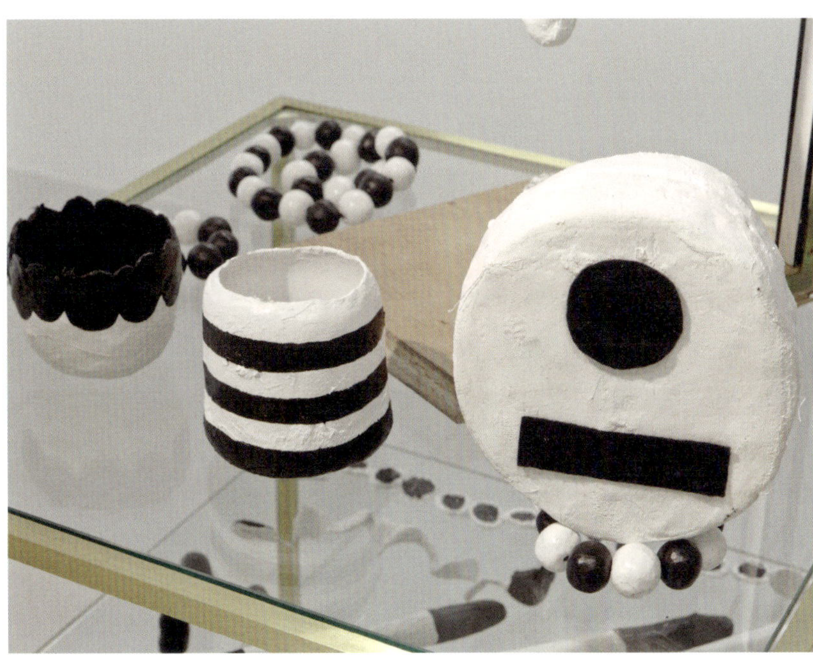

DR: For me that piece doesn't have anything to do with Buren, it's the last thing I think about. I know I should in a way, but for me it's a little like *The Story of Stripes and Dots* forced themselves on to you, or through you, and then on to us. There is something of an inner necessity to the fact that it has to be like this—it's a beautiful symbol of how things exist objectively in the world that we do not have any power over. There is a facticity to the world that we are just subject to, and we are not the subject of it, or the master of it. That's why I like public art, those things that suddenly plop down in. Like these acorns here. Public art has a way of telling you: *you know what, we're here. You're just going to have to make peace with that. You're not running the show, you're actually sharing the world, not just with other people, but mostly with objects*. In a way, good art can be a very strong allegory of that relationship.

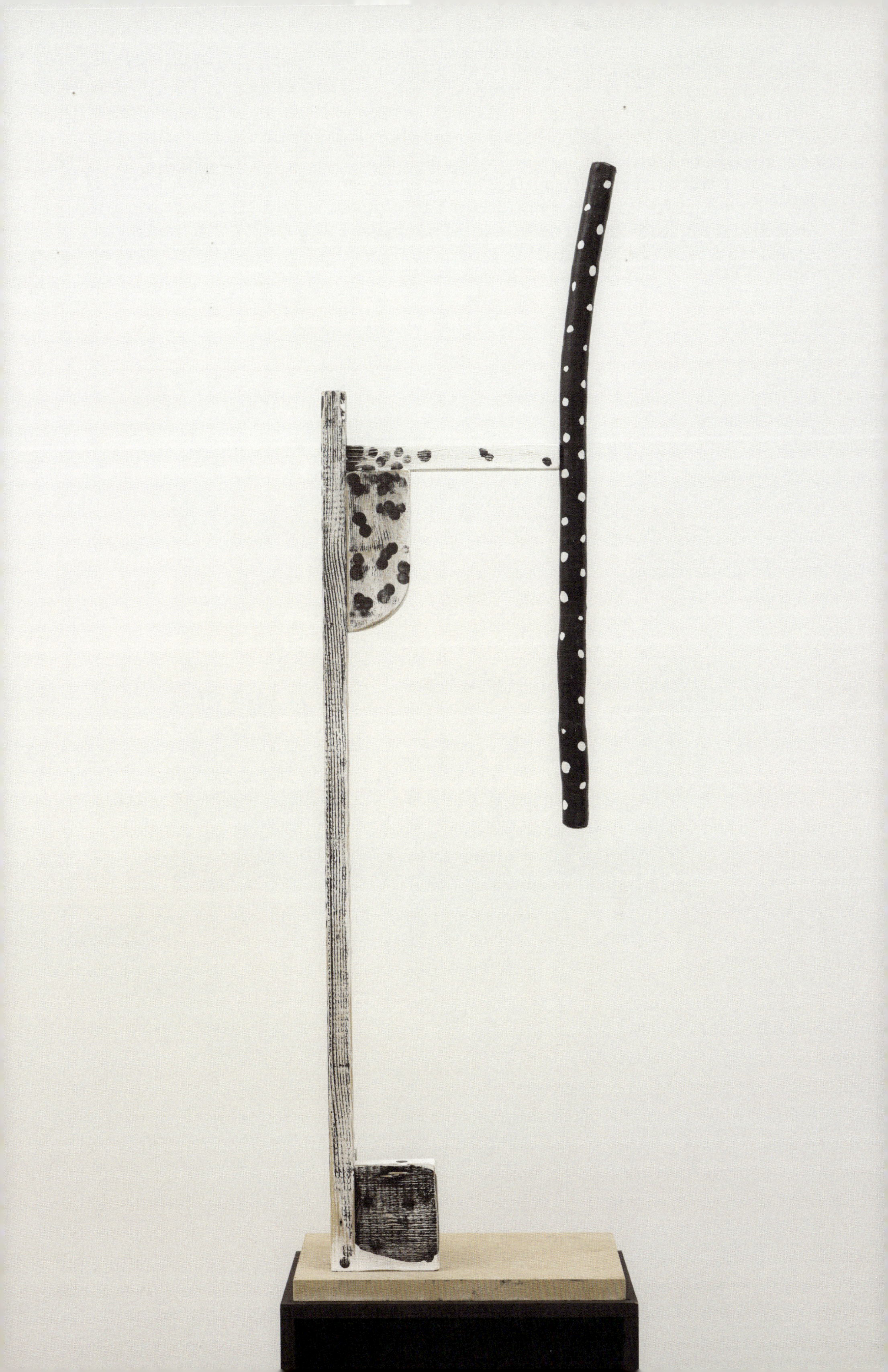

There is something that I like as a mantra, or a motto. It's from *The Way of the Samurai*, which is an amazing book, and *Ghost Dog* (an adaptation), which is an amazing movie. I bought *The Way of the Samurai* book, the little treatise. It has this terrific passage, when the samurai in training is instructed to treat the matters of greatest concern with utmost lightness, and treat the matters of smallest concern with utmost gravity. I like that, because your work is funny and light in a great way. I like walking into an exhibition and laughing out loud because I see something really completely wonky and nuts.

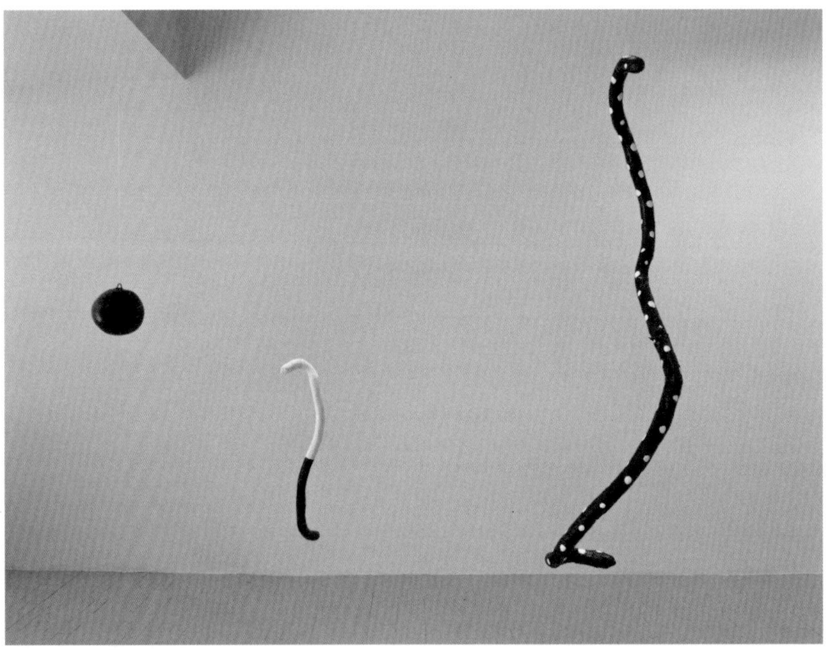

ZT: Like a video showing a piece of wood trying to make a piece of bread? Absurdity is a great communication tool in that way. A thought that is so abstract and out-there that it becomes funny, but in doing so is able to communicate differently. I watch a lot of comedy, watching the way a comedian works, the way they can polish a story into a humorous thing. Performers use humour to communicate incredibly complex opinions very quickly, opening you up to following that track of thought. As I was trying to make these works that are somehow interesting in a complex way, they became complex because they were trying to be too interesting, and humour became a way of opening it up, of putting viewers at ease so they could follow the narrative a bit more. It's part of the pitch, to get you interested.

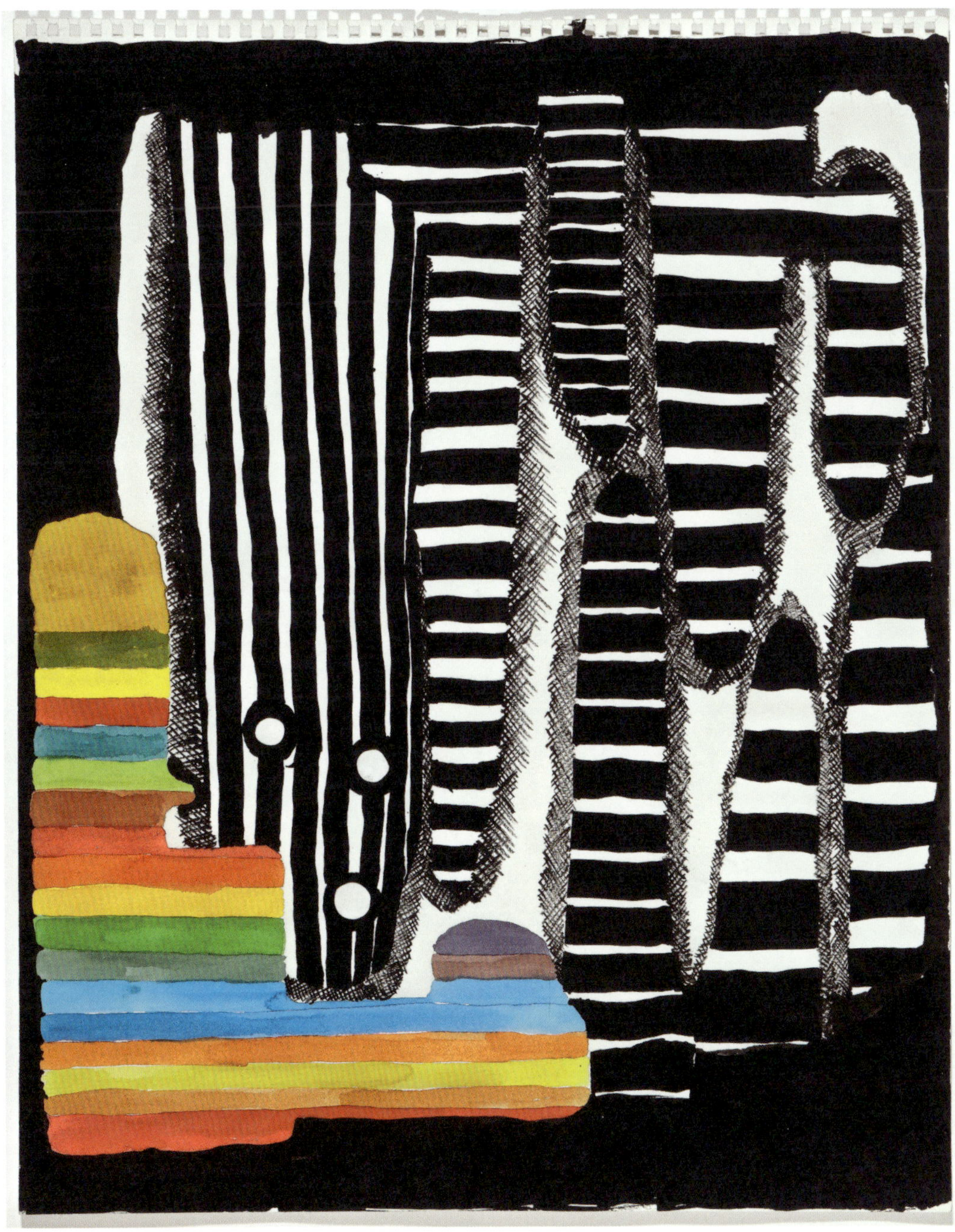

DR: It's a really lame cliché, but poetry, words arranged in a certain fashion on the page, is a kind of sculpture. Poetry is also in the way you hang things for a gallery show, the way you decide this is where the line break is—it becomes a matter of rhythm. I think that for me, an exhibition is like an essay. When I write an essay, it's words on paper; when I curate a show, it's objects in space. The goal is comparable: the formulation of a hypothesis. It's a very speculative enterprise. That's why the word "essay" is so important: the essay, to try, to attempt. There is zero authority in it. Using an artwork, and using artists, to tell your own story, or to articulate your own theories reeks of instrumentalization. But we've talked about that. There's nothing wrong with instrumentalization if you are honest about it. What a curator should do, I think, is to go out there and tell an artist, "Listen, I have this idea. I need your work to make it happen; I need your work to lend it oomph." The invitation needs to be gracious and it's an expression, it's basically saying that as a curator there is no other way of telling your story than by works of art. It shows an amazing appreciation for the work of art. It's a real admission that words can't do it all, or, that words sometimes aren't that interesting to make your point.

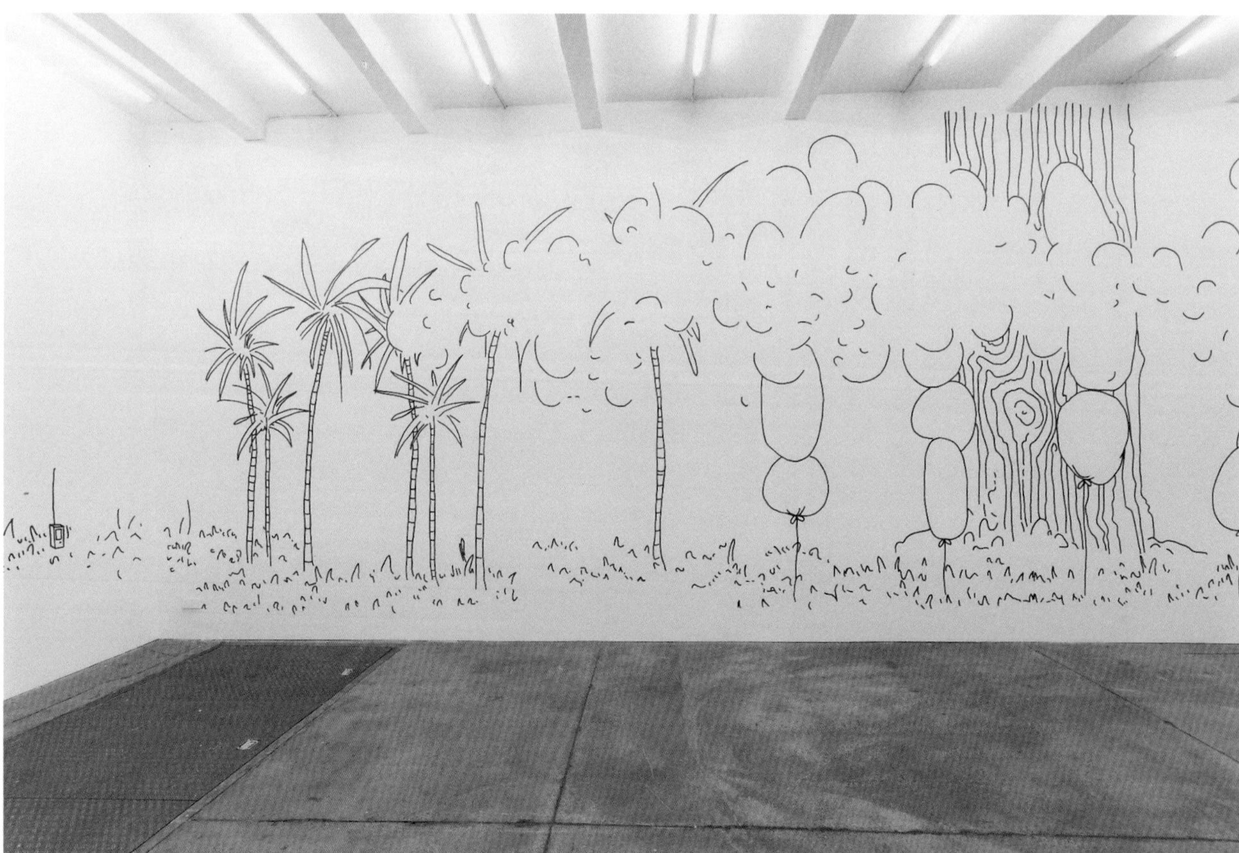

ZT: That there's a difference between forms of communication. There's the visual, then there's the textual. There is the thinking, and then how that thinking turns into a form.

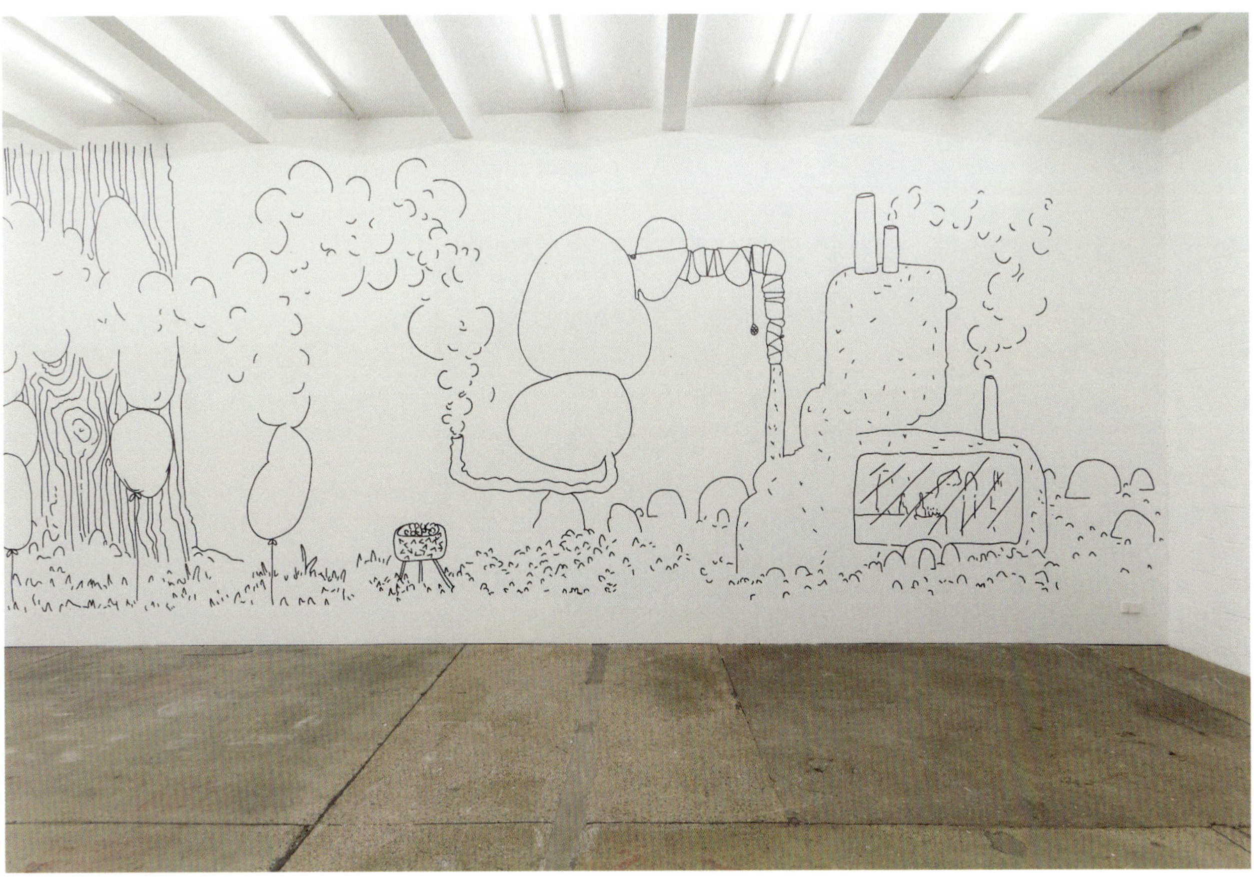

DR: Here we hit upon the crux of where maybe our interests intersect: you use the word thinking very often, and I do too. I think a lot. I was trained as a philosopher, I'm not an artist. I've never had any kind of curatorial training in a strict sense, so I'm interested in the thought process, how thoughts are formed. Those are words that are completely crucial to the way you conceive of your own work. How thoughts are formed. The really deep sense that you get when looking at your work is that you're witnessing the mental emergence of ideas as forms and shapes and material facts. It's quite powerful. Some works are allegories of that very event, such as *The Bakery of Blok* and the *Stripes and Dots* saga. [...]

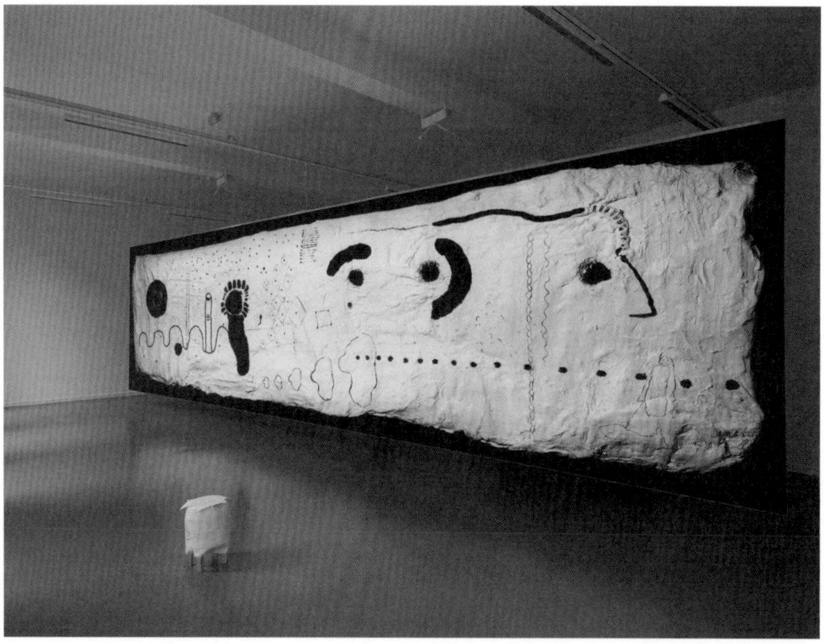

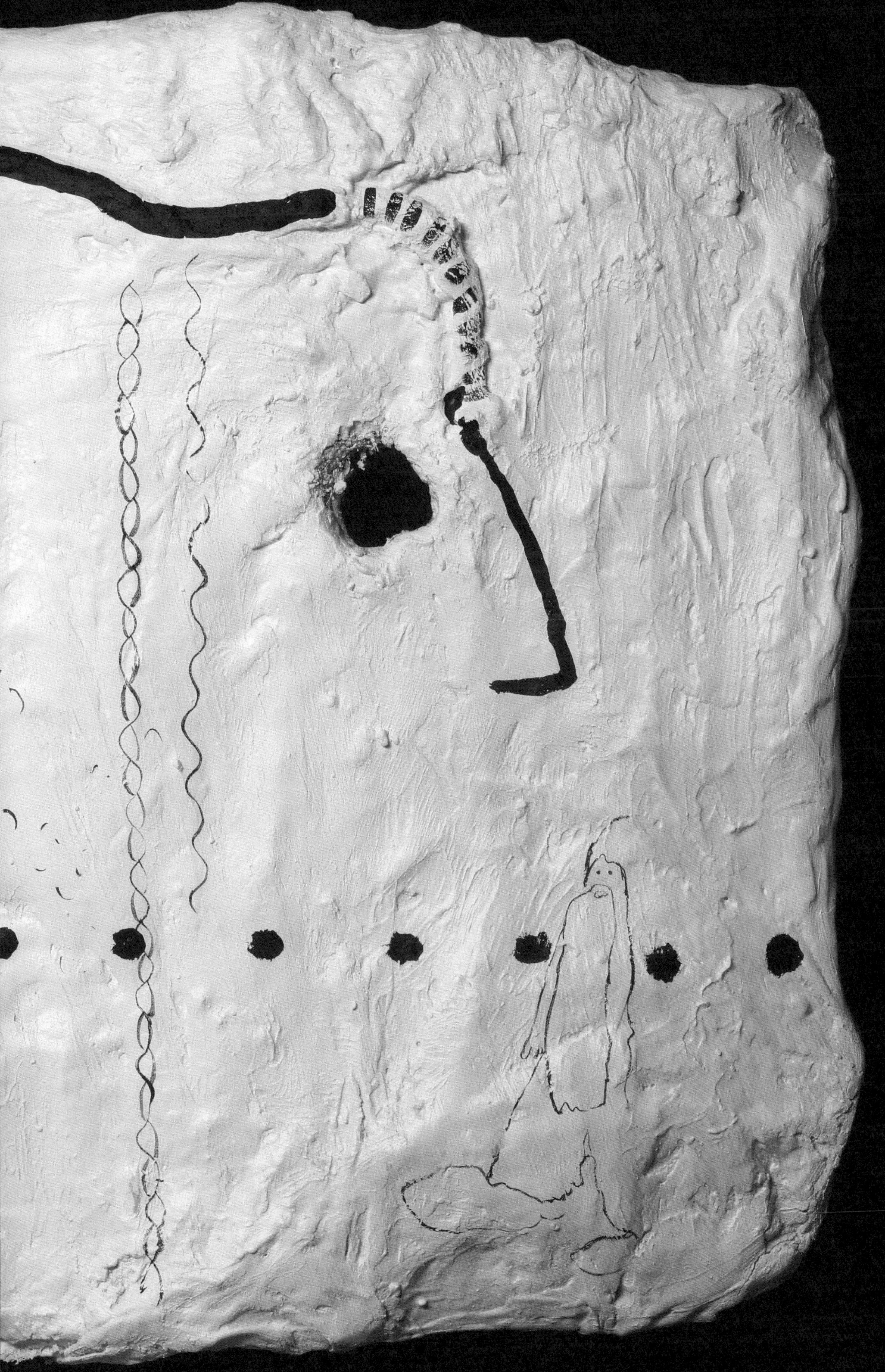

Those are histories of formation. You're not an art-about-artists person, in the sense that you don't make art about other artists. You've done that with Kippenberger and Broodthaers, but that was different. Your art is about art as this slightly miraculous creative ability in people to put things into the world that really don't mean anything, but that do, at their deepest goal, make clear that the making of meaning from the arbitrary is possible. That's a powerful way of thinking about art. [...]

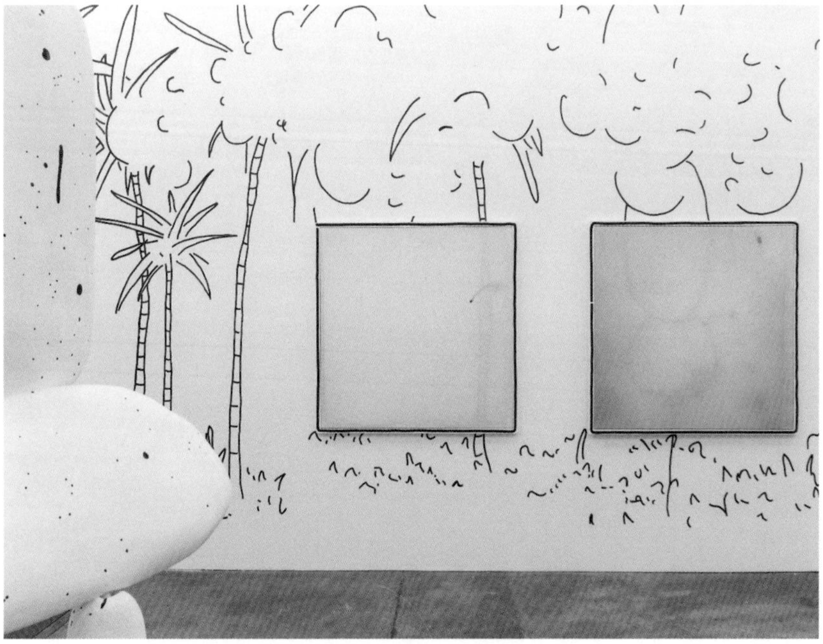

We talked about Paul Klee earlier, about how I want to write a short article that points out how he is the producer of the most popular images in the history of modern philosophy to grace book covers of philosophical thought. I look at these books and it's amazing how often Adorno, Horkheimer, Benjamin, Sartre, Foucault, or Wittgenstein, feature a Klee on their covers. If you are looking for a campaign image for the venture of philosophy in the twentieth century, Paul Klee is your go-to man. It's like Caspar David Freidrich from the German romantic period of early nineteenth-century philosophy. There is clearly something in Paul Klee's work that isn't philosophical, but lends itself incredibly well to the illumination of these very abstract concepts: time, existence, faith, critique, all these things. I can imagine a lot of your work would do well on book covers like that. That's an incredibly powerful place. It's like making record covers. For me, as somebody who studied philosophy and for whom philosophy is very important for thinking about art, there is something so elemental about the images you produce. [...]

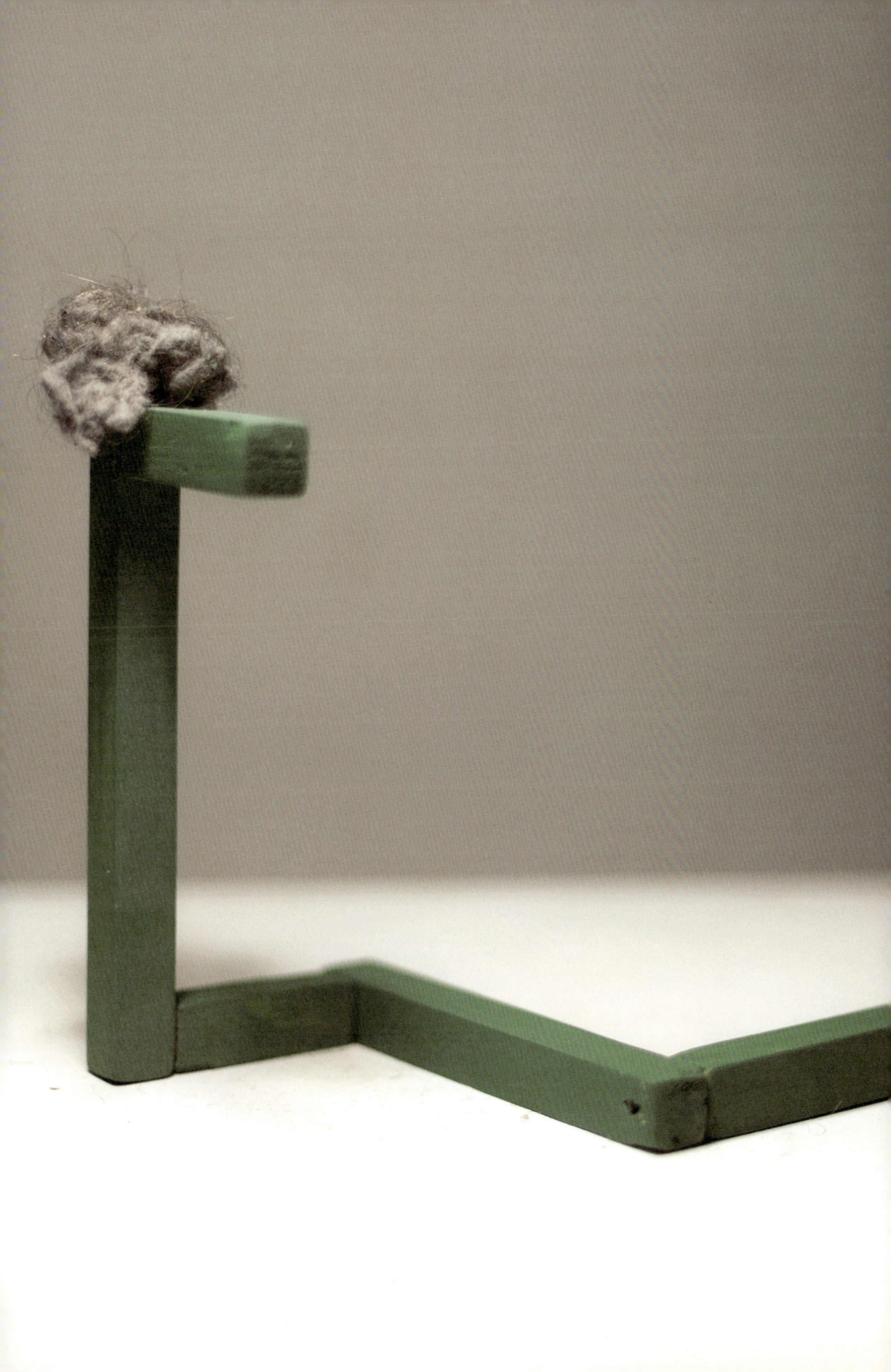

I was thinking a little bit about absence, vacuums, holes, emptiness, absence of language. I like that your work isn't too heavy, there's lightness. There's an element of application in your work. This is something that I learned to think about through Liam Gillick. For him, of all the things that he really contests, it's this historical divide between applied arts and the other arts—high art versus the decorative and applied, art versus design, sculpture versus architecture. I remember Gillick giving this lecture, and he's given many since this one, where he talks about that false dichotomy by referencing the history of Josef and Anni Albers. To him, Anni Albers is the more interesting artist. Josef is the pure artist who paints squares, and she's the applied artist who, using the same squares, shapes the world with tea towels, or wallpaper. So application is something I'm really quite interested in. It may have something to do with seeing my father, who is a sculptor, leave the realm of pure sculpture to make objects of use, like tables, in order to make a living. For me it was a moment when the art became a bit stronger as well. Wallpaper, costumes... this is another moment where the notion of instrumentalization comes up. What's so wrong with that?... It's a good point. That you can think of artworks as tools, as a means to an end.

ZT: It's an idea that runs into a use. You've got the world of ideas, and you have the world of use. This is a little like Theory versus Practice. What engages about the world of use, or the world of application, is that if the application is not useful, then it's not purchased, thought about, or interacted with. Another story will not be built. The wonderful thing about the translation of a thought into a tool is that it undergoes a transformation enabling collision with other kinds of information. An idea running up against other kinds of information can stimulate a dialogue with multiple contributors. I think anyone would agree that the more brains you have talking about a subject, the further that subject can move away from a static and fixed position. The more it can develop into something very different and important, possibly even poignant. So with application, the work is a tool to do something else with, but never the end point. I prefer overlap, carryover, dialogue between older works and newer works and subject matter as well. [...]

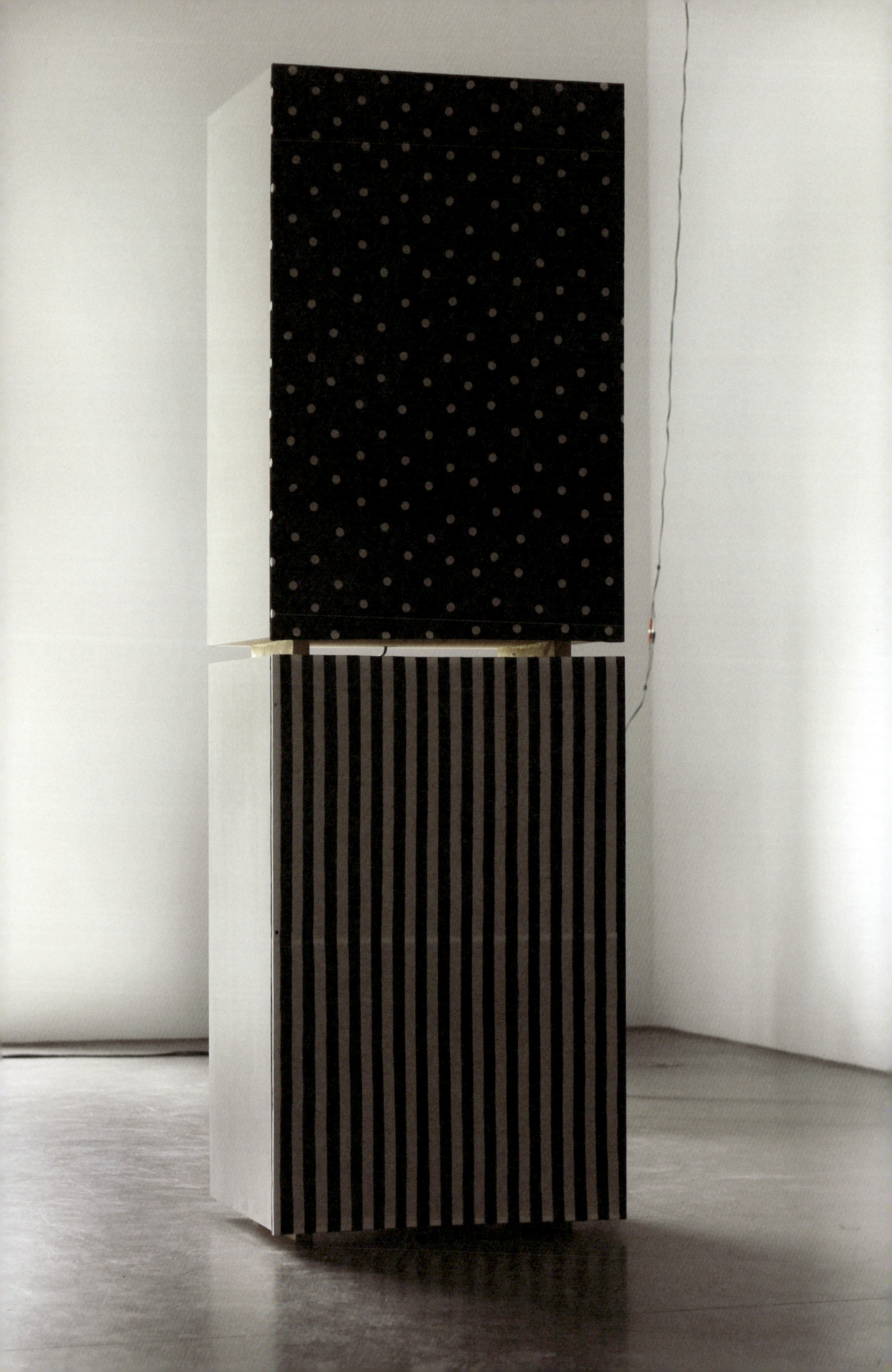

The *Lichen Voices* video was made at the same time as the *Lichen Wall*, which at the time I thought was a little weak, I thought I should have been able to come up with another idea, but it seemed to work. This was an extreme example of that program I'm trying to do of producing multiplicities for a singular thing in order to grow alternate definitions for a subject. Here are two works exhibiting in different parts of the world, yet all coming from the same source, and instrumentalized, or used, in a different way to tell a different kind of story based on that situation and point in time. They looked different because the intention was different, yet the source was the same. It's the form as a portal, a screen of thought that augments the reality you are looking at; the lavender glass that you look through.

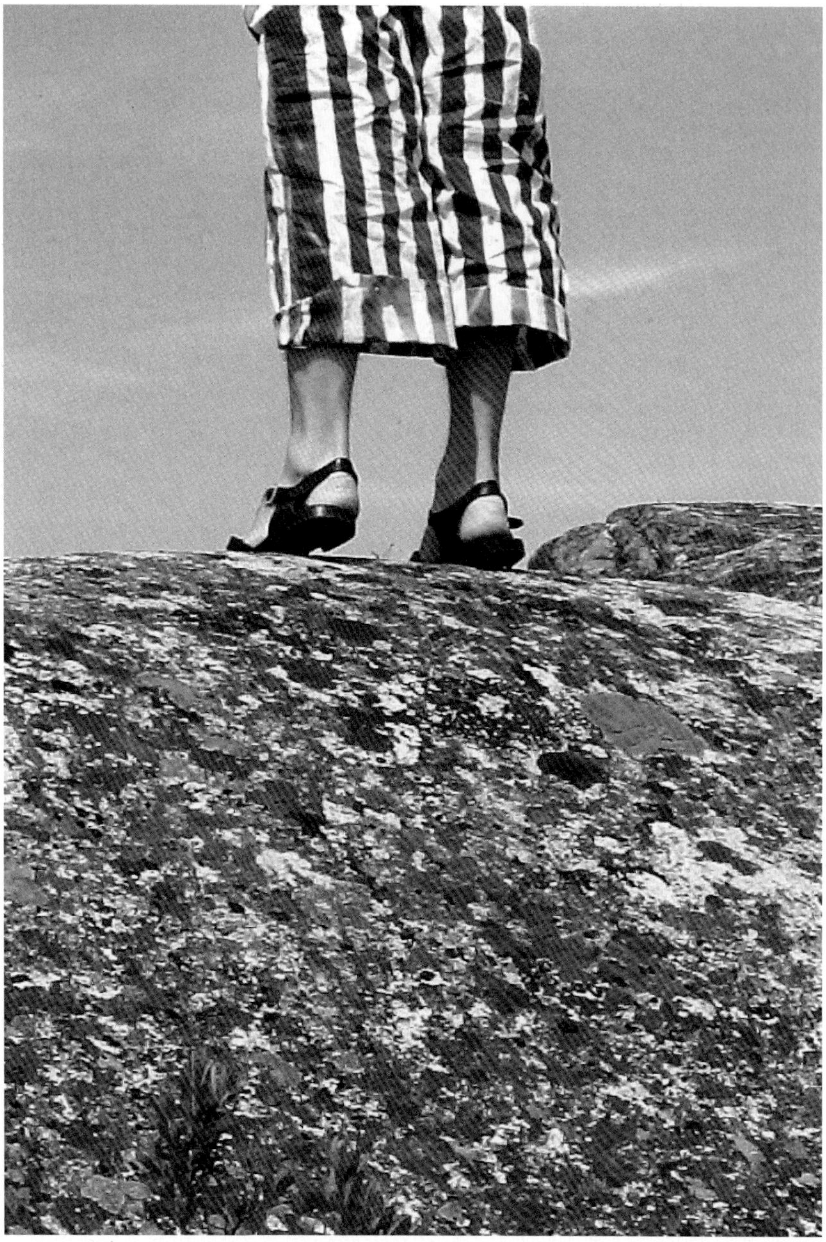

This book is a uniquely beautiful and thoughtful monograph on the work of Zin Taylor, an artist of significant merit whose practice is as sharp and insightful as it is dreamy and droll. Zin's art often explores the nature of meaning and the epistemological processes by which it takes form – including its manifestation as the very book before you. It follows, then, that the essay accompanying this publication similarly reflects a process of sense making; in this instance, through an extended, informal and unscripted dialogue between the artist and Dieter Roelstraete, a renowned curator, writer and long-time enthusiast of Zin's work. Further, the selection and placement of images, as compelling and exquisite as they are, is exceedingly deliberate and generate additional meaning beyond merely illustrating the text.

On behalf of the Southern Alberta Art Gallery, we wish to extend our gratitude to Dieter Roelstraete for his enthusiastic participation, inquisitive voice and commitment to Zin's practice. For the brilliant and apposite design of this monograph, our sincere thanks go to the much-celebrated artist and designer Boy Vereecken. We are grateful to Shannon Anderson who edited the contents of this publication with a watchful and discerning eye.

I would like to thank the dedicated staff, board members and volunteers who helped realize the exhibition, *The Story of Stripes and Dots* (Chapter 6), which ultimately led to the development of this publication. We express our appreciation to our major funders: the Canada Council for the Arts, the Alberta Foundation for the Arts, and the City of Lethbridge all of which are instrumental in providing the support SAAG requires to deliver our programming.

Special acknowledgement must be given to the RBC Emerging Artists Project and in particular to Robin Anthony, Art Curator with the Royal Bank of Canada, who was instrumental in advocating on behalf of Zin Taylor and the Southern Alberta Art Gallery to secure a large part of the funding for this endeavour. This program provided significant support, financially and otherwise, without which a book of this stature would not have been possible.

Finally, we extend our deepest gratitude to Zin Taylor. An exemplary artist, Zin has been gracious, generous, enthusiastic, professional and nothing short of inspirational throughout this process. His vision has guided the conception of this extraordinary new book resulting in the most comprehensive and considered look at his expansive practice to date, balanced with a compelling collection of images and thoughtful design that embed Zin's uniquely talented voice within these pages.

Ryan Doherty
Director/Curator, Southern Alberta Art Gallery

Zin Taylor
Lavender Glass

Taylor Made: Zin Taylor and the Story of Form
Originally published in *Mousse*, no. 27, February - March 2011

CONVERSATION
Dieter Roelstraete & Zin Taylor

DESIGN
Boy Vereecken
with Antoine Begon

COPY EDITOR
Shannon Anderson

PHOTO CREDITS
Isabelle Arthuis
Nick Ash
Sam Drake
Cassan der Eeftinck-Schattenkerk
Torben Eskerod
Linda Fuchs
Toni Hafkenscheid
Miguel Abreu Gallery
MuHKA - Museum of Contemporary Art Antwerp
Zin Taylor

PRINTING
Cassochrome, Belgium

ISBN
978-88-6749-327-2

Southern Alberta Art Gallery
601 – 3rd Avenue South
Lethbridge, Alberta T1J 0H4
www.saag.ca

Mousse Publishing
Corso di Porta Romana, 63,
20122 Milano, Italy
www.moussepublishing.com

WITH SUPPORT BY
RBC Foundation; RBC Emerging Artist Program
Canada Council for the Arts
Alberta Foundation for the Arts
City of Lethbridge

Library and Archives Canada Cataloguing in Publication

Taylor, Zin, 1978-
[Works. Selections]
Zin Taylor : lavender glass.

Published in conjunction with the exhibition "The Story of Stripes and Dots (Chapter 6)" held at the Southern Alberta Art Gallery from December 7, 2013 to February 2, 2014. Co-published by Mousse Magazine and Publishing.
ISBN 978-8-86749-327-2 (hardcover)

1. Taylor, Zin, 1978- --Exhibitions.
2. Exhibition catalogs--
I. Roelstraete, Dieter, 1972-, writer of added commentary II. Doherty, Ryan, 1974-, writer of added commentary III. Southern Alberta Art Gallery, issuing body, host institution IV. Title. V. Title: Lavender glass.

N6549.T395A4 2018
709.2
C2018-901388-5

SOUTHERN ALBERTA ART GALLERY — Canada Council for the Arts / Conseil des Arts du Canada — RBC Emerging Artists Project — Alberta Foundation for the Arts

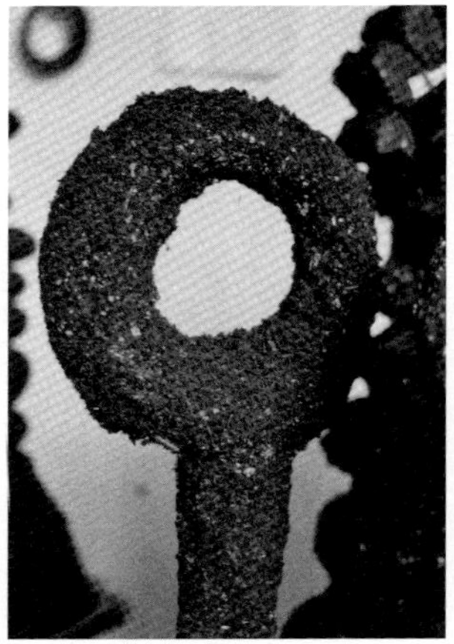

The Allegorical Function of Dirt: a discussion with Aki Tsuyuko's Ongakushitsu, studio detail, 2004

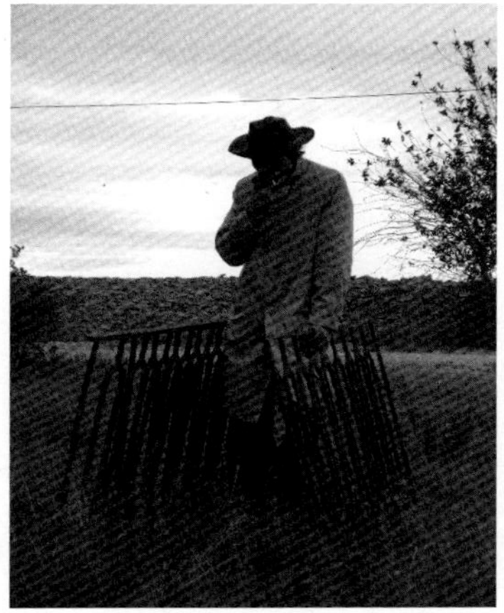

Put Your Eye in Your Mouth: a conversational documentary recording Martin Kippenberger's Metro-Net Station in Dawson City, Yukon, (Chris as Kippi on the Island of Syros, Greece), 2007

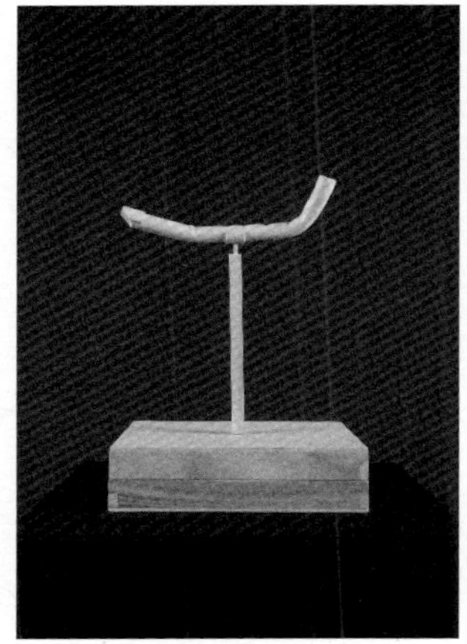

The Flute of Sub, 2007

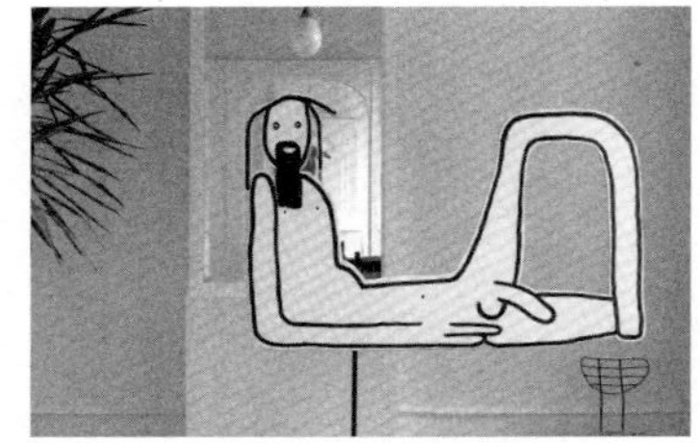

The Reclining Hippy, 2015

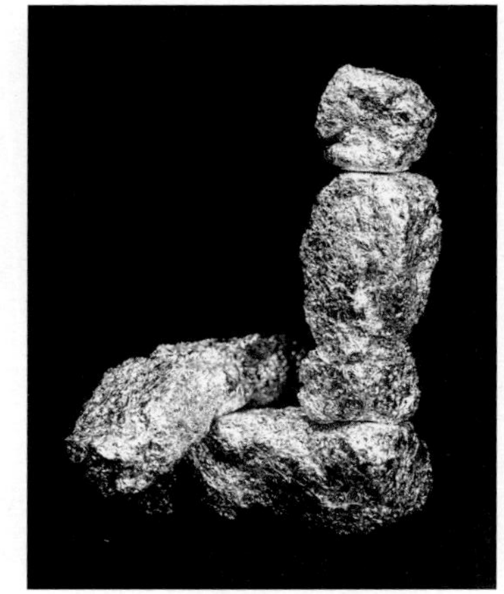

The Crystal Ship, 2008

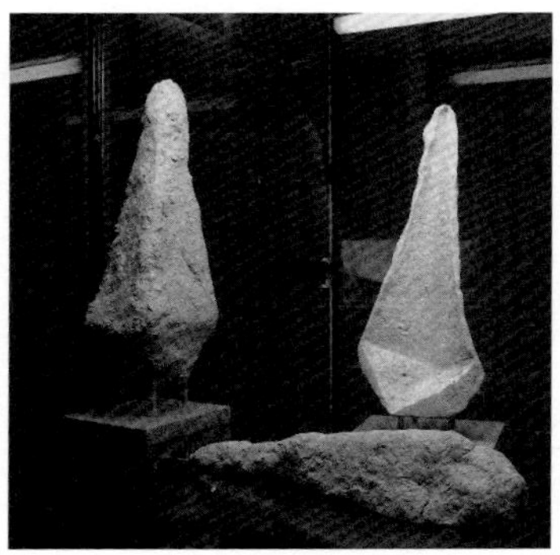

The Crystal Ship, installation at BELvue Museum, Brussels, Belgium, 2008

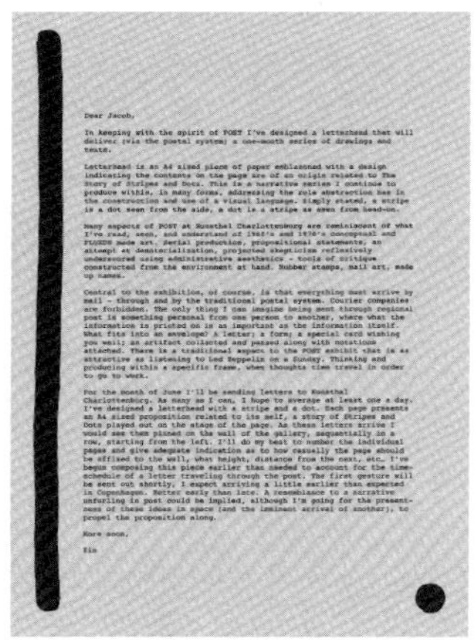

Letterhead (Letter to Jacob Fabricius), 2013

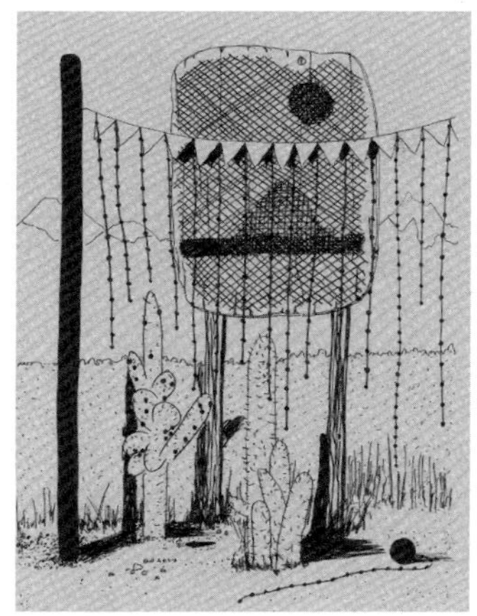

Letterhead, 2013

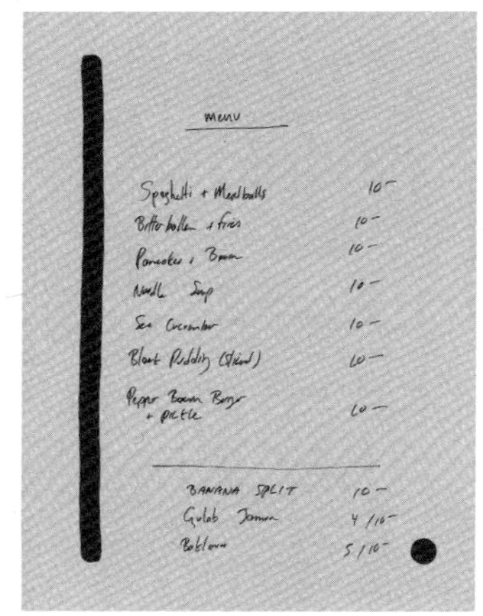

Letterhead, 2013

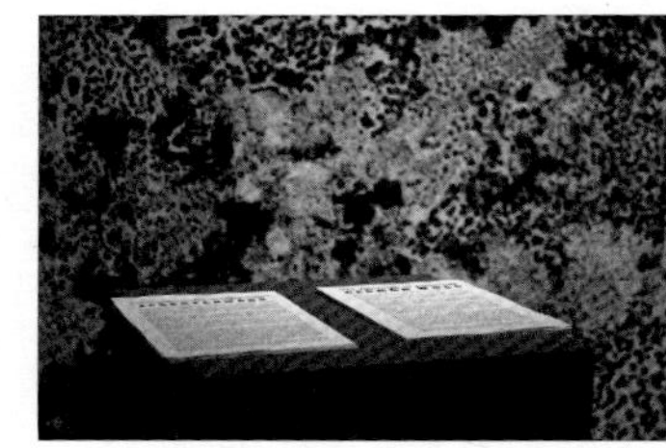

The Proposal of a Surface (Lichen Wall), A4 text in English and German, 2013

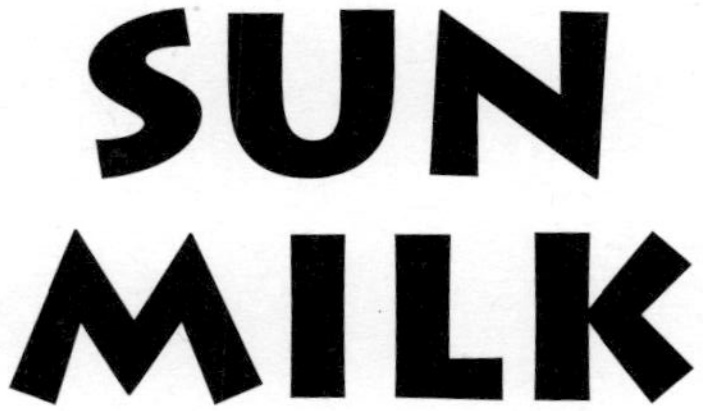

Portals (Sun Milk), Invitation card, 2014

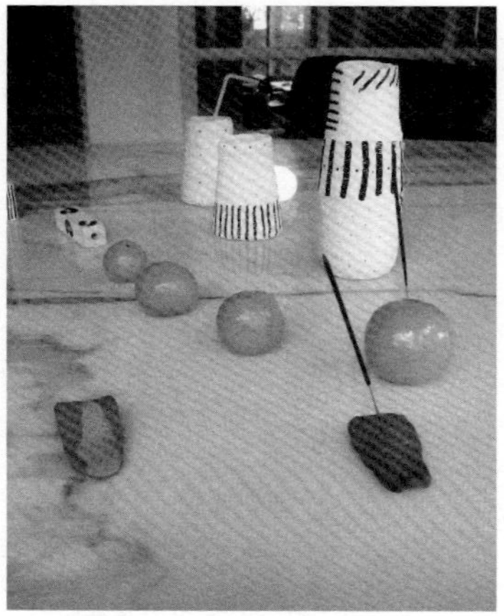

Portals (Sun Milk), installation at Maison Gregoire, Brussels, Belgium, 2014

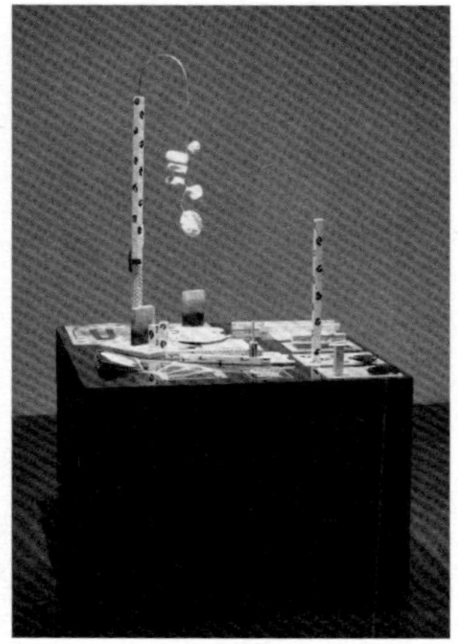

Thoughts Related to Elements on a Field, Where the Field is a Ruin in Arles, France, 2013

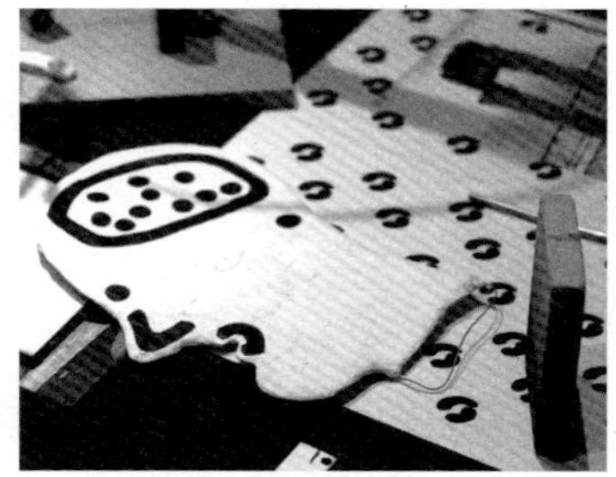

Thoughts Related to Elements on a Field, Where the Field is a Ruin in Arles, France, (detail), 2013

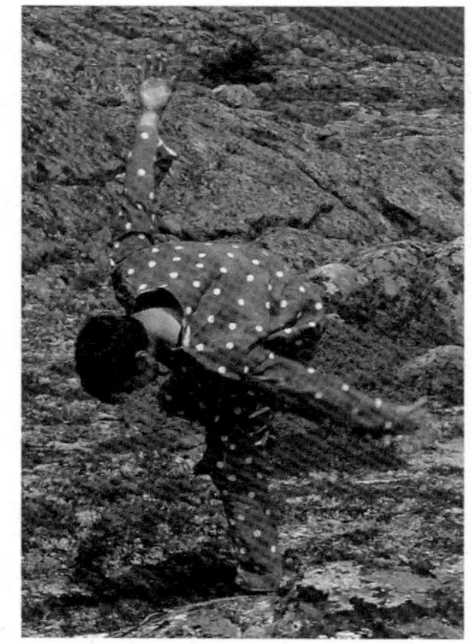

Lichen Voices / Stripes and Dots, 2013

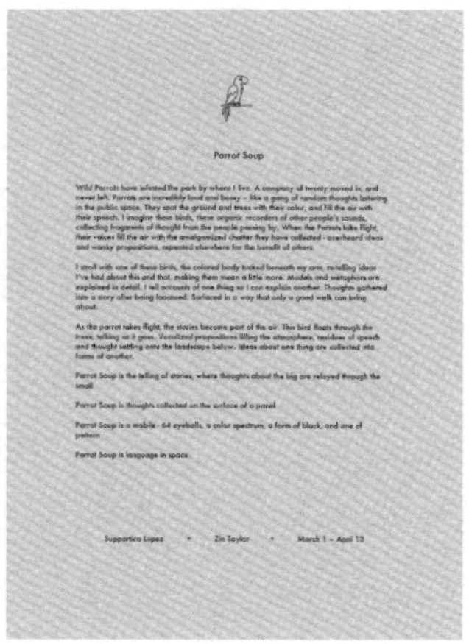

Parrot Soup press release, 2013

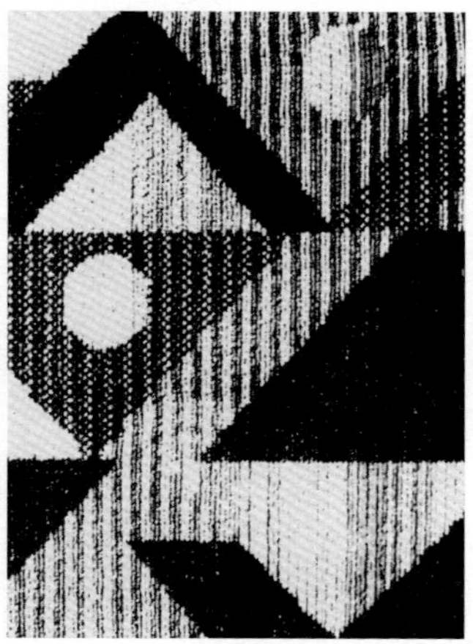

Parrot Soup press release (verso), 2013

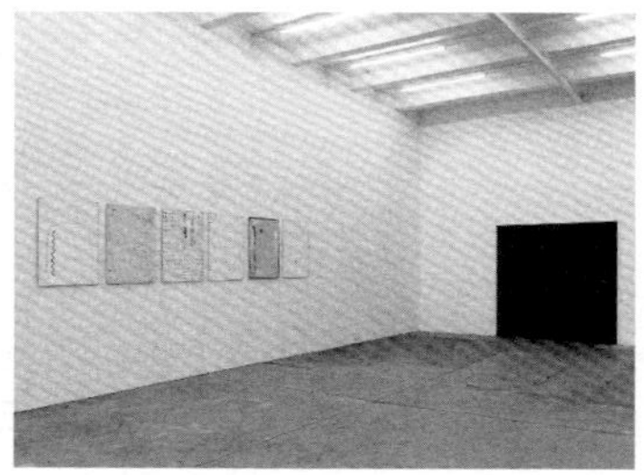

Parrot Soup, installation at Supportico Lopez, Berlin, Germany, 2013

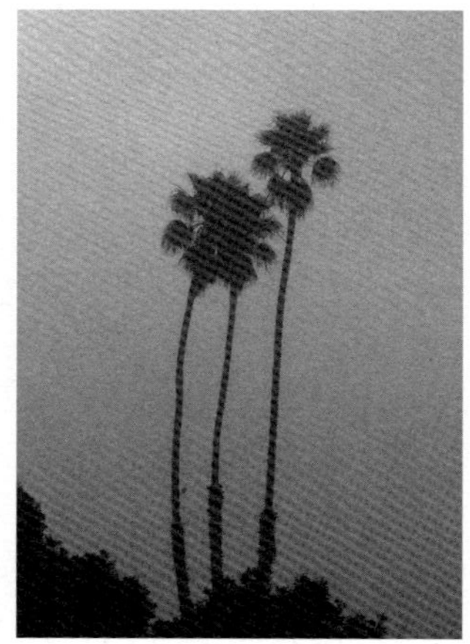

Living Systems / Narrative Haze, 2013

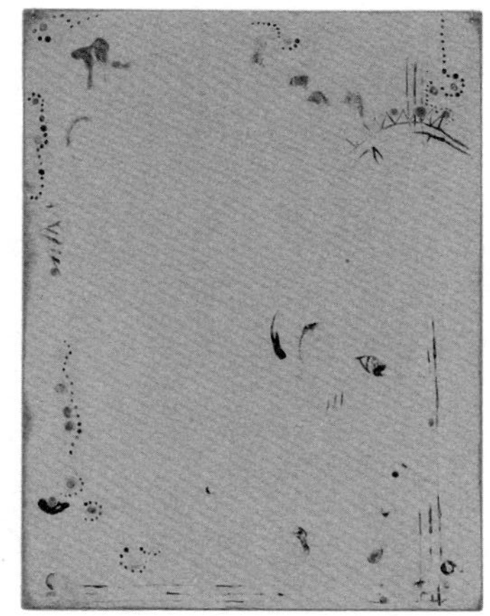

Thoughts Collected on the Surface of a Panel (a motif of pattern related to the psych-naturalism of 2004), 2013

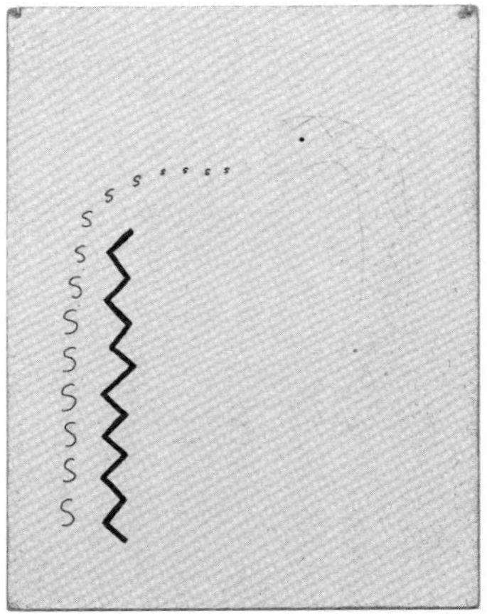

Thoughts Collected on the Surface of a Panel (snake speaking a pattern), 2013

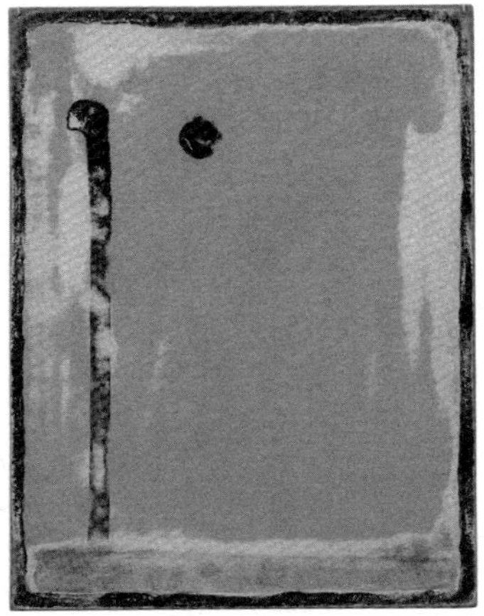

Thoughts Collected on the Surface of a Panel (the line, the dot, a haze of pink), 2013

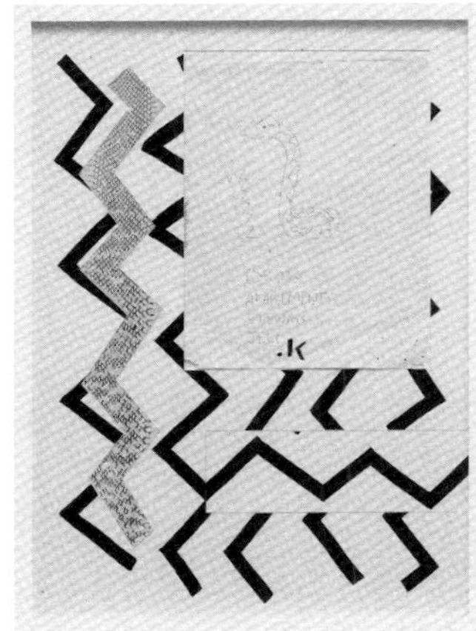

The Hiss of a Snake, the Sound of a Form, 2014

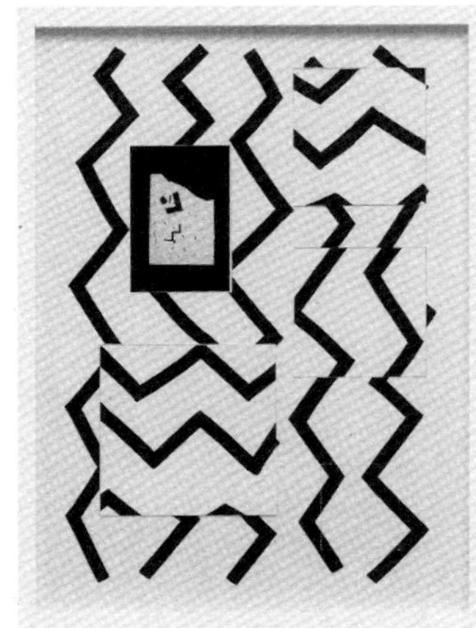

A Diagram, 2014

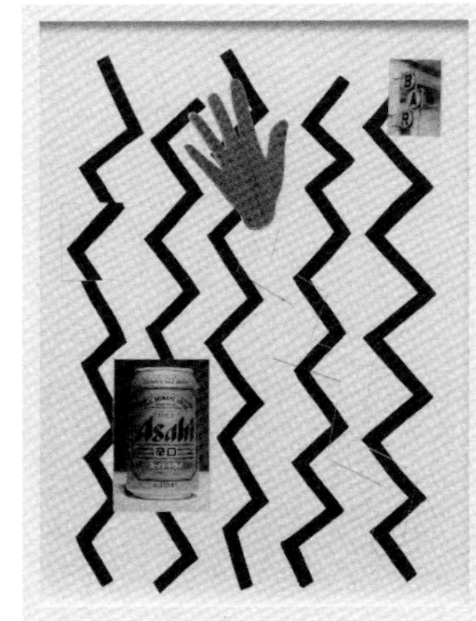

Bar of the Lavender Hand, 2014

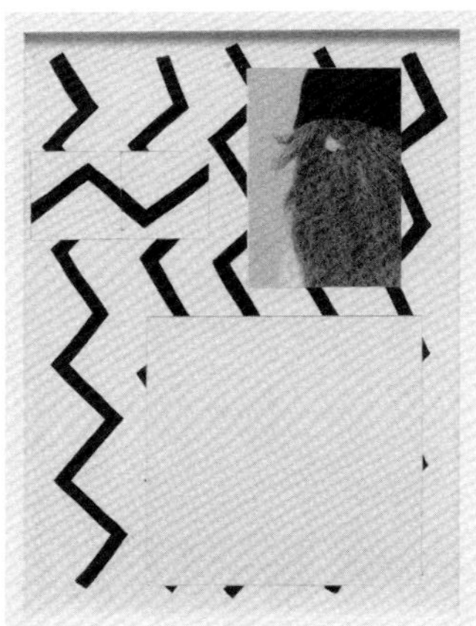

Bzzzz, said Zig Zag, in the Presence of Solid Foam, 2014

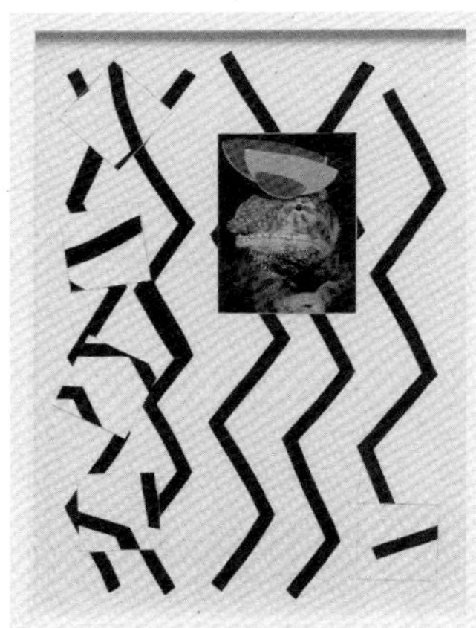

Segments and Surfaces (Miami Iguana), 2014

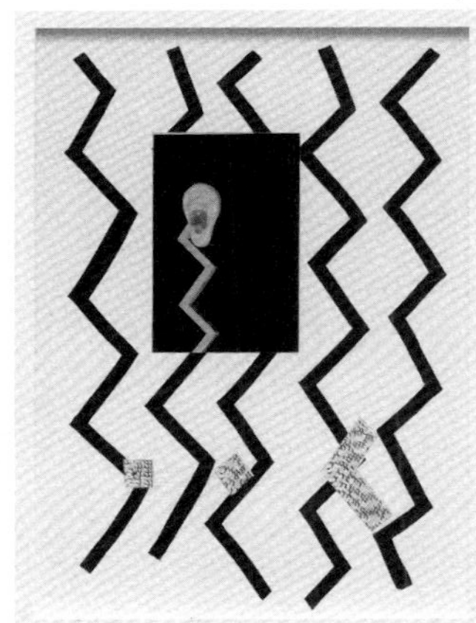

Sound Forms (Square, Diamond, ZigZag), 2014

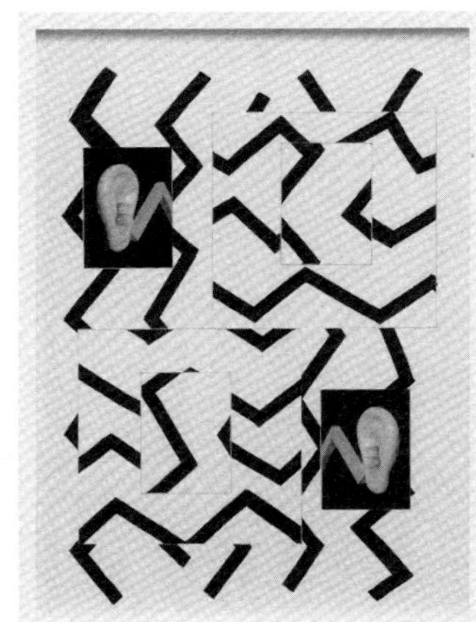

The Brain, 2014

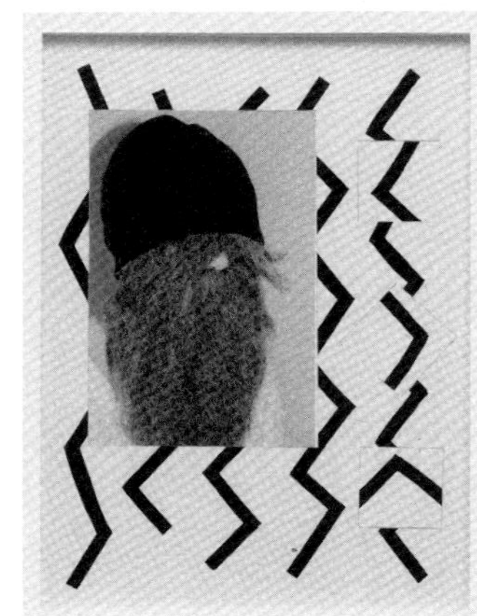

ZigZag/Solid Foam - Thoughts Throwing Shapes, 2014

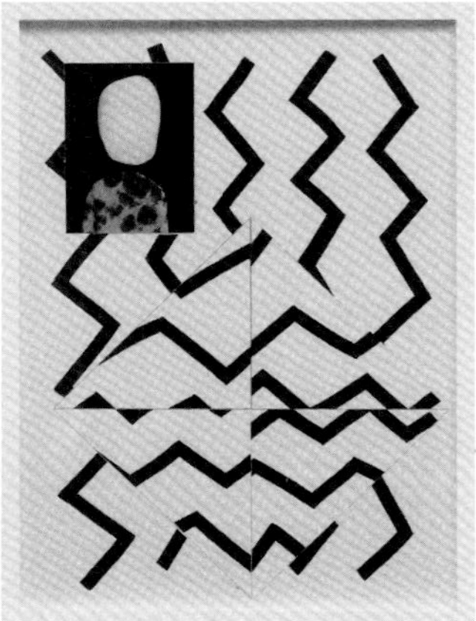

The Mystic, 2014

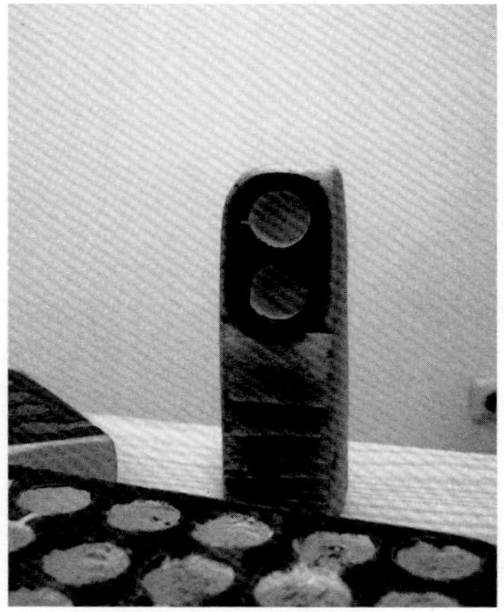

The Bakery of Blok (Arrangement IV), Salt, 2010

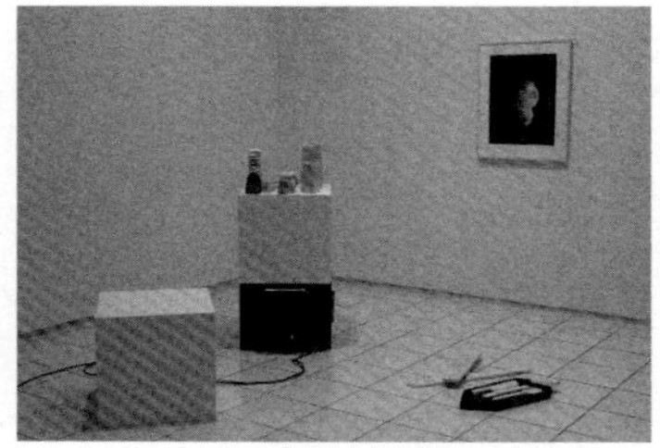

The Bakery of Blok (Arrangement III), installation at Miguel Abreu Gallery, New York, USA, 2009

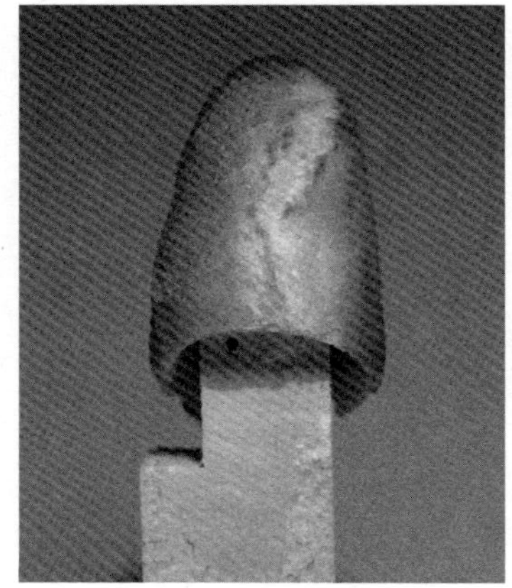

Arrangement for Bread and Wood (Bread Hat), 2009

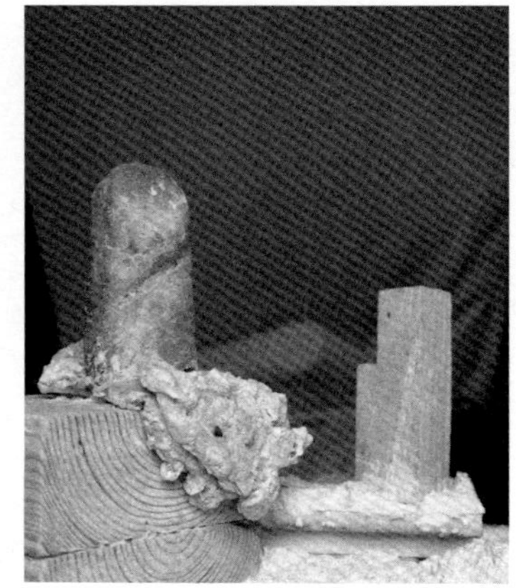

Arrangement for Bread and Wood (Upstairs, Downstairs), 2009

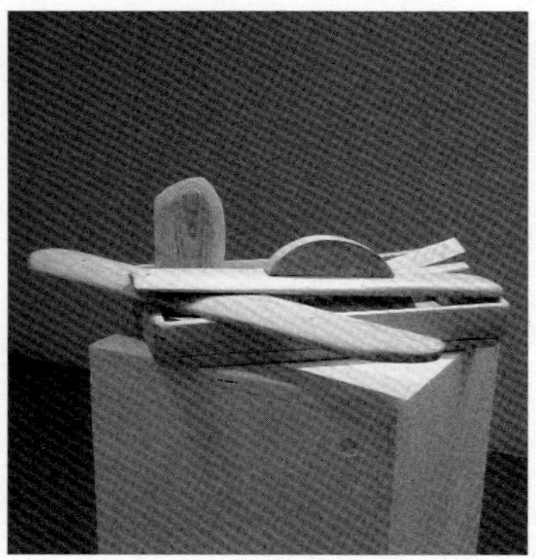

Tools of the Blok, installation at Jessica Bradley Gallery, Toronto, Canada, 2009

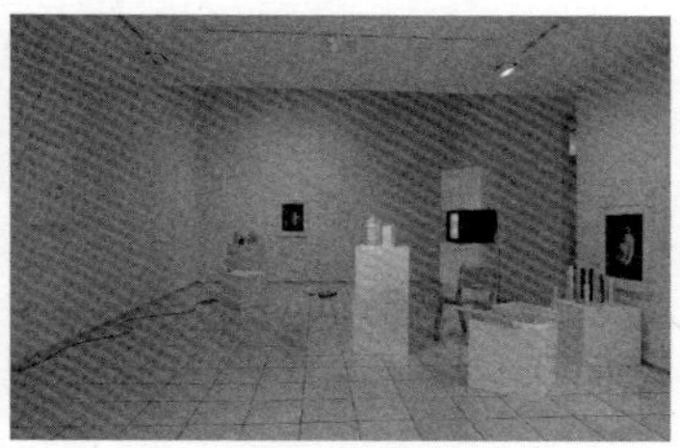

The Bakery of Blok and the Three Forms of Unit, installation at Miguel Abreu Gallery, New York, USA, 2009

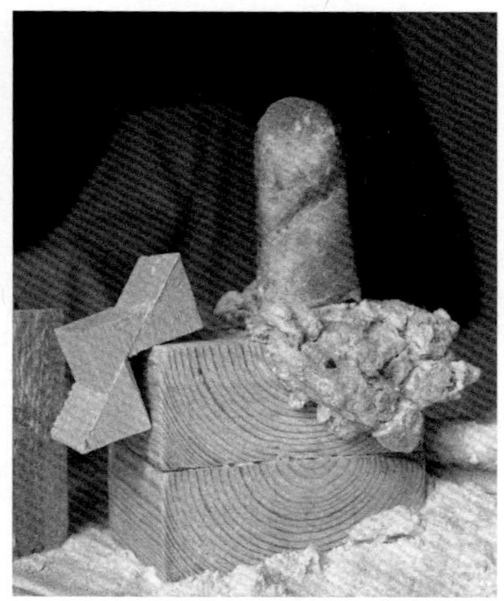

Arrangement for Bread and Wood (Bread and Salt), 2009

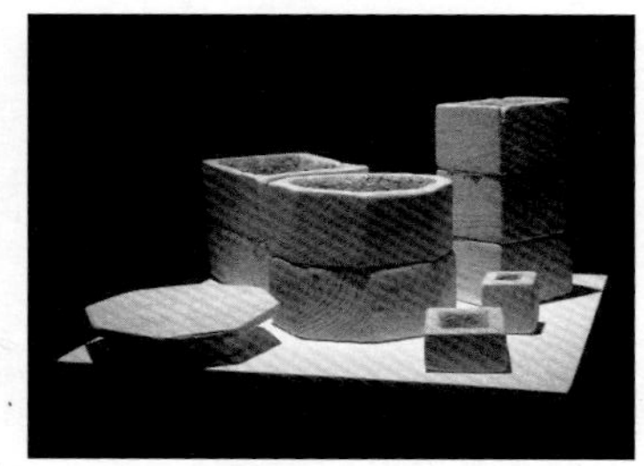

Containers of the Blok, installation at Jessica Bradley Gallery, Toronto, Canada, 2009

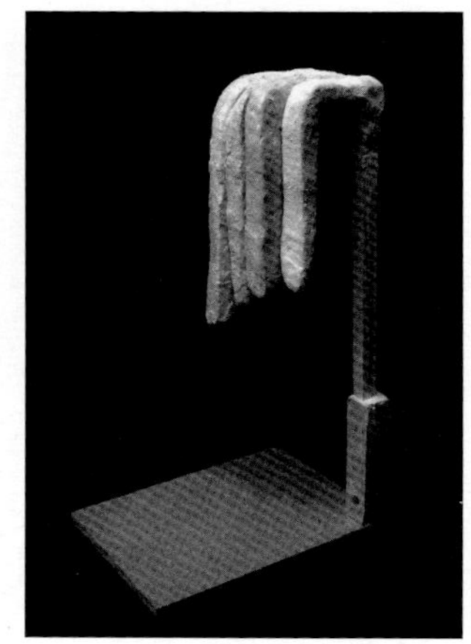

The Purple Hand, 2011

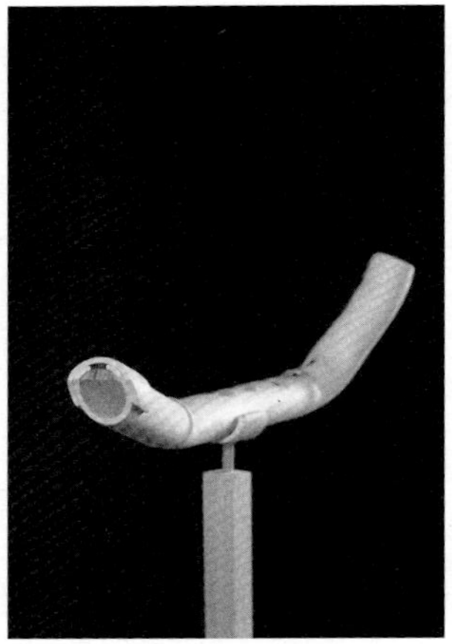

The Flute of Sub, 2007

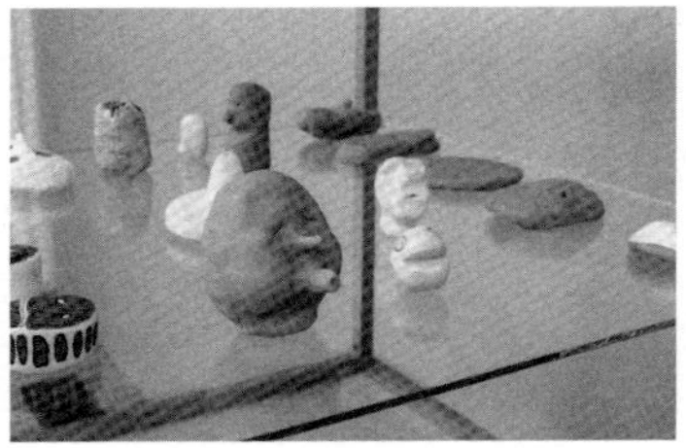

36 Thoughts About a Little Head Manifested into a Form, Displayed Within a Vitrine Made of Brass and Glass, 2012

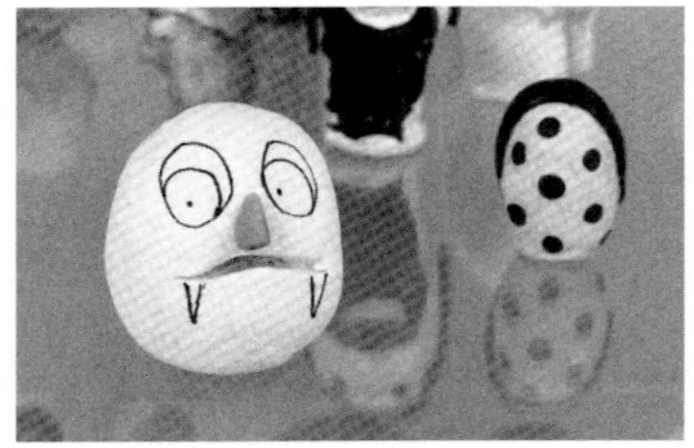

36 Thoughts About a Little Head Manifested into a Form, Displayed Within a Vitrine Made of Brass and Glass, 2012

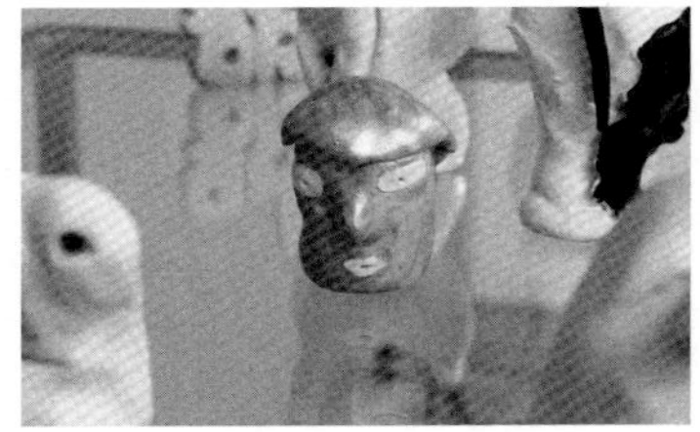

36 Thoughts About a Little Head Manifested into a Form, Displayed Within a Vitrine Made of Brass and Glass, 2012

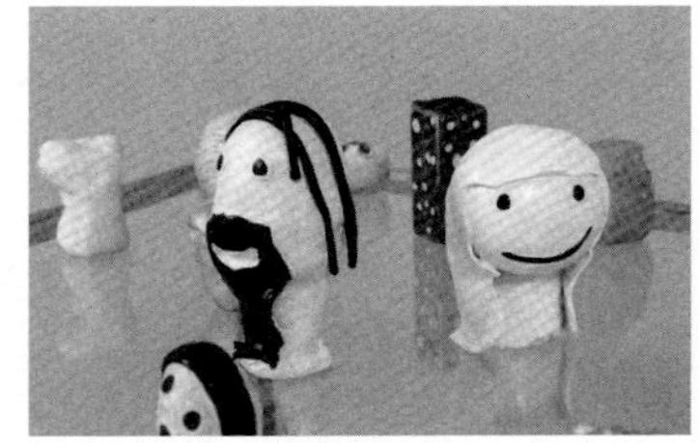

36 Thoughts About a Little Head Manifested into a Form, Displayed Within a Vitrine Made of Brass and Glass, 2012

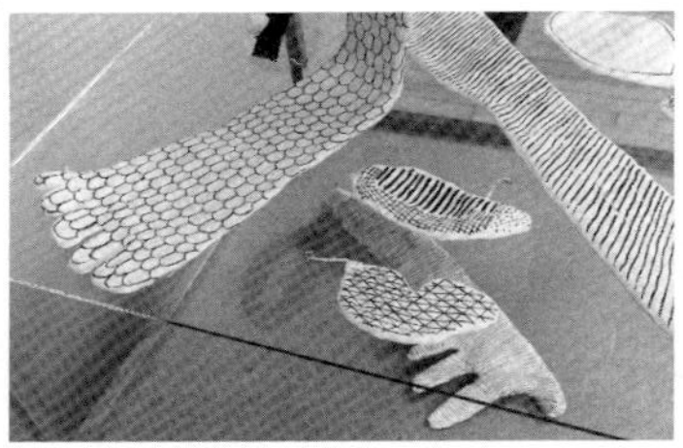

19 Thoughts About the Parts of a Character Manifested into a Form, Displayed Within a Vitrine Made of Brass and Glass, 2012

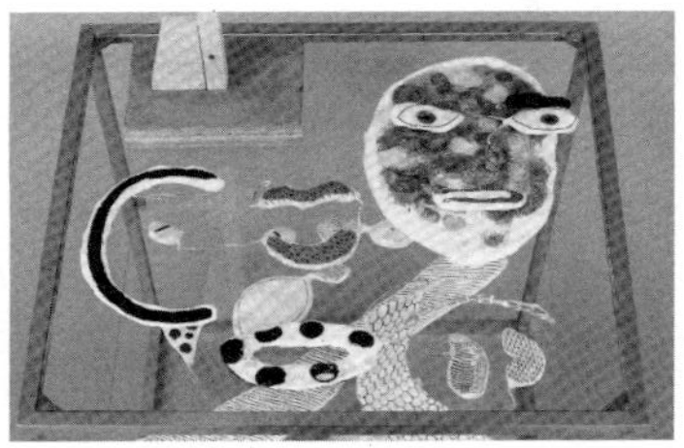

19 Thoughts About the Parts of a Character Manifested into a Form, Displayed Within a Vitrine Made of Brass and Glass, 2012

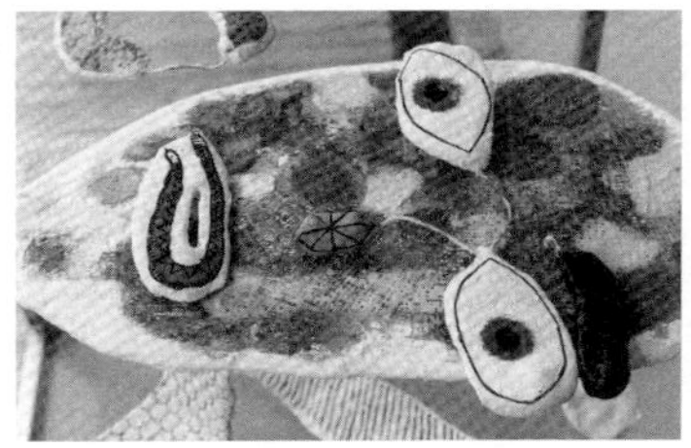

19 Thoughts About the Parts of a Character Manifested into a Form, Displayed Within a Vitrine Made of Brass and Glass, 2012

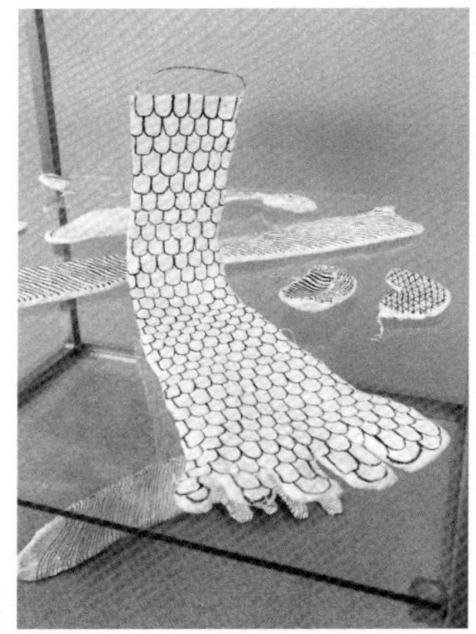

19 Thoughts About the Parts of a Character Manifested into a Form, Displayed Within a Vitrine Made of Brass and Glass, 2012

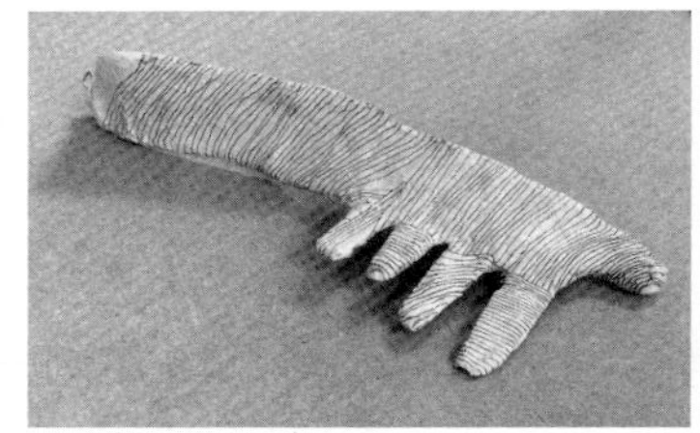

19 Thoughts About the Parts of a Character Manifested into a Form, Displayed Within a Vitrine Made of Brass and Glass, 2012

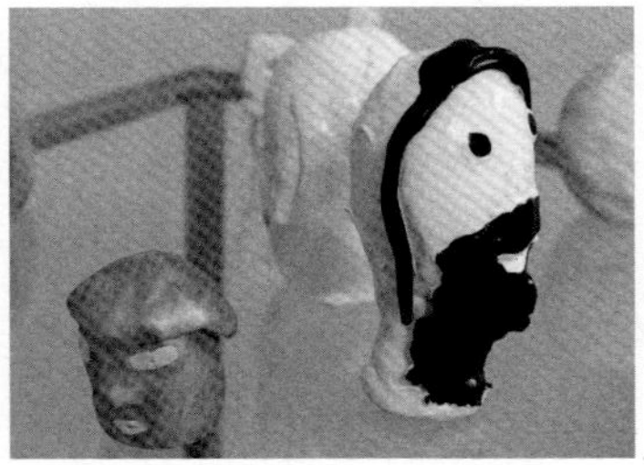

36 Thoughts About a Little Head Manifested into a Form, Displayed Within a Vitrine Made of Brass and Glass, 2012

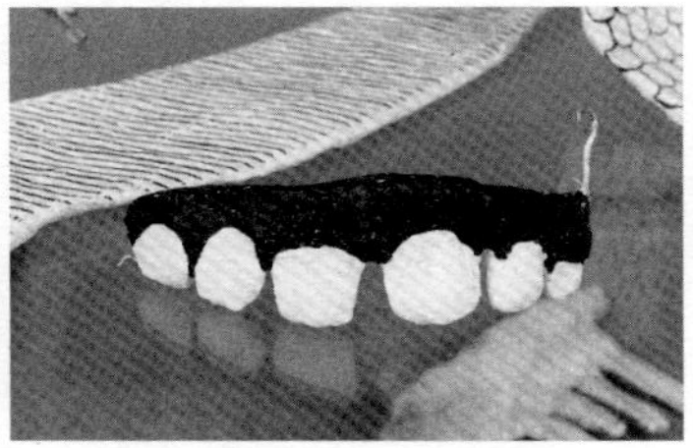

19 Thoughts About the Parts of a Character Manifested into a Form, Displayed Within a Vitrine Made of Brass and Glass, 2012

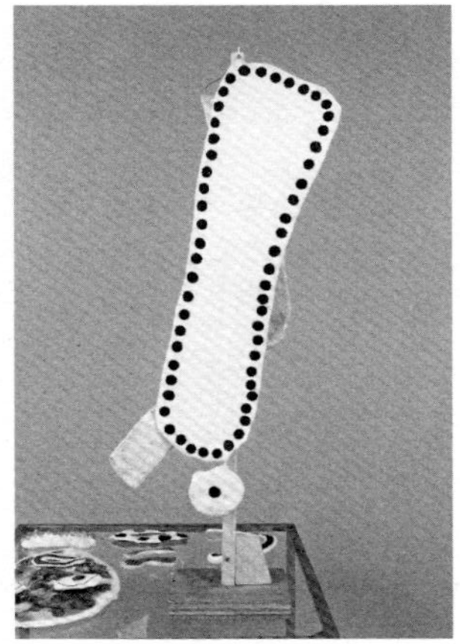

19 Thoughts About the Parts of a Character Manifested into a Form, Displayed Within a Vitrine Made of Brass and Glass, 2012

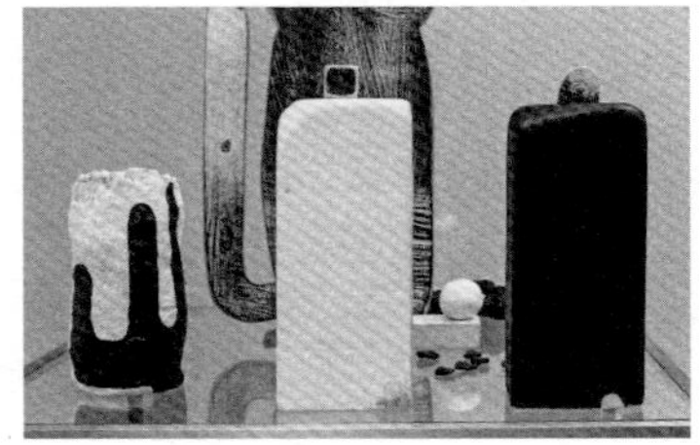

24 Thoughts about Stripes and Dots Manifested into a Form, Displayed Within a Vitrine Made of Brass and Glass, 2012

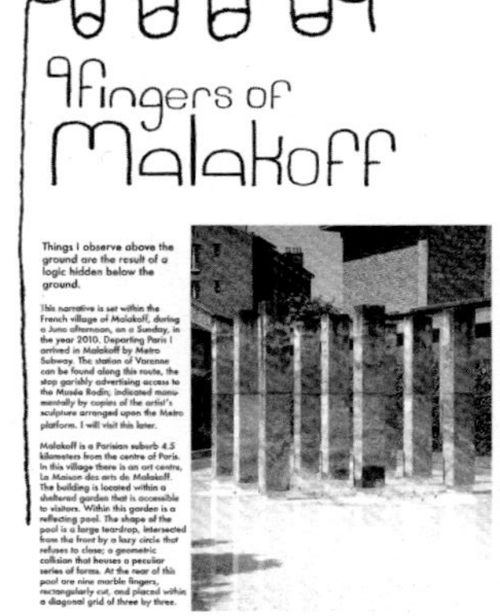

The 9 Fingers of Malakoff, 2010

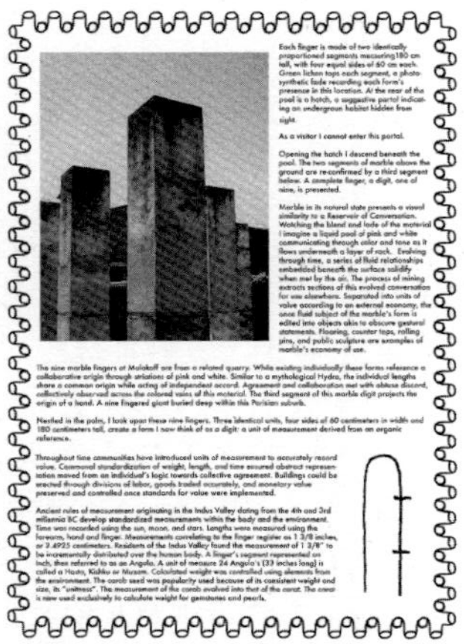

The 9 Fingers of Malakoff, 2010

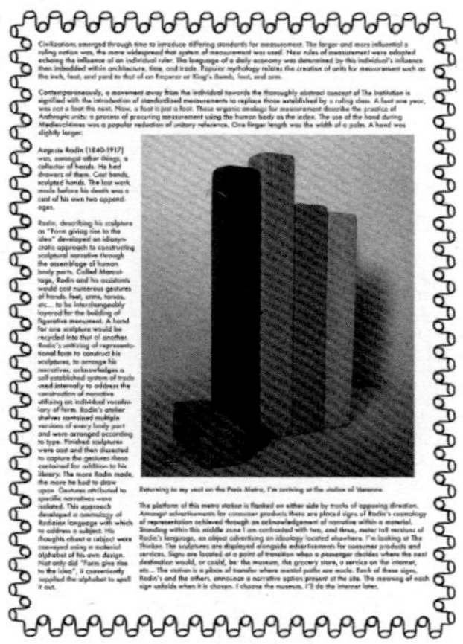

The 9 Fingers of Malakoff, 2010

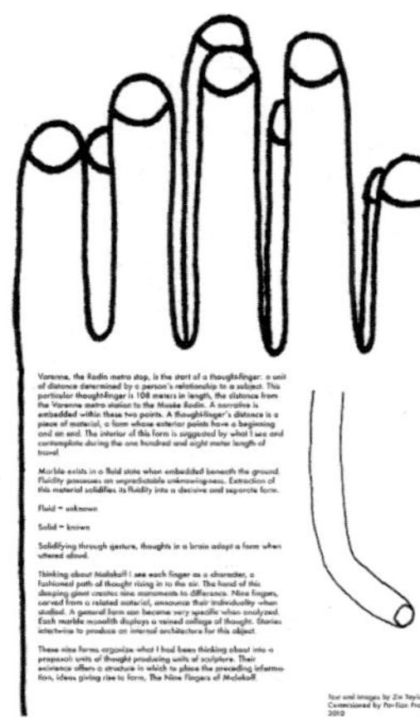

The 9 Fingers of Malakoff, 2010

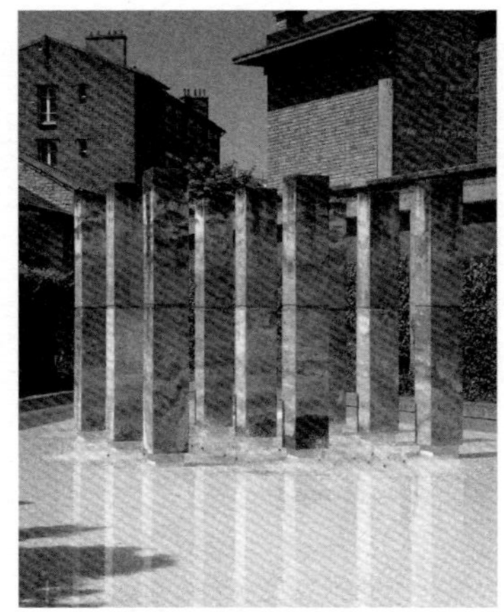

Fountain at the Art Centre of Malakoff, Malakoff, France, 2010

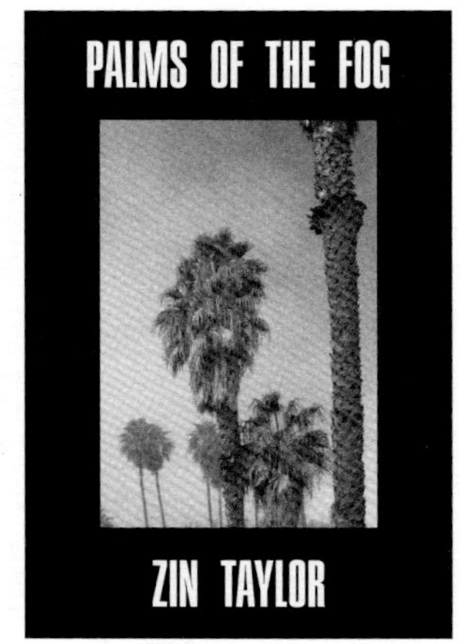

Palms of the Fog, Mousse Publishing, 2013

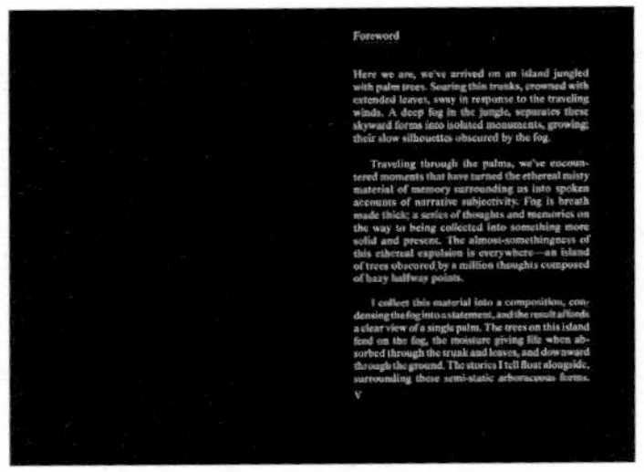

Palms of the Fog, foreword, 2013

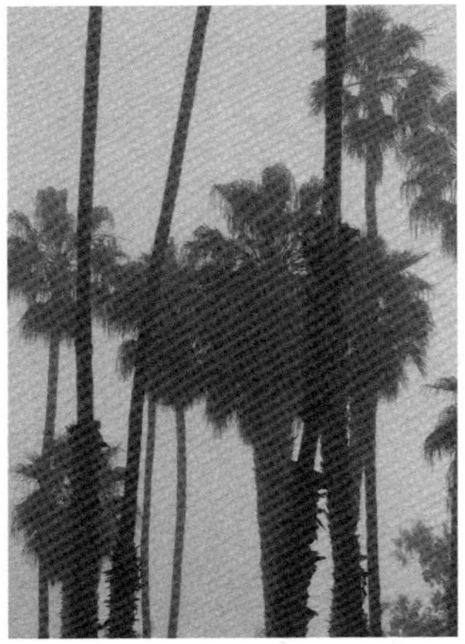

Living Systems/Narrative Haze, 2013

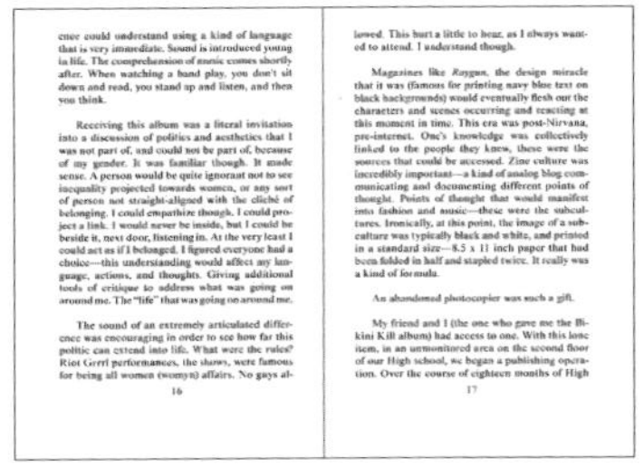

Palms of the Fog, excerpt, 2013

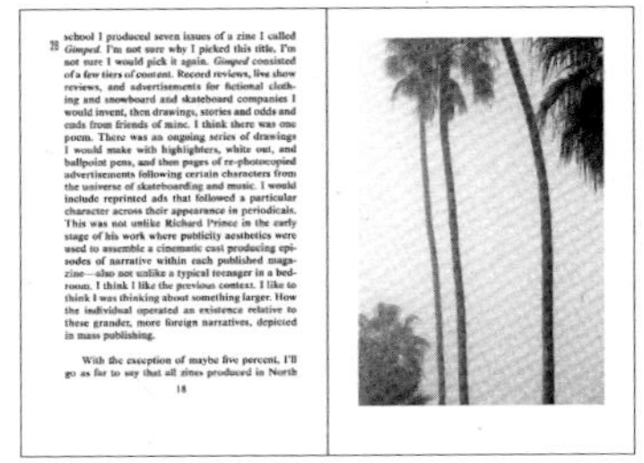

Palms of the Fog, excerpt, 2013

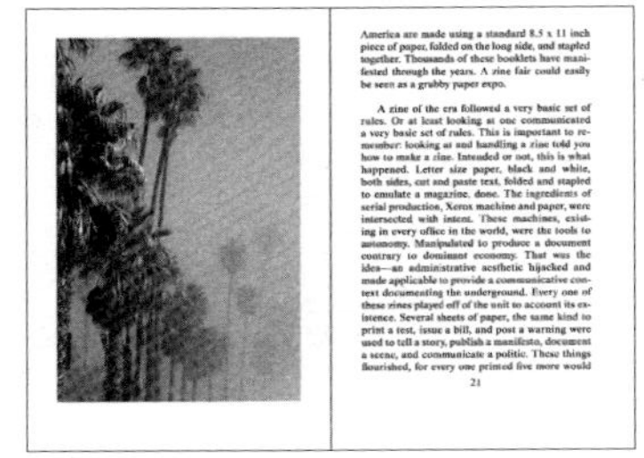

Palms of the Fog, excerpt, 2013

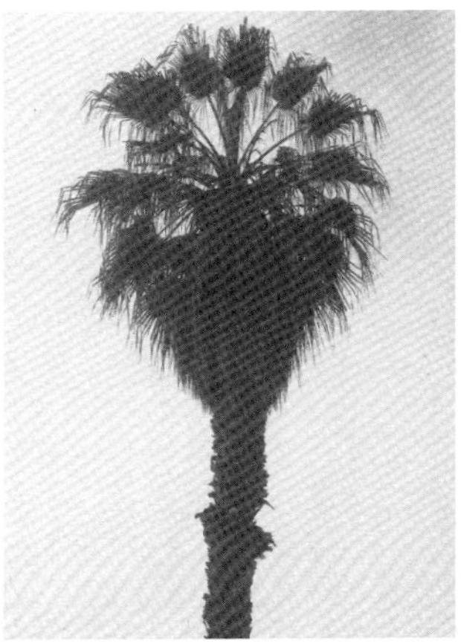

Living Systems/Narrative Haze, 2013

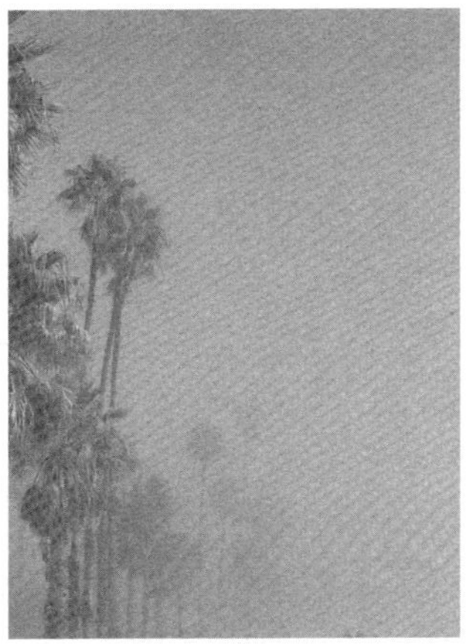

Living Systems/Narrative Haze, 2013

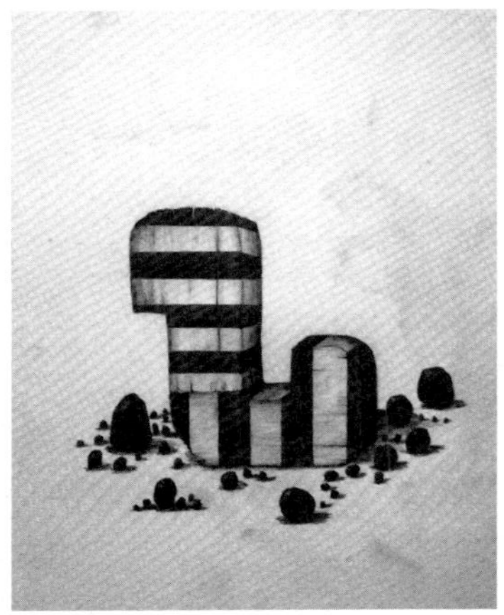

Growth on a Form (Z), 2010

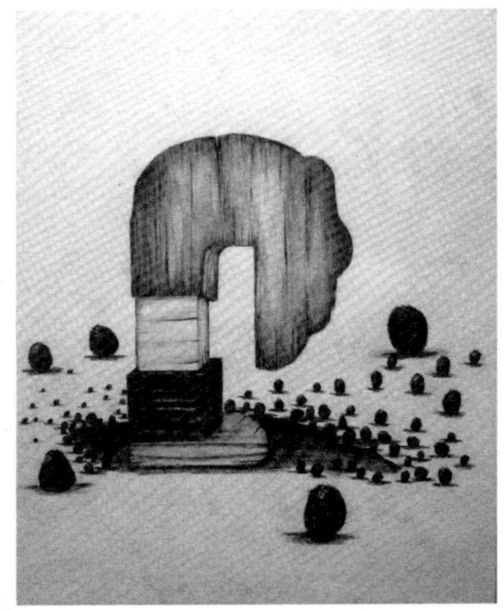

Growth on a Form (Hook Nose), 2010

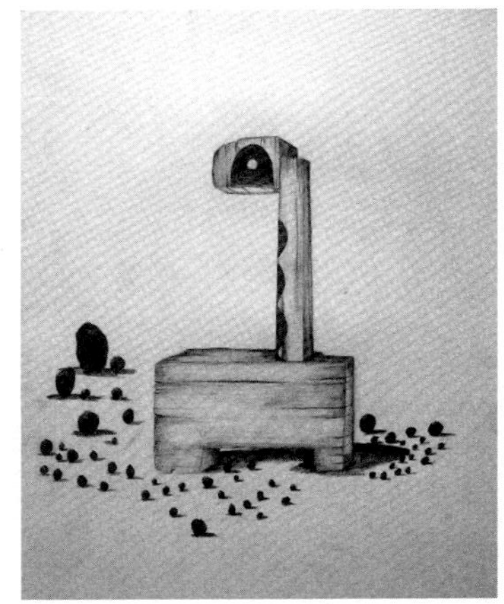

Growth on a Form (Giraffe), 2010

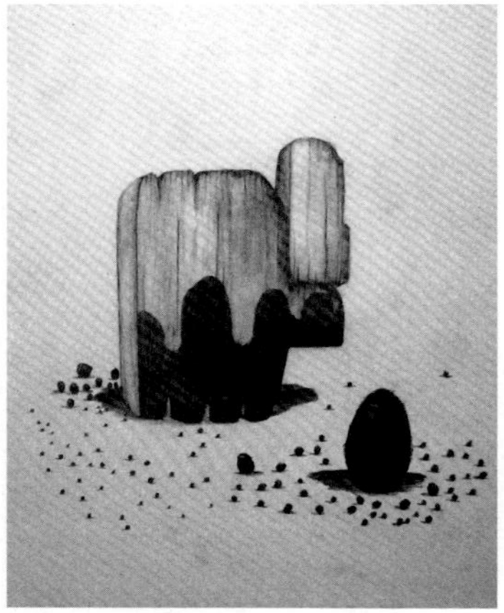

Growth on a Form (Wave Pool), 2010

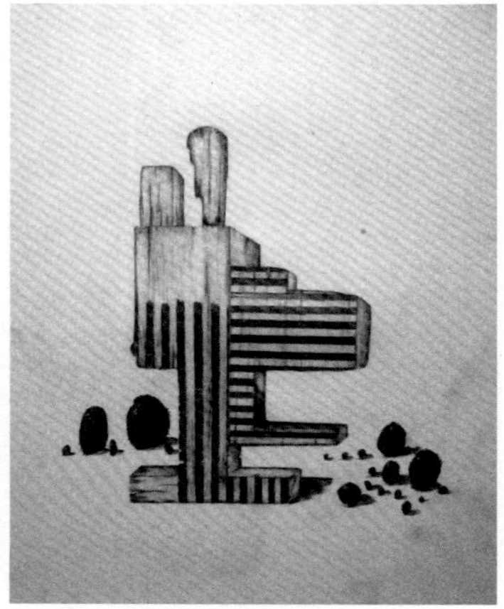

Growth on a Form (That Zebra is a Radio), 2010

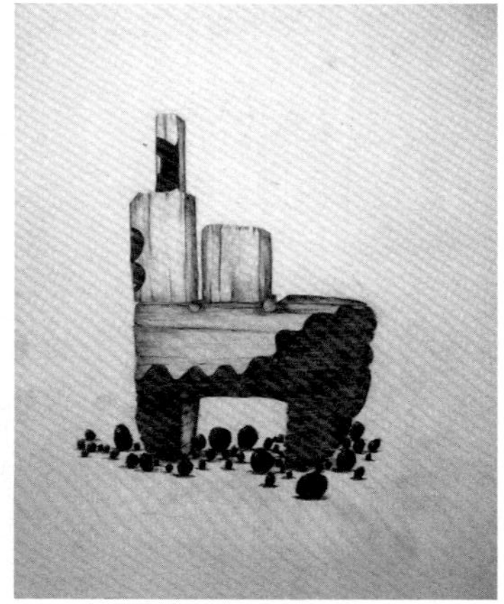

Growth on a Form (The Pack Horse), 2010

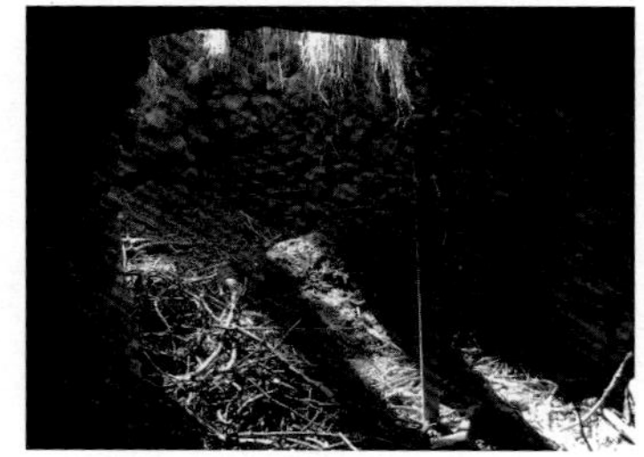

The Flute of Sub, production detail, 2007

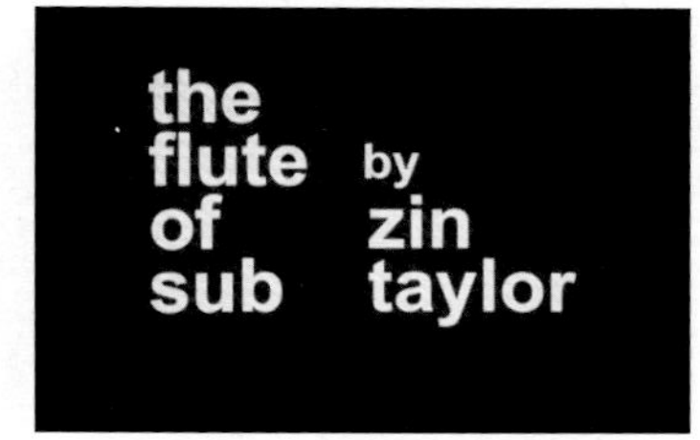

The Flute of Sub, video still, 2007

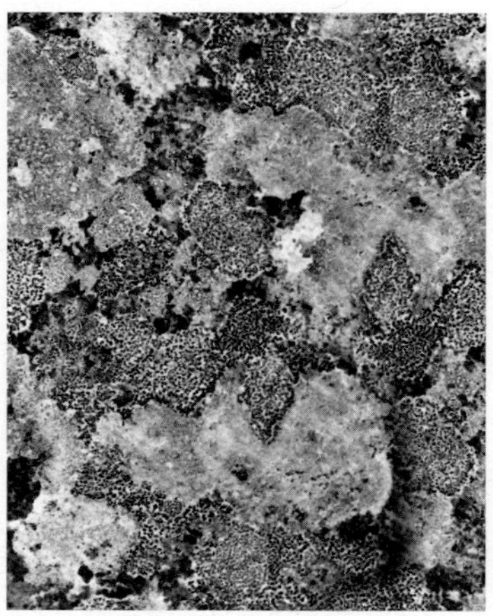

The Proposal of a Surface (Lichen Wall), 2013

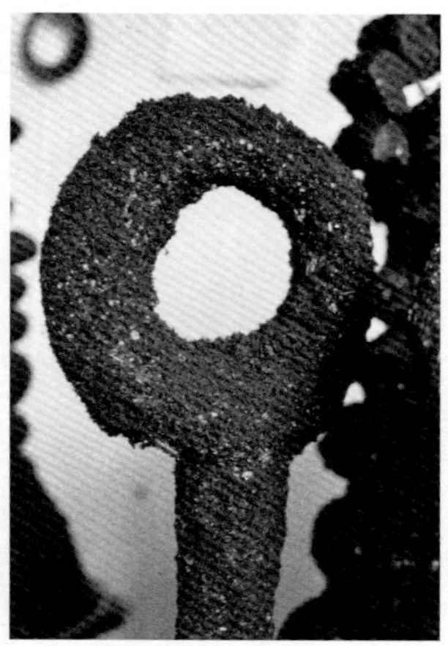

The Allegorical Function of Dirt: a discussion with Aki Tsuyuko's Ongakushitsu, studio detail, 2004

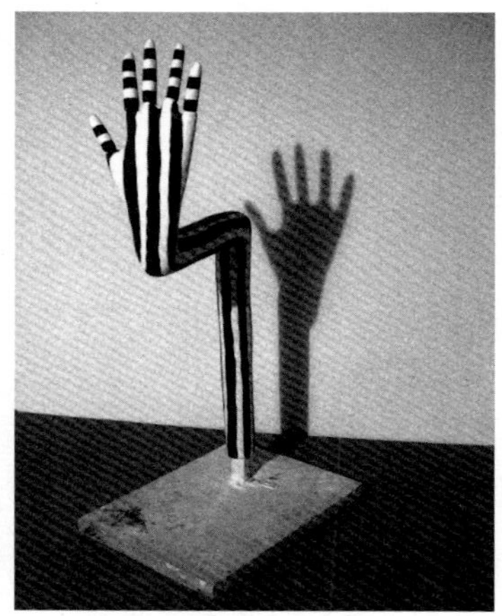

The Voids, invitation card, 2011

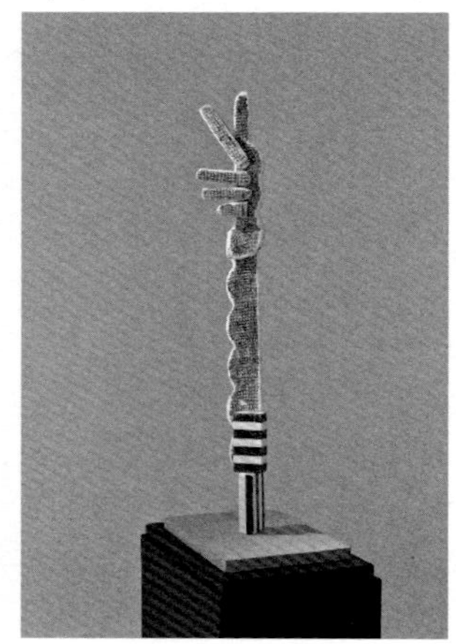

An Haze of Influence Choreographed into an Arm (Stripes and Dots), 2012

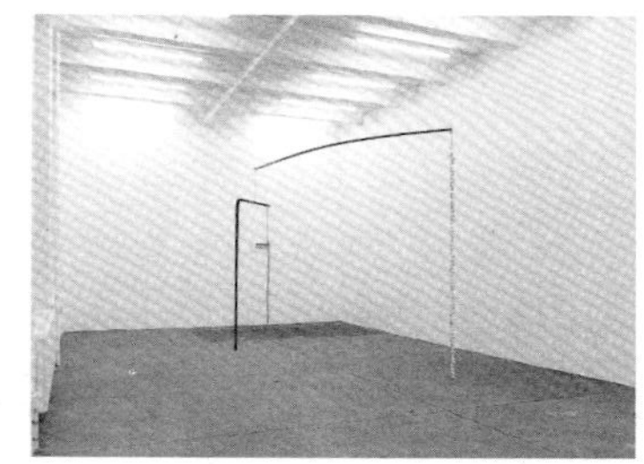

A String of Eyeballs, a Spectrum of Colour, a Structure of Form in Black and White, 2013

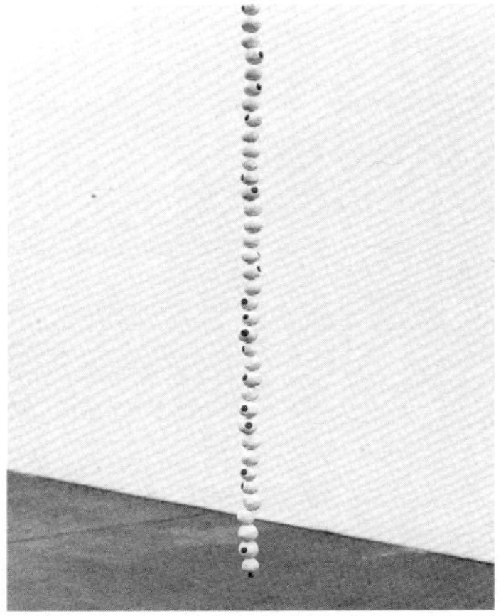

A String of Eyeballs, a Spectrum of Colour, a Structure of Form in Black and White, 2013

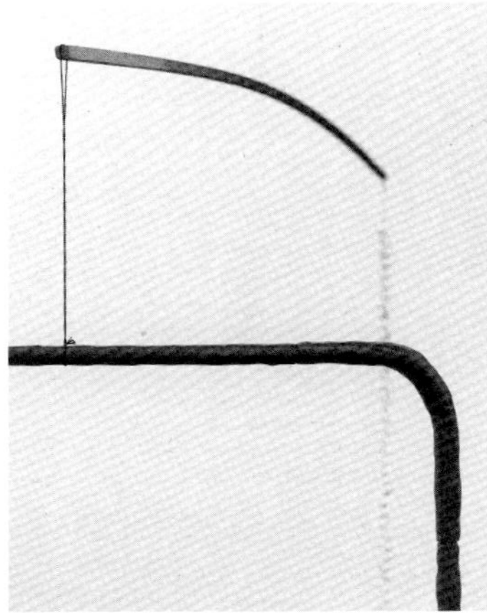

A String of Eyeballs, a Spectrum of Colour, a Structure of Form in Black and White, 2013

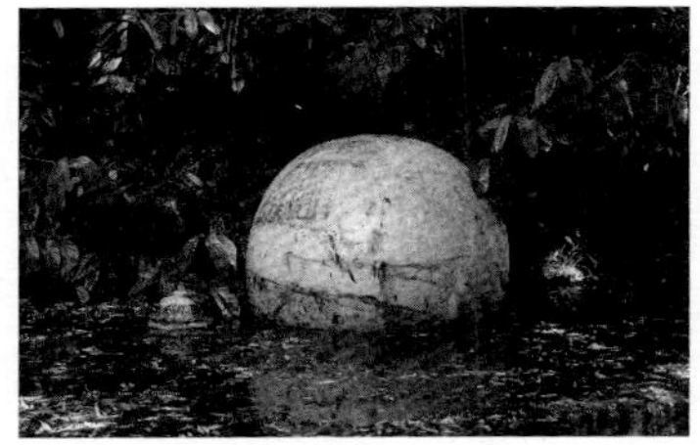

White Pearl Sunshine Summoning Charm, 2007

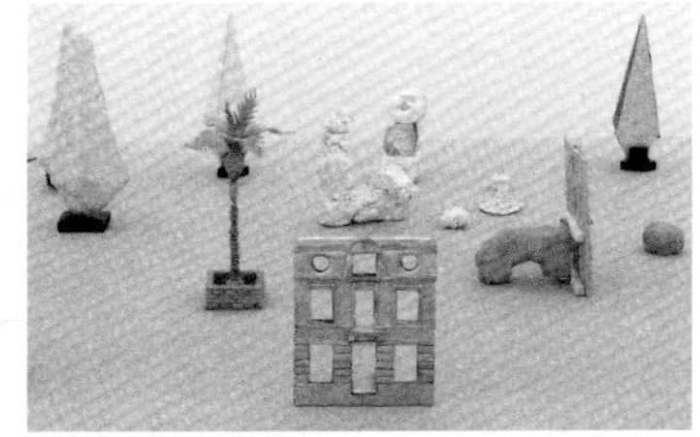

The Crystal Ship, installation at Mendes Wood DM, Sao Paulo, Brazil, 2015

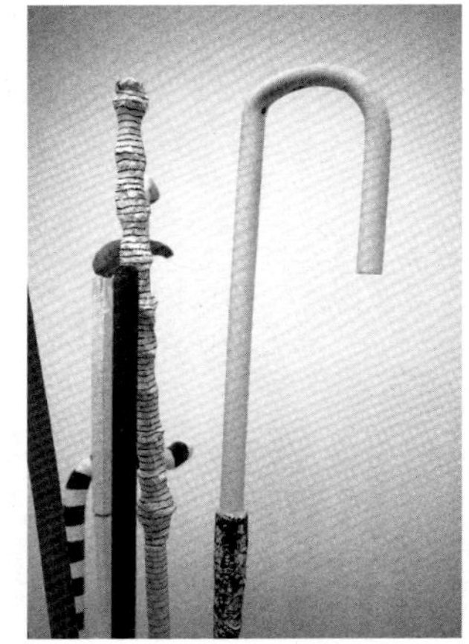

16 Thoughts About a Cane Manifested into a Form, Displayed Within a Vitrine Made of Brass and Glass, 2012

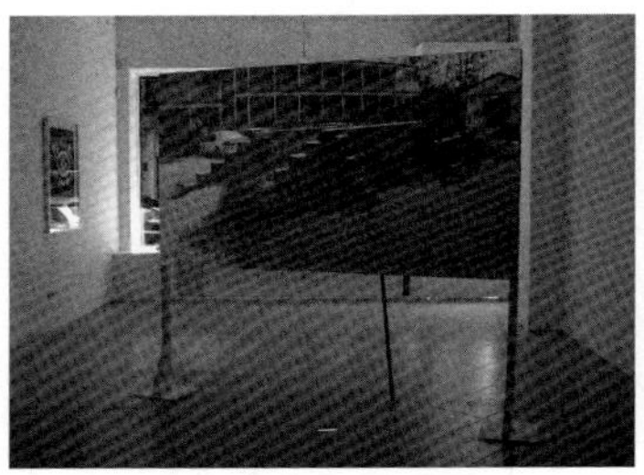

Put Your Eye in Your Mouth: a conversational documentary recording Martin Kippenberger's Metro-Net Station in Dawson City, Yukon, installation at Etablissement d'en face projects, Brussels, 2007

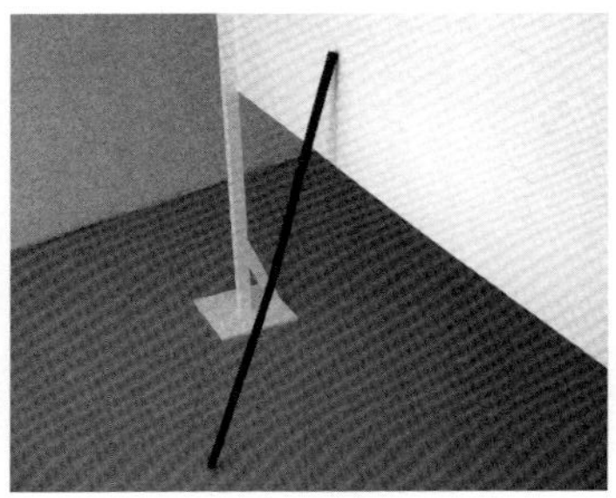

Put Your Eye in Your Mouth: a conversational documentary recording Martin Kippenberger's Metro-Net Station in Dawson City, Yukon, installation at Etablissement d'en face projects, Brussels, 2007

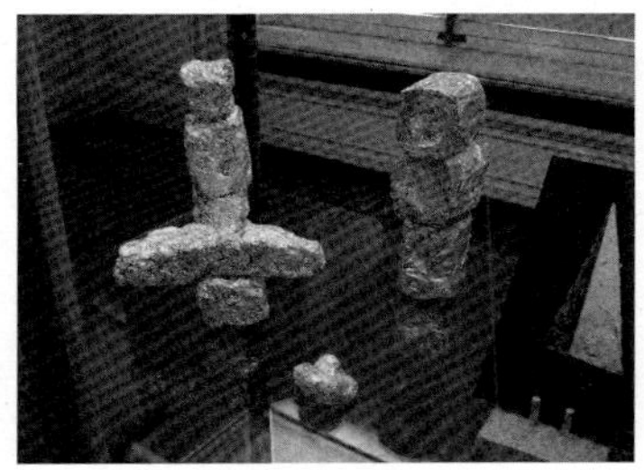

The Crystal Ship, installation at BELvue Museum of Belgian History, Brussels, Belgium, 2008

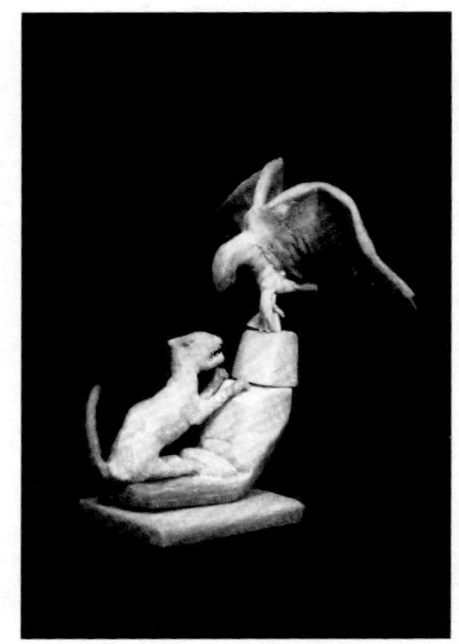

Cat and Eagle from *The Crystal Ship*, 2008

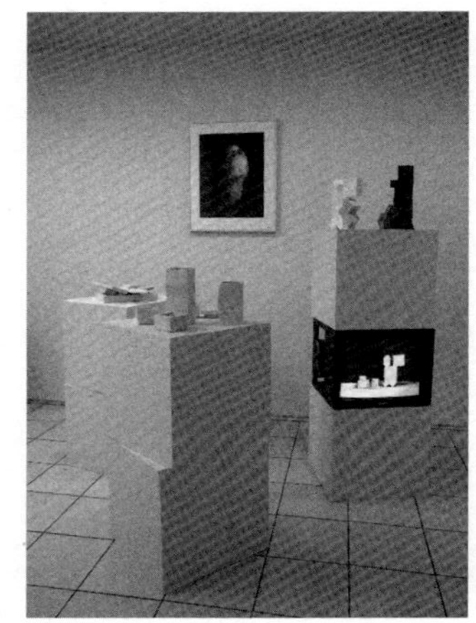

The Bakery of Blok (Arrangement I), installation at Miguel Abreu Gallery, New York, USA, 2009

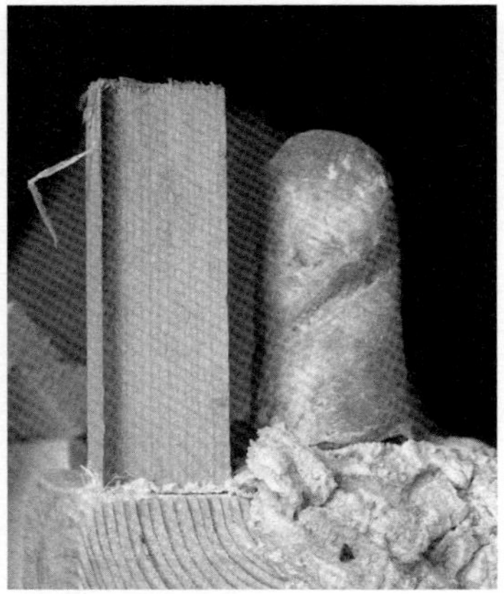

An Arrangement for Bread and Wood (Red Stripe and Second Loaf), 2009

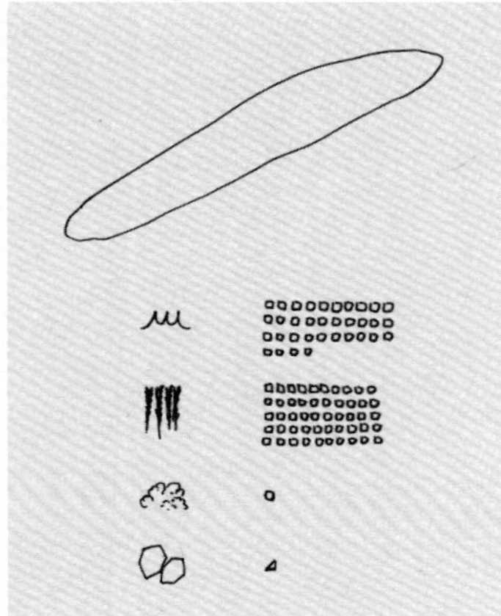

The Recipe of Bread, 2009

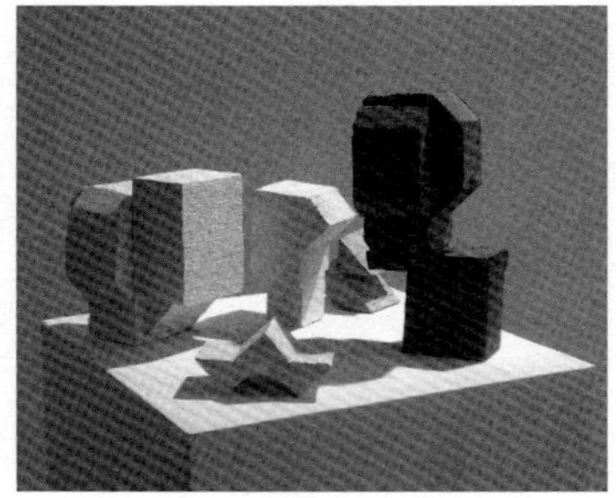

Weights of The Blok, installation at Jessica Bradley Gallery, Toronto, Canada, 2009

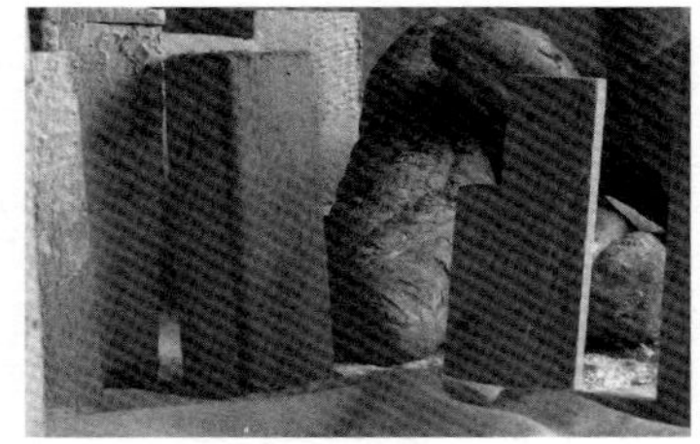

Eight Pilot Episodes for The Bakery of Blok, video still, 2009

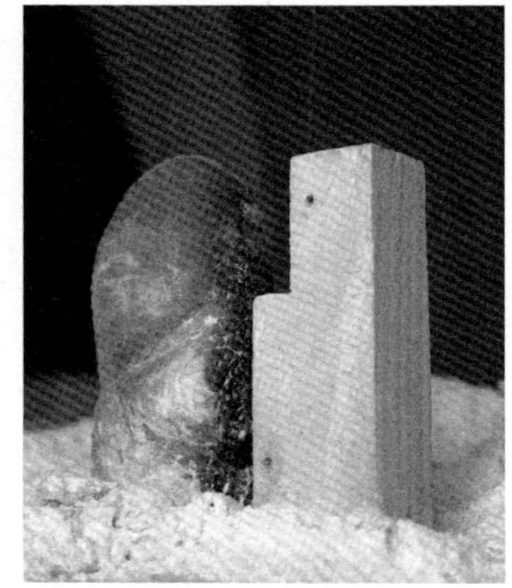

An Arrangement for Bread and Wood (One Eye and Second Loaf), 2009

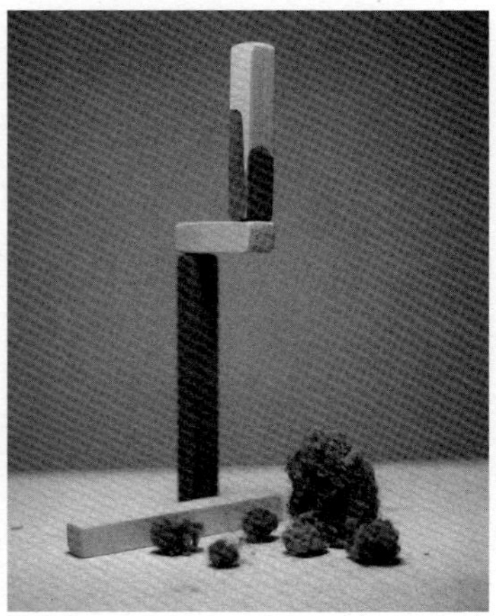

Wood and Dust (Enacting an Image Previously Drawn), 2010

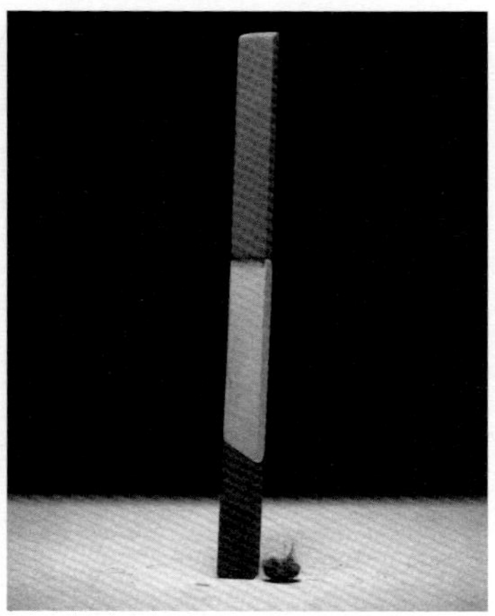

Wood and Dust (A Tower and its Rock), 2010

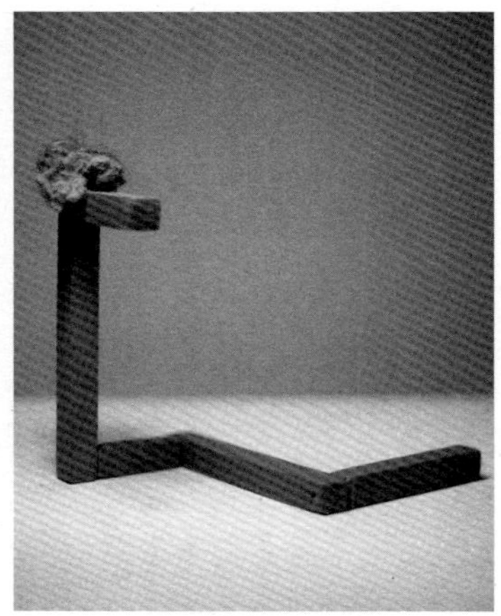

Wood and Dust (Snake and Wig), 2010

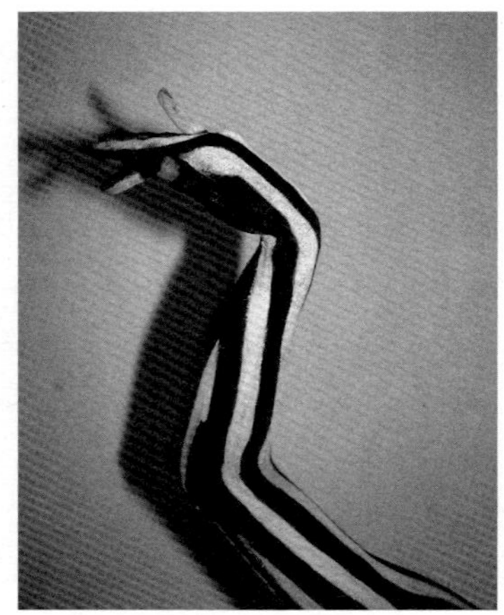

A Structure for Language onto an Organic Form (#09), 2011

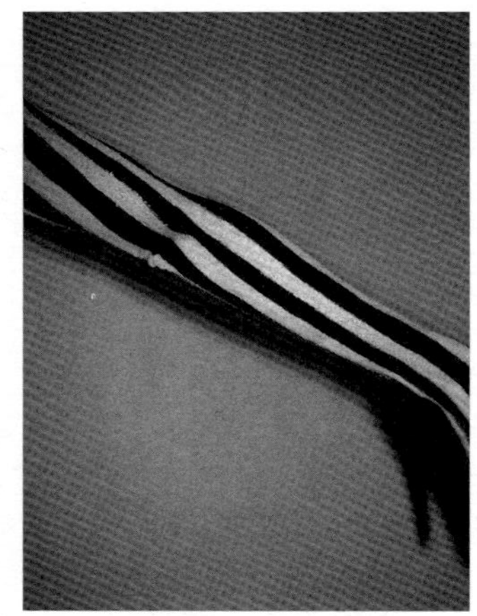

A Structure for Language onto an Organic Form (#22), 2011

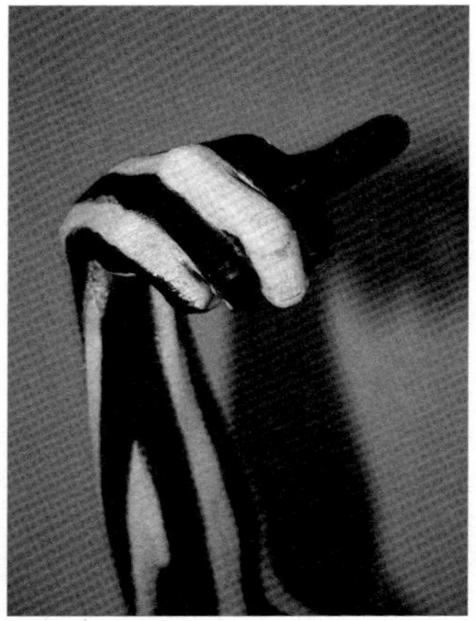

A Structure for Language onto an Organic Form (#21), 2011

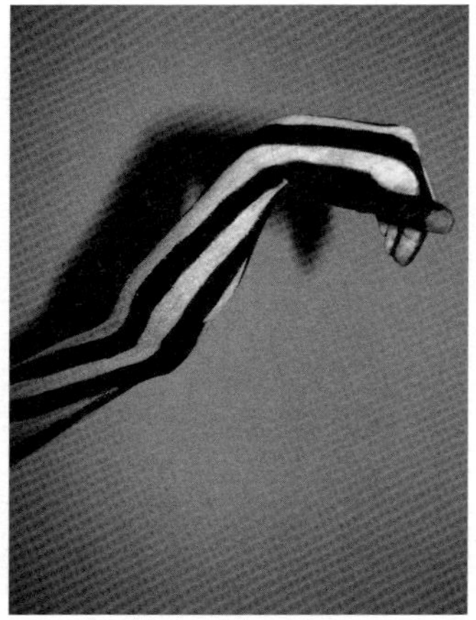

A Structure for Language onto an Organic Form (#12), 2011

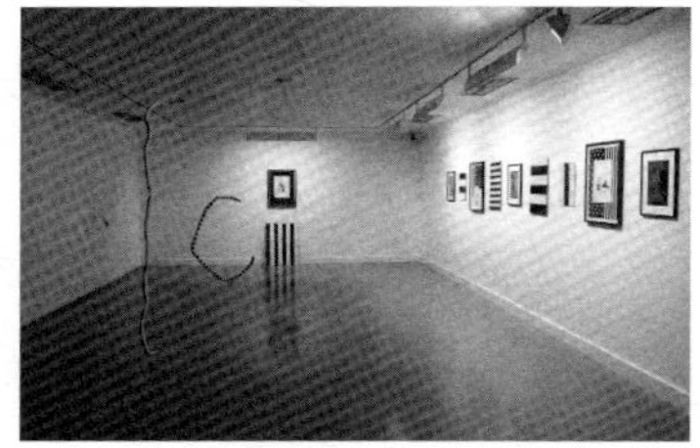

The Story of Stripes and Dots (Chapter 1), installation at MuHKA, Antwerp, Belgium, 2012

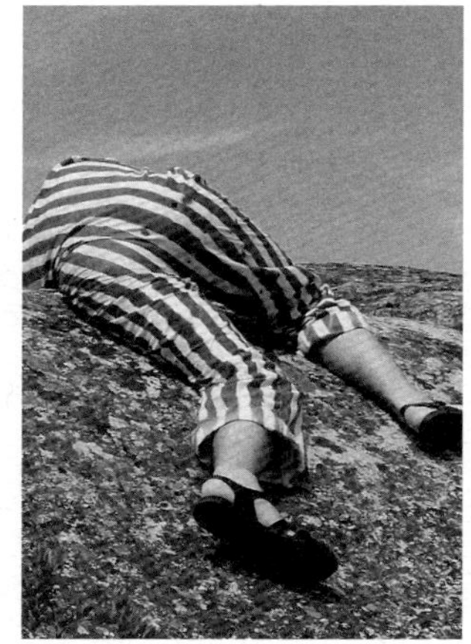

Lichen Voices/Stripes and Dots, video still, 2013

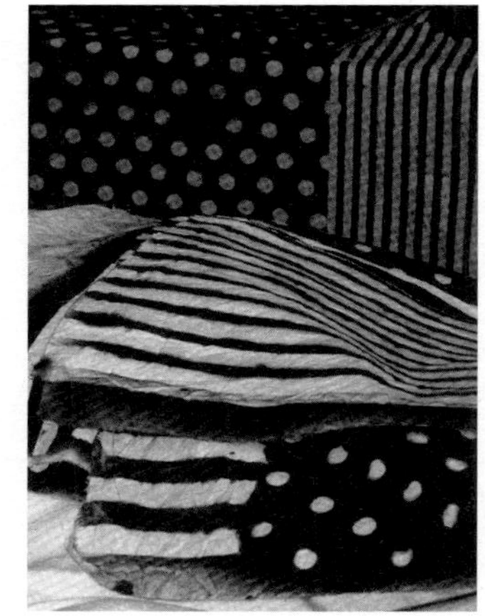

Fabric (Stripes and Dots), 2011

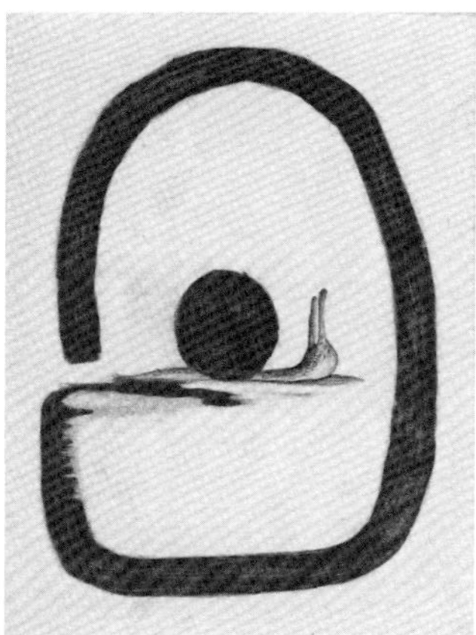

The Story of Stripes and Dots (A round shelled snail and the trail it made), 2012

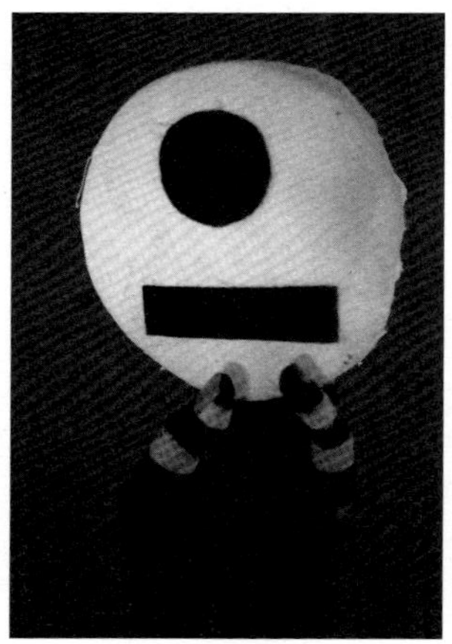

The Creature of Stripes and Dots (#1), 2012

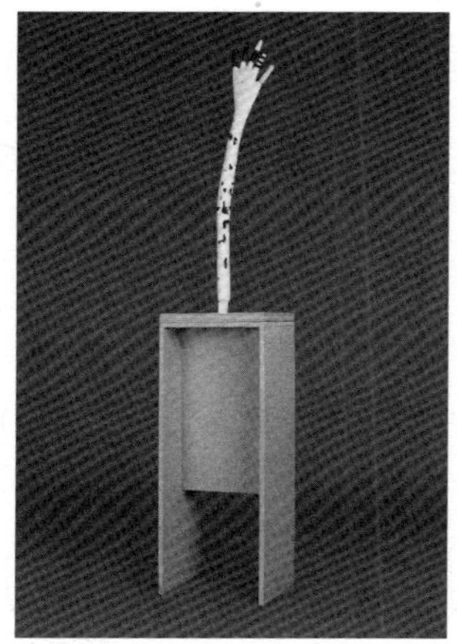

A Haze of Influence Choreographed into an Arm (#4), 2011

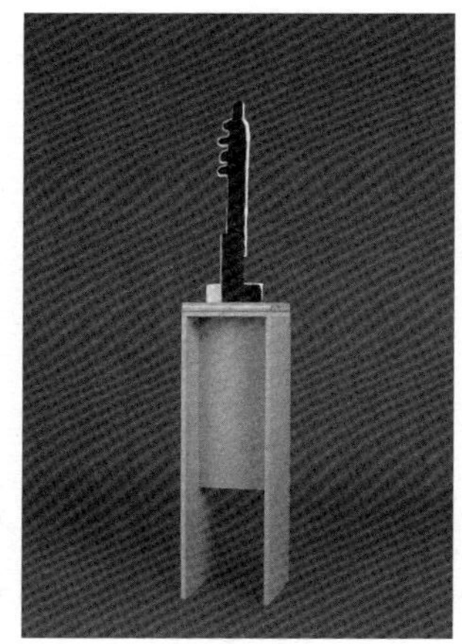

A Haze of Influence Choreographed into an Arm (#1), 2011

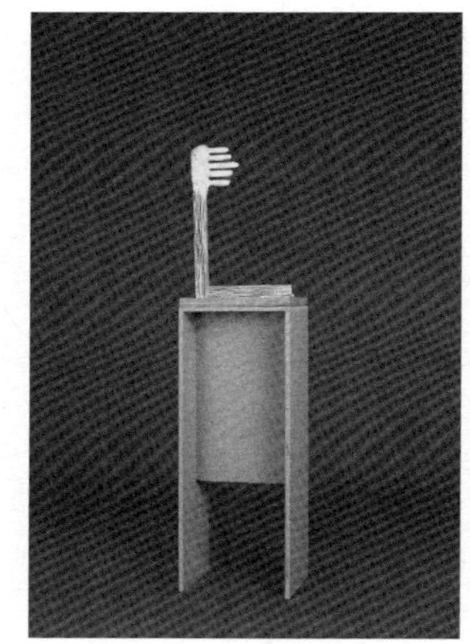

A Haze of Influence Choreographed into an Arm (#2), 2011

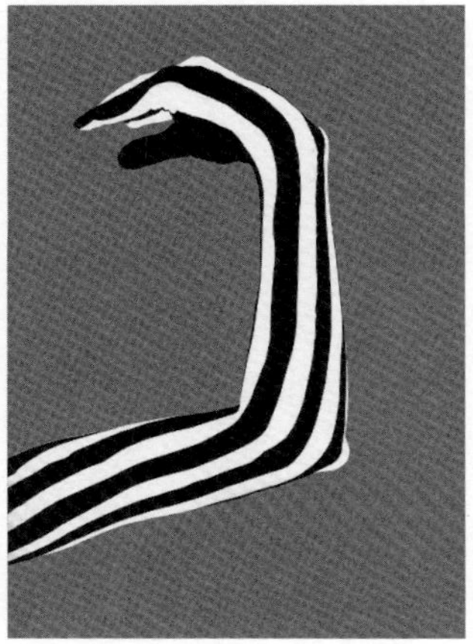

Growth, Sternberg Press and Ursula Blickle Stiftung, 2011

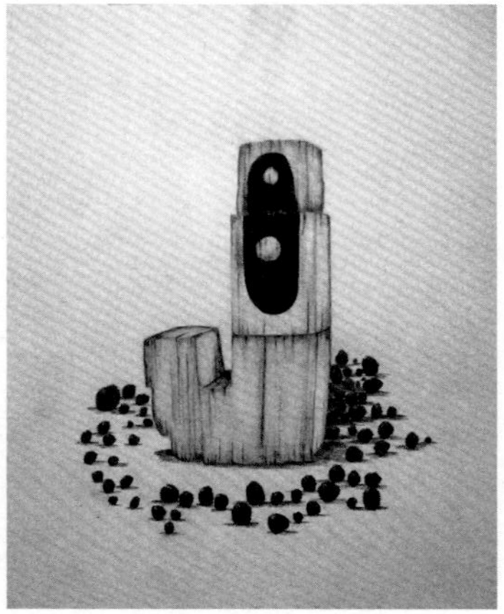

Growth on a Form (The Robot), 2010

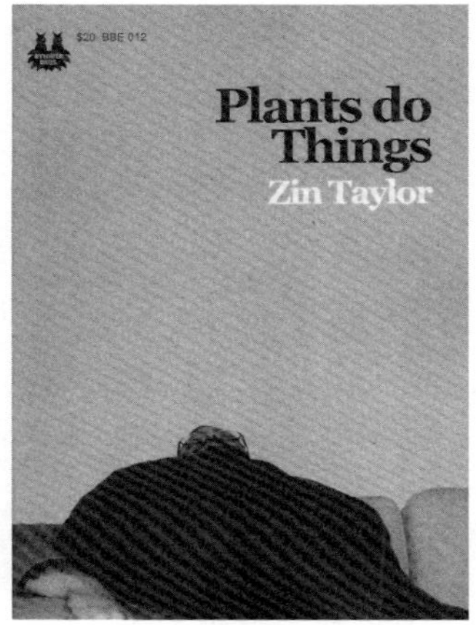

Plants do Things, Bywater Bros., 2010

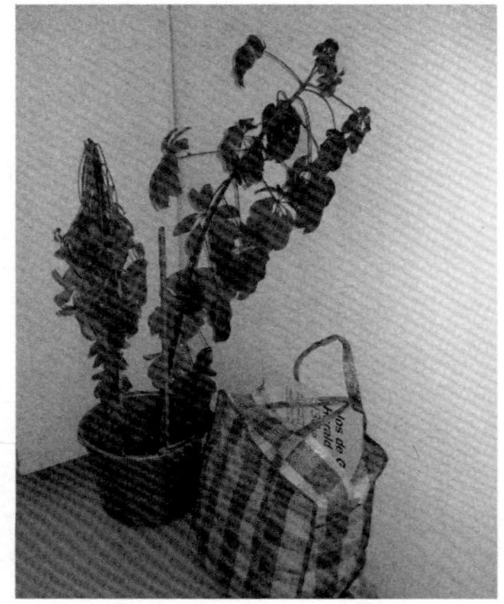

Plants do Things, 2010

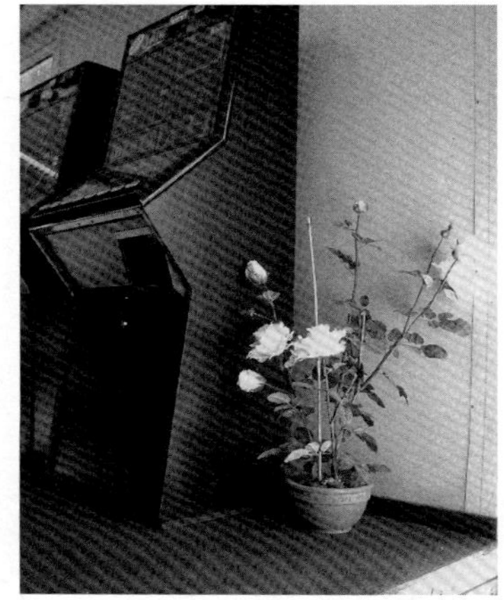

Plants do Things, 2010

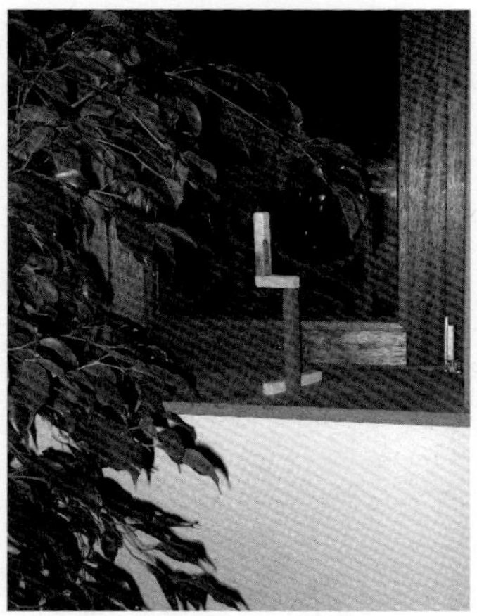

Plants do Things, 2010

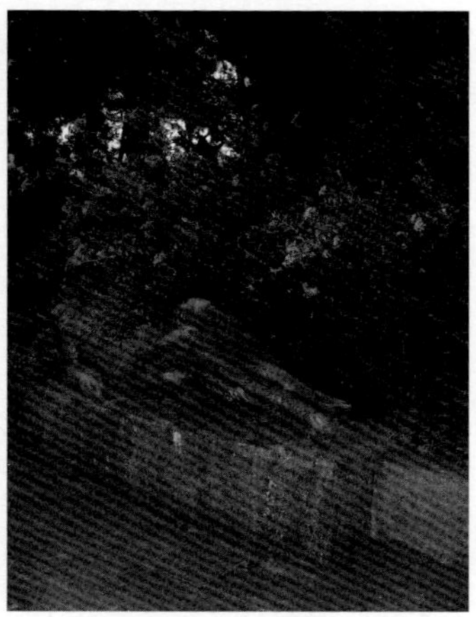

Plants do Things, 2010

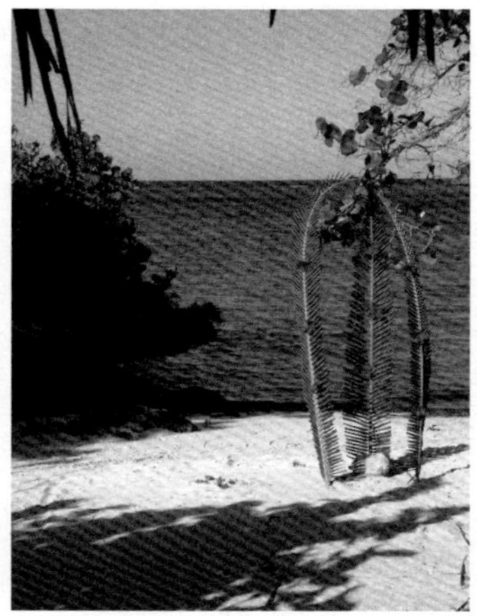

Plants do Things, 2010

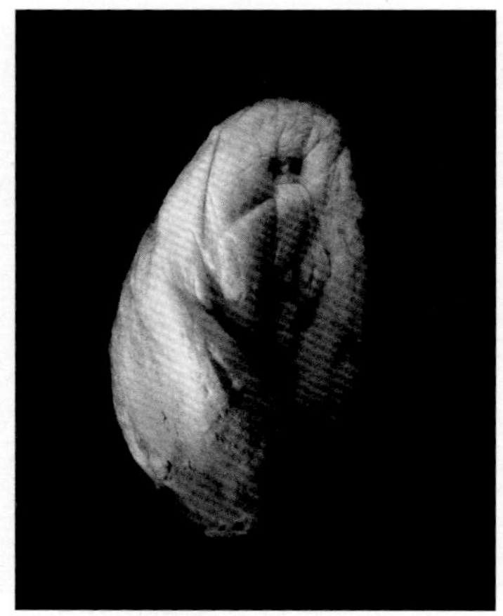

15th Organism, 2009

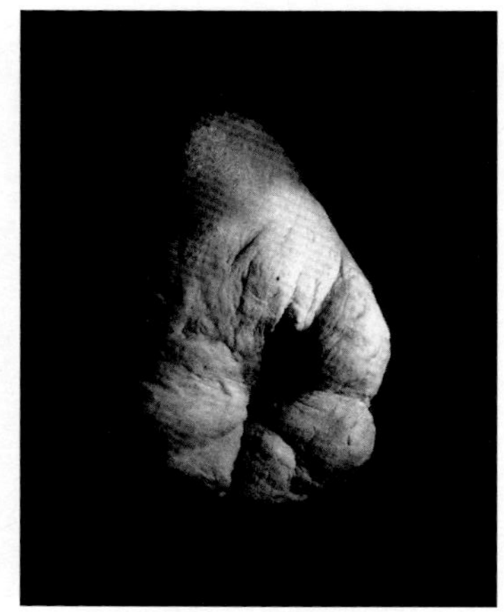

17th Organism, 2009

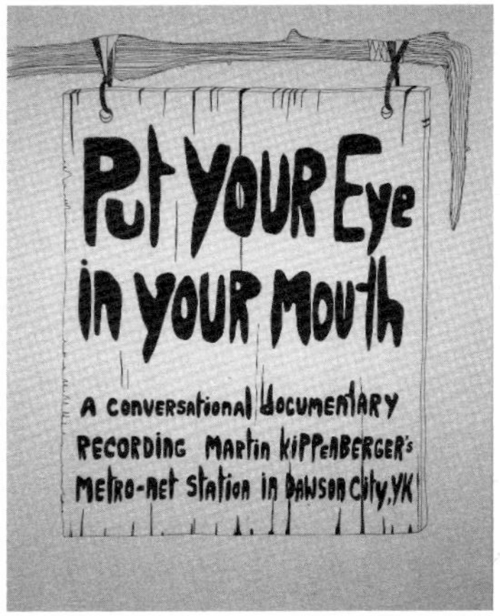

Poster No.4 (Put Your Eye in Your Mouth), 2007

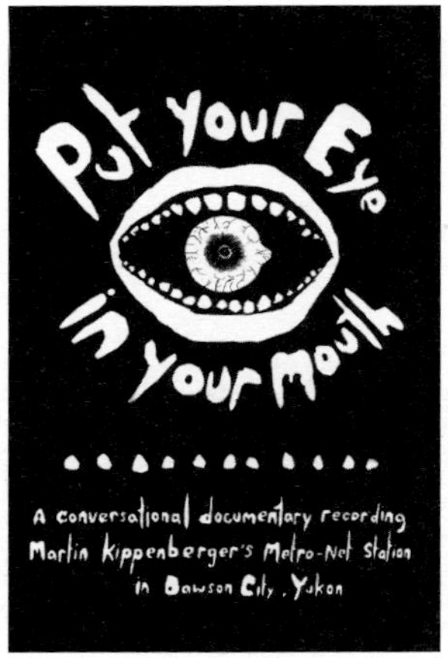

Poster No.1 (Put Your Eye in Your Mouth), 2006

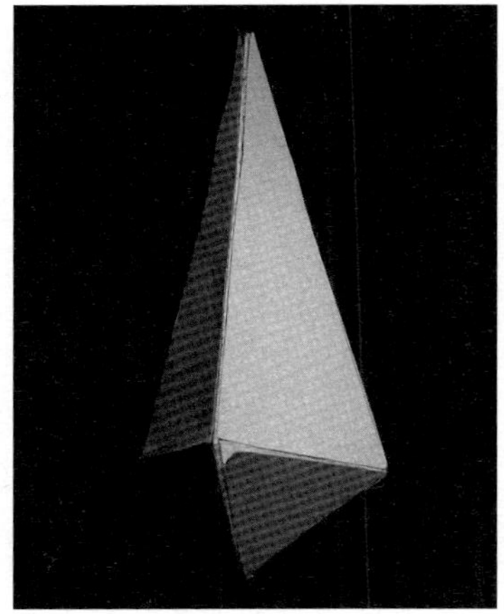

Coloured Crystal from *The Crystal Ship*, 2008

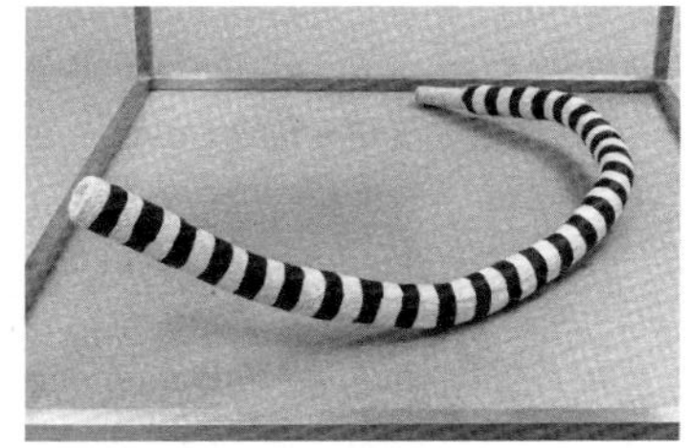

24 Thoughts About Stripes and Dots Manifested into a Form, Displayed Within a Vitrine Made of Brass and Glass, detail, 2012

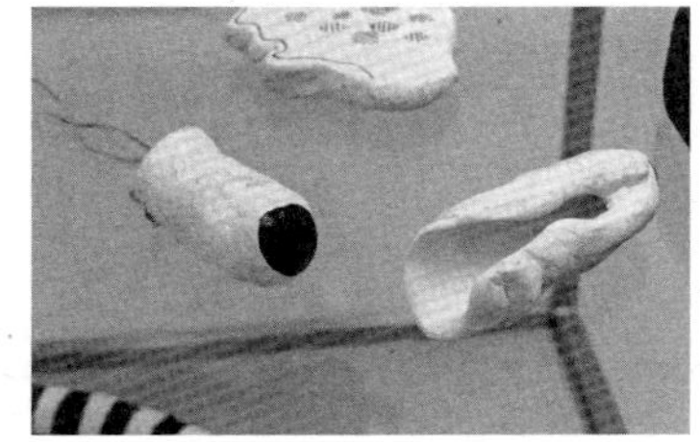

24 Thoughts About Stripes and Dots Manifested into a Form, Displayed Within a Vitrine Made of Brass and Glass, 2012

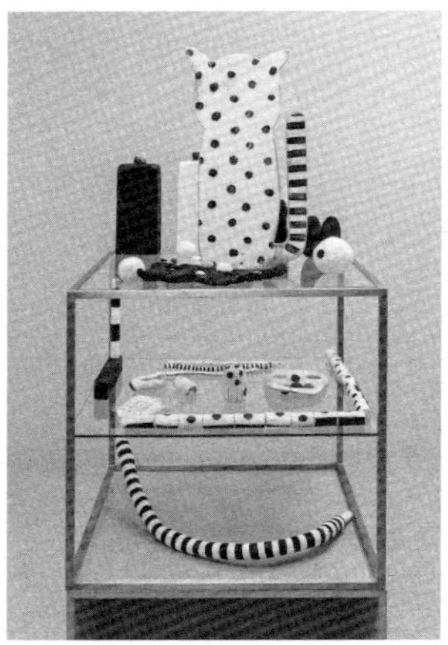

24 Thoughts About Stripes and Dots Manifested into a Form, Displayed Within a Vitrine Made of Brass and Glass, 2012

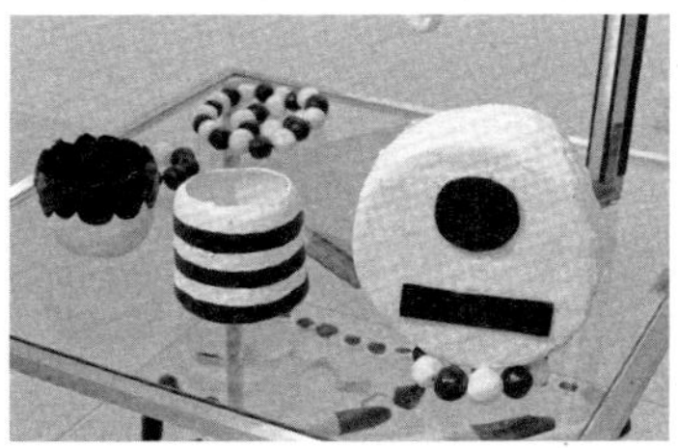

22 Thoughts About Stripes and Dots Manifested into a Form, Displayed Within a Vitrine Made of Brass and Glass, 2012

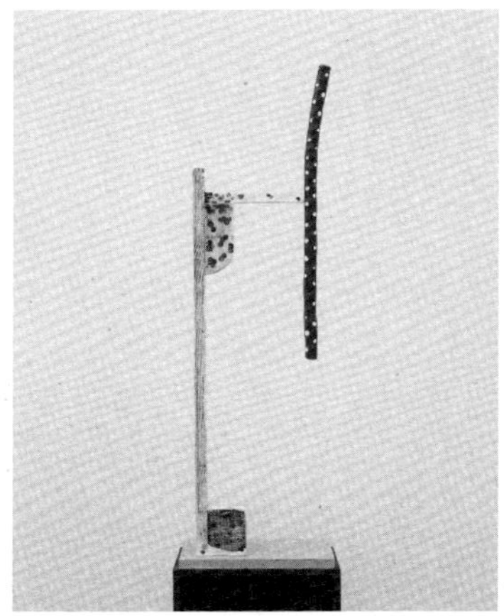

A Tool for Stripes and Dots (the elephant/the elements of the base collect into an appendage), 2012

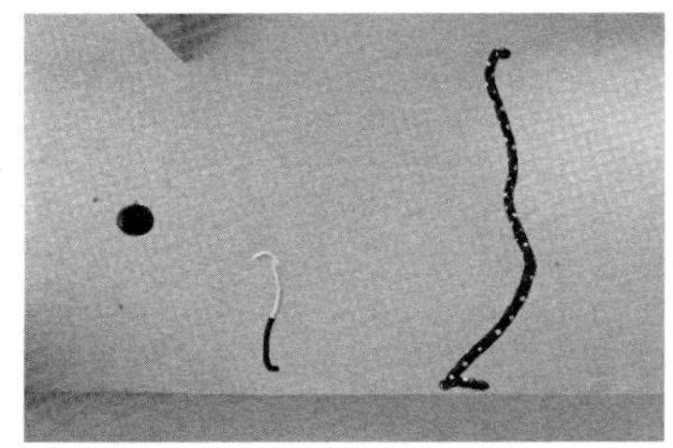

A Structure to Filter a Room (Two Snakes and a Dot), 2012

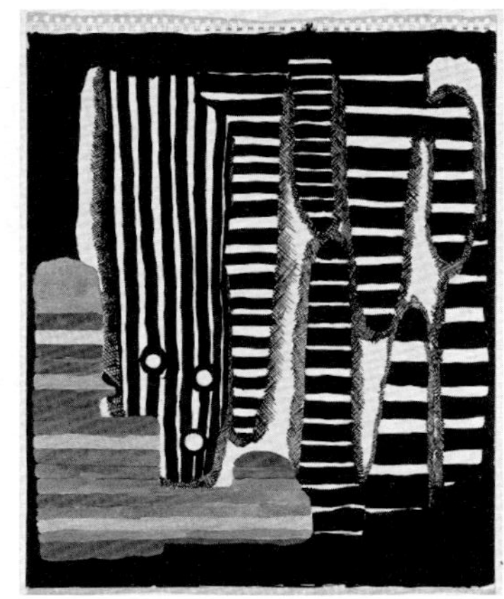

The Horizontals and The Verticals (a record cover), 2012

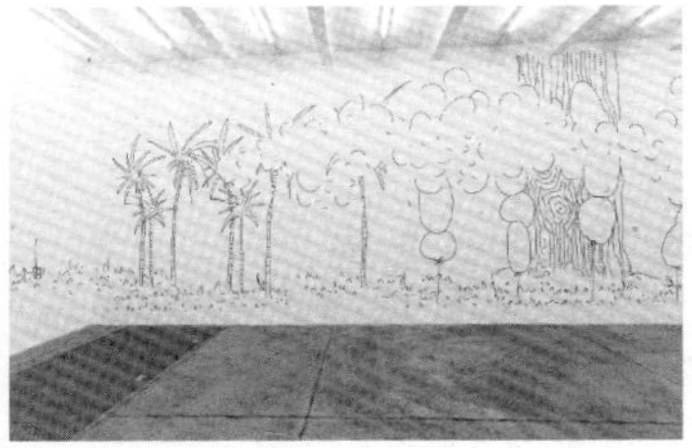

Thoughts of a Dot as it Traverses a Space (Lost Coast Haze Retreat), 2015

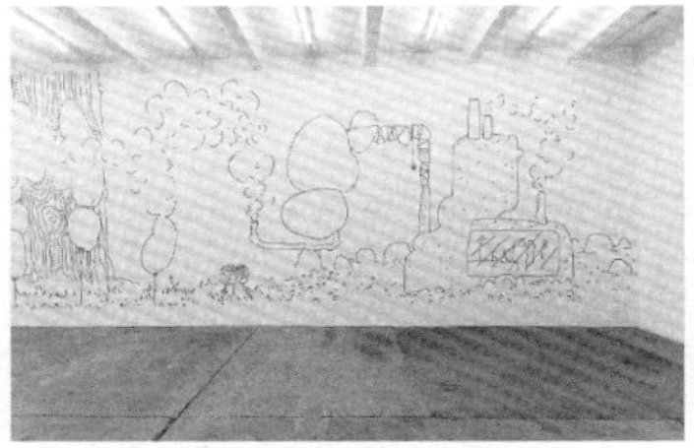

Thoughts of a Dot as it Traverses a Space (Lost Coast Haze Retreat), 2015

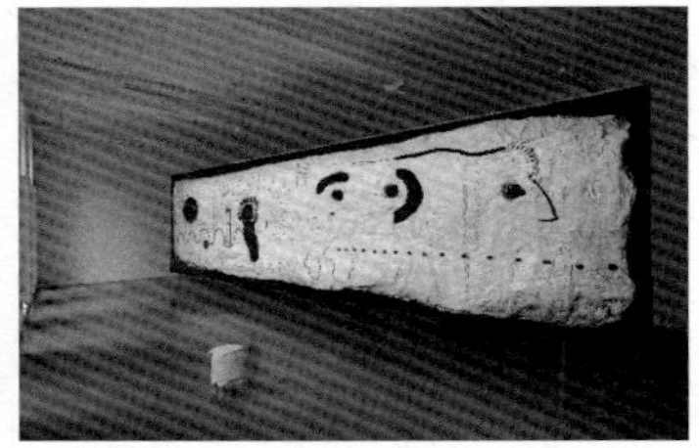

A Segment of Translation (F. Kiesler's Mind Form), Witte de With - Center for Contemporary Art, Rotterdam, The Netherlands, 2015

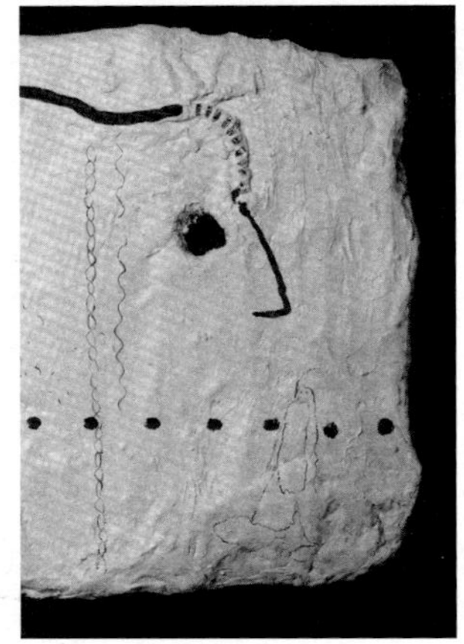

A Segment of Translation (F. Kiesler's Mind Form), detail, 2015

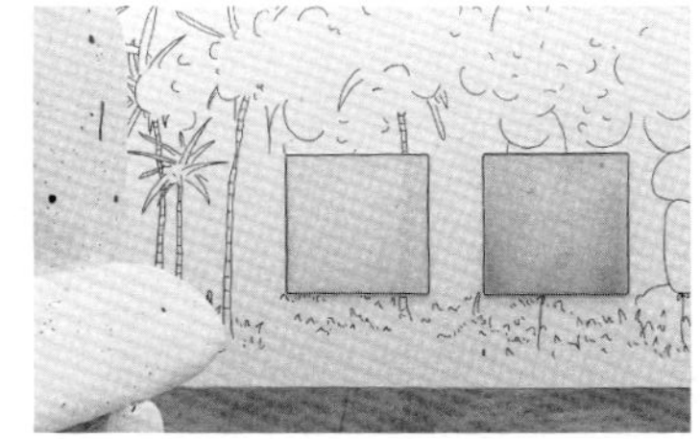

Three Units of Haze, Installation at Supportico Lopez, Berlin, Germany, 2015

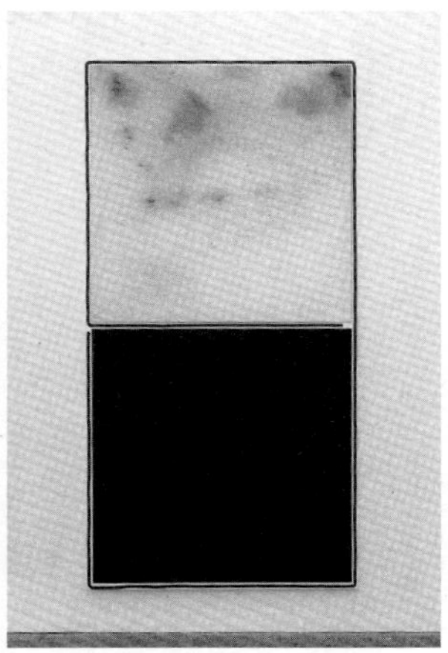

A Stripe of Thought Navigating a Void of Haze VI, 2015

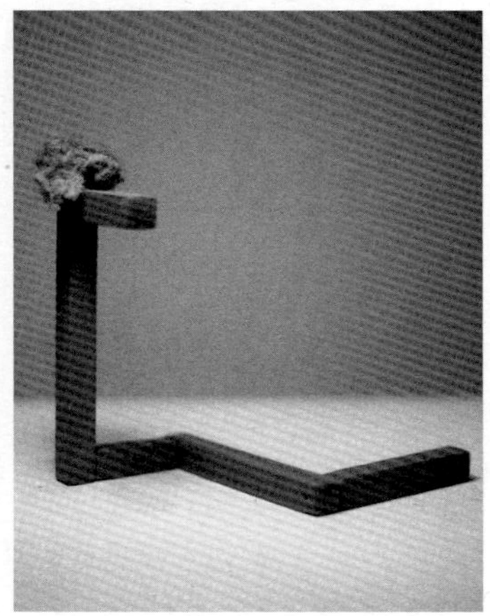

Wood and Dust (Snake with a Wig), KIOSK members edition, 2010

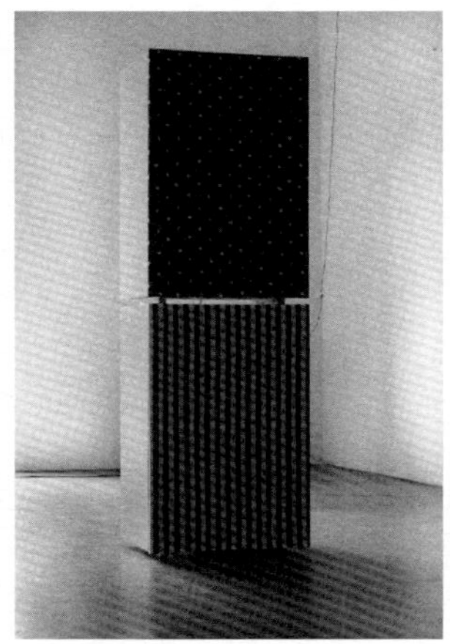

The Story of Stripes and Dots on the Isle of Portikus (Two Speakers), Installation at Portikus, Frankfurt, Germany, 2015

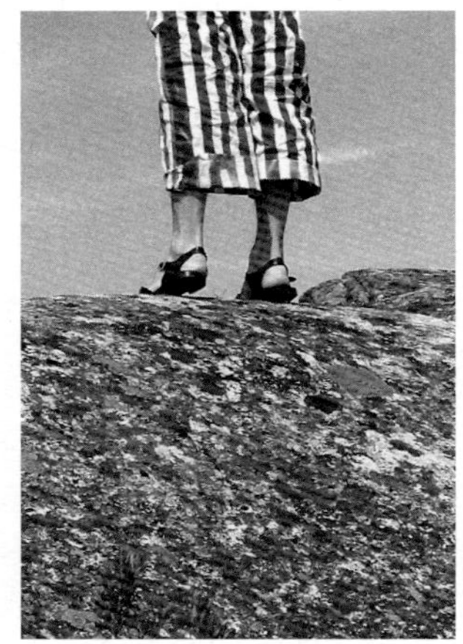

Lichen Voices/Stripes and Dots, video still, 2013

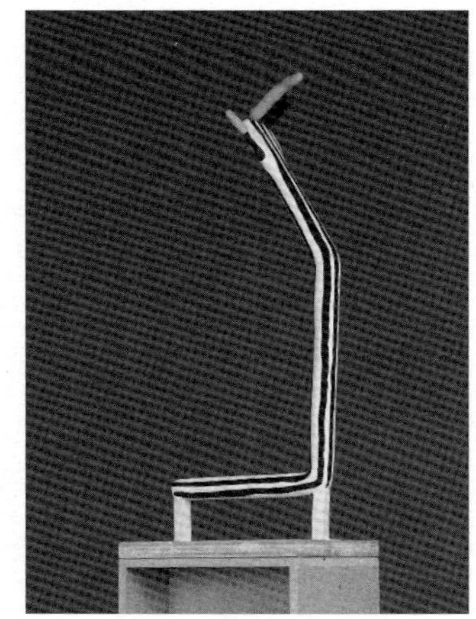

A Haze of Influence Choreographed into an Arm (#3), 2011